BREAKING NON-TARIFF BARRIERS

Insights to Concepts, Regulations for Exports to other Countries & Indian Regime

BREAKING NON-TARIFF BARRIERS

Insights to Concepts, Regulations for Exports to other Countries & Indian Regime

Tanu Singh

PENTAGON PRESS LLP

First published in 2023 by

PENTAGON PRESS LLP
206, Peacock Lane, Shahpur Jat
New Delhi-110049, India
Contact: 011-64706243

Typeset in Palatino, 10.5 Point
Printed by Aegean Offset Printers, Greater Noida, U.P.

ISBN: 978-93-90095-68-1 (HB)

www.pentagonpress.in

To Odie

The explorer who crossed the rainbow bridge.
You will always be loved.

Contents

Preface

For exporters, timely knowledge and anticipation of market changes is power. It helps in planning production based on demand-supply changes. Awareness of a change in customs duty is power. It helps prevent unnecessary confusion among importers. The ability to deliver goods on time by choosing the right freight carrier is power. It helps in earning a reputation to grow business. Staying updated with non-tariff measures is power. It helps in smoother market access for exports and prevent uncertainties.

Which exporter does not want this kind of situation?

Working for more than five years in the Non-Tariff Measures (NTMs) field has given me a chance to understand these concepts from both the regulators' as well as the exporters' perspectives. Each product sector has its own dynamics and unique features. To an exporter, these concepts may, at times, appear alien but they are part of the export package and must be known beforehand. Working from the regulators' side has led me to know the best practices used by other countries to improve their regulatory regime. How are effective technical regulations prepared and what are the methods to overcome them and how and where to raise issues that are hurting the industry are some of the questions, answers to which I have learnt over time. Each regulation is a new learning experience.

Why should you read it

This book attempts to aid an Indian exporter understand the concepts of NTMs and their practical aspects: how are they made; their form across major export destinations mapped in different sectors, and how the regulatory regime can be strengthened in India given the current trade environment. This will help Indian exporters play an active role in their formulation which will be to their advantage.

For beginners, this book explains the concepts of NTMs, with details of agencies involved at the global and national levels. The more important aspect of what existing regulations are in countries in different sectors is of larger interest to exporters. Compliance with these regulations will ensure smoother market access for their products in both developed and developing countries.

Reasons to write this book

There are a number of NTMs under the WTO framework but Sanitary and Phyto-Sanitary (SPS) Measures and Technical Barriers to Trade (TBT) are the most common. SPS Measures broadly cover agricultural goods while TBT covers non-agricultural goods. Moreover, the export of agricultural goods from India was only USD 39.75 billion (2020-21) as compared to non-agricultural goods that accounted for 86 per cent.

Given the export value and that the WTO SPS Agreement is in itself, a complete field for which a separate discussion and research is required, the focus of this book, thus, was laid on TBT.

Another limiting factor for choosing to write on TBT was that the regulations in agricultural goods are primarily aimed at protecting plant, animal, and human health and, hence, any and all measures are covered under them, leaving little room to innovate on technical regulations.

TBT varies from sector to sector due to the risks associated with various products. From a broader perspective, for agricultural goods, the risk is associated with a fairly consistent level as it affects health at all times, whereas in non-agricultural goods, the risk associated varies. It may be high for toys but may not be the same for furniture. This leaves some room for regulators to innovate and make technical regulations with varying focus.

About the book

The book is divided into three sections. The first is purely conceptual and explains the concepts of SPS and TBT WTO Agreements. Thereafter, the focus shifts to the TBT Agreement-related environment giving way to its implementation at the global level in terms of introduction of the agencies involved, their functioning and rule-making processes in standards, conformity assessment, and technical regulations. The book also gives a sneak-peak into the Indian regulatory set-up with details of the organizations involved; how technical regulations are made and how they are enforced by agencies.

The second section of the book is more sector-focused and is oriented towards exporters. This is a more useful segment from the export point of view. It has details of the regulatory regimes of developed and developing countries and draws out the disparities between them. The challenges faced by exporters of developing countries like India in exporting to developed and other countries and a possible way out is also covered in this section.

The last section of the book focuses on ways to strengthen India's regulatory regime. Rather than suggesting various initiatives and recommendations, it focuses on two major aspects of the regulatory regime to make NTMs more effective: market surveillance and regulatory impact assessment.

The information in this book is based on secondary data, including an extensive literature search, scrutiny of government and other websites from a number of countries as well from the WTO and international organisations, both public and private, and some so-called 'grey' (not officially published). The views expressed by the author in this book are personal and not necessarily that of the Government of India.

Tanu Singh

ACKNOWLEDGEMENTS

This book is inspired by the work done by our team that met at 10 a.m. for a cup of coffee to discuss NTBs like national newspaper headlines. Without the team members, this book would not have been possible. It was a great learning experience with our team leader. He not only encouraged a positive discussion but also encouraged us to explore new ideas.

The legal expert, Shruthi, and economics expert, Pallavi, were two pillars of the team. It is commendable how they came out of their comfort zone to study and work in a completely new area.

I am thankful to my father who kept nagging me to complete what I had started; my mother who inspires us with her will to study even at this age and my sister who took care of me during and after my tough days while I worked.

I am grateful to Dr. Amiya Chandra for guiding me through the experience and providing useful feedback to improve the book and preventing the focus from digressing.

Despite being accused of repetition, I have to state that last but not the least, I am glad to have worked under the guidance of Shri Darpan Jain who constantly encouraged the seeking of knowledge.

Tanu Singh

List of Abbreviations

ACA	Accredited Certification Agents
AISC	Automotive Industry Standards Committee
ALOP	Appropriate Level of Protection
ANVISA	Brazilian Health Surveillance Agency
AQSIQ	General Administration of Quality Supervision, Inspection and Quarantine
ARAI	Automotive Research Association of India
ARECS	Act on the Registration and Evaluation of Chemicals
BEVs	Battery Electric Vehicles
BIS	Bureau of India Standards
BLA	Biologic Licence Application
BRRA	Business Regulatory Review Agency
CABs	Conformity Assessment Bodies
CAP	Conformity Assessment Procedure
CBP	Customs and Border Protection
CCA	Chemicals Control Act
CCC	China Compulsory Certification
CCPSA	Canada Consumer Product Safety Act
CDSCO	Central Drugs Standard Control Organization
CFR	Code of Federal Regulations
CHMP	Committee for Medicinal Products for Human Use
CIBRC	Central Insecticides Board and Registration Committee
CLP	Classification, Packaging and Labelling

CMR	Carcinogenic, Mutagenic or toxic to Reproduction
CMV	Central Motor Vehicles Rules, 1989
CMVR-TSC	CMVR: Technical Standing Committee
CNAS	China National Accreditation Service for Conformity Assessment
CNCA	Certification and Accreditation Administration of the People's Republic of China
CoC	Certification of Compliance
CPC	Children's Product Certificate
CPSIA	Consumer Product Safety Improvement Act
CRS	Compulsory Registration Scheme
CSCL	Chemical Substances Control Law
CSO	Central Standards Office
DAV	Drug Administration of Vietnam
DCGI	Drug Controller General of India
DCPC	Department of Chemicals and Petrochemicals
DoC	Declaration of Conformity
DoT	Department of Transportation
DPIIT	Department for Promotion of Industry and Internal Trade
ECHA	European Chemicals Agency
EEA	European Economic Area
EFPIA	European Federation of Pharmaceutical Industries and Associations
EMA	European Medical Agency
ENCS	Existing and New Chemical Substances
EPA	Environment Protection Agency
EPAR	European Public Assessment Report
EU	European Union
EVs	Electric Vehicles
FCEVs	Fuel Cell Electric Vehicles
FDA	Food and Drug Administration
FMCS	Foreign Manufacturers Certification Scheme
FMVSS	Federal Motor Vehicle Safety Standards
FPLA	Fair Packaging and Labelling Act

FSSAI	Food Safety and Standards Authority of India
FTC	Federal Trade Commission
GAC	General Administration of Customs
GAMR	General Administration of Market Supervision
GMP	Good Manufacturing Practices
GRP	Good Regulatory Practices
GTR	Global Prescription Regulations
HEV	Hybrid EVs
IAF	International Accreditation Forum
ICE	Internal Combustion Engine
IEC	International Electrotechnical Commission
IECSC	Inventory of Existing Chemical Substances in China
ILAC	International Laboratories Accreditation Cooperation
INMETRO	National Institute of Metrology, Quality, and Technology
INSS	Indian National Strategy for Standardization
IPPC	International Plant Protection Convention
IRCA	Indian Railway Conference Association
ISGRs	International Standards, Guidelines, and Recommendations
ISH	Industrial Safety and Health Act, 1972
ISO	International Organization for Standardization
JAS	Japanese Agricultural Standard
JCIA	Japan Cosmetic Industry Association
JFSL	Japan Food Sanitation Law
JMF	Japan Machinery Federation
JSIC	Japan International Standards Committee
JTA	Japanese Toy Association
KOSHA	Korea Occupational Safety and Health Agency
KPTA	Korean Pharmaceutical Traders Association
MAFF	Ministry of Agriculture, Forestry and Fisheries
MAFRA	Ministry of Agriculture, Food and Rural Affairs
MAH	Marketing Authorization Holder
MAPA	Ministry of Agriculture, Livestock and Food Supply

METI	Ministry of Economy, Trade and Industry
MFDS	Ministry of Food and Drug Safety
MHLW	Ministry of Health, Labour and Welfare
MIIT	Ministry of Industry and Information Technology
MLITT	Ministry of Land, Industry, Transport and Tourism
MoE	Ministry of Environment
MOH	Vietnam Ministry of Health
MoRTH	Ministry of Road Transport and Highways
MRL	Maximum Residue Limit
MSAs	market Surveillance Authorities
MVA	Motor Vehicles Act, 1988
NABCB	National Accreditation Board for Certification Bodies
NABL	National Accreditation Board for Testing & Calibration Laboratories
NAFTA	North American Free Trade Agreement
NALTEC	National Agency for Automobile and Land Transport Technology
NAQS	National Agricultural Products Quality Management Service
NDA	New Drug Application
NHFPC	National Health and Family Planning Commission
NHTSA	National Highway Transport Safety Administration
NMPA	National Medical Product Agency
NPOP	National Programme for Organic Production
NRTL	Nationally Recognized Testing Laboratory
NTBs	Non-tariff Barriers
NTMs	Non-tariff Measures
OEM	Original Equipment Manufacturer
OIE	World Organization for Animal Health
OSHA	Occupational Health and Safety Administration
OTC	Over-the-counter Drugs
PBT	Persistent, Bio-accumulative and Toxic
PEMSAC	Platform of European Market Surveillance Authorities for Cosmetics

PHA	Preliminary Hazard Analysis
PHEVs	Plug-in Hybrid Electric Vehicles
PIC/S	Pharmaceutical Inspection Cooperation Scheme
PIF	Product Information File
PMDA	Pharmaceuticals and Medical Devices Agency
PPE	personal Protective Equipment
QCO	Quality Control Orders
QP	Qualified Person
RDSO	Research Design & Standards Organization
RIA	Regulatory Impact Assessment
RTRC	Railway Testing Research Centre
SA	Safety Assessment
SAC	Standardization Administration of the People's Republic of China
SAMR	State Administration for Market Regulation
SAWS	State Administration on Work Safety
SCOE	Standing Committee on Implementation of Emission Legislation
SDO	Standards Developing Organization
SGAS	Cosmetic Automation System
SIC	Standard Industrial Classification
SITC	Standard International Trade Classification
SPS	Sanitary and Phyto-Sanitary
STCs	Specific Trade Concerns
SVHC	Substance of Very High Concern
TAA	Type Approval Authority
TBT	Technical Barriers to Trade
TC	Technical Committee
TCCA	Toxic Chemical Control Act
TRs	Technical Regulations
TSCA	Toxic Substances Control Act
UKCA	UK Conformity Assessment
UNECE	United Nations Economic Commission for Europe

USDA	US Department of Agriculture
USMCA	United States-Mexico-Canada Agreement
VCRP	Voluntary Cosmetic Registration Program
vPvB	very Persistent and very Bio-accumulative
WP.29	World Forum for Harmonization of Vehicle Regulations
WTO	World Trade Organization

List of Figures and Tables

FIGURES

TABLES

Chapter One

WTO and Non-Tariff Measures

Getting familiar with ABCs of Non-Tariff Measures (NTMs)

This section has details about when and how NTMs came into being in the global trade environment and what role has the WTO played in benefitting developed and developing countries in being active trading countries.

It highlights the governing agreements and rules under the WTO for NTMs and their types. The WTO Agreements are worded in legal language and hence, may be too overwhelming to read at the first instance. Therefore, this section de-mystifies the concepts in the agreements hidden behind the legal language.

The implementation of the agreements by different agencies at global and national levels is intended to give a complete picture starting from the concepts in the agreements to their implementation by countries. This includes discussion on the working of standard setting bodies such as the ISO, accreditation bodies, and conformity assessment bodies, and how these organizations have helped build a sturdy regulatory environment over decades.

Rising importance of Non-tariff Measures in international trade

The advent of globalization of trade has given rise to a complex network of economic, political, social, and cultural interactions and these intense linkages have diluted borders to create a 'global economy'. The creation of the World Trade Organization (WTO), its rules and regulations were indeed a response to regulate the increasingly integrated global economy.

The WTO Agreements provide frameworks to ensure trade liberalization which means removing or reducing restrictions or impediments to the free movement of goods between countries. This includes removing or reducing tariff barriers such as surcharges and duties as well as non-tariff measures. The trade liberalization policy under the WTO regime has three fundamental components. They include:

1. Expansion of market access by requiring the conversion of all non-tariff barriers to tariffs (tariffication) and the binding and reduction of these tariffs
2. Reduction of trade-distorting domestic subsidies or support
3. Reduction of both the volume of and expenditures on subsidized exports

Expansion of market access means access to the foreign market for exporters. At the time of formation of the WTO, use of NTMs was not in vogue as tariffs (or custom duties) were the dominant method to control imports in a country. With the formation of the WTO, focus further intensified on tarrifs because developing countries had high tariffs and at the same time, they were growing markets. Since the developed countries wanted access to these markets, efforts of trade liberalization focussed more on binding tariff and their reduction, than on NTMs.

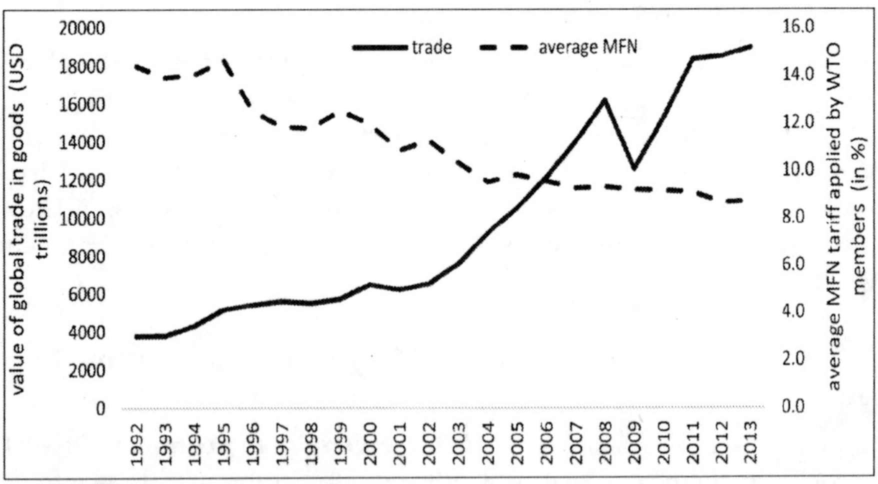

Figure 1: Tariff applied by WTO members and global trade in goods (1996-2013)

In a brochure published by the WTO on completing 20 years of its existence, one of the points highlighted was the trend of increase in global trade while average MFN tariffs reduced. This trend has gained momentum with the increasing number of FTAs being signed by various countries to facilitate trade. FTAs tend to reduce or eliminate tariff to facilitate trade and enhance market access between signing countries. Thus, bringing down overall MFN tariff.

> ***Tariffs***
>
> *Customs duties on merchandise imports are called tariffs. Tariffs give a price advantage to locally-produced goods over similar goods that are imported, and they raise revenues for governments. One result of the Uruguay Round was the commitments of countries to cut tariffs and to "bind" their customs duty rates to levels that are difficult to increase.*

In the early 1990s, tariff was the main policy measure for countries to regulate trade, especially imports. With trade liberalization brought about by the WTO, the developed countries reduced their customs duties drastically whereas developing countries had more relaxed rules and higher transition period to reduce tariffs. Although it was done with the justification of liberalization and creating a level playing field for all countries, the developed countries felt stifled for not being able to use tariffs as a tool to regulate trade because the tariffs were bound and the countries could not increase them beyond the bound rate or it would be a violation of the WTO. No country wants to give away the power of regulating inflow and outflow of goods as it is a revenue generating activity.

What are Non-tariff Measures?

With little to play around with tariffs, countries started shifting the focus of their policies to non-tariff measures (NTMs), to retain their flexibility to regulate trade, and more so, imports. NTMs are well within the scope of the WTO. A formal definition mentions NTMs as "policy measures other than ordinary customs tariffs that can have an economic effect on international trade in goods, change in quantities traded, or prices or both".

A single measure may be trade restrictive for some and trade-facilitative for others.

MRL

The maximum permissible limit of a pesticide, fungicide, insecticide or a biocide, also called Maximum Residue Limit (MRL) is set to prevent its excessive usage that may be harmful to humans when consumed. Any amount below the MRL is considered safe for human use. Of course, the MRLs vary from chemical to chemical.

For example, a country *Alpha* exports carrots to both Japan and the European Union (EU). It also uses a biocide 2-phenylphenol during its farming of carrots. This biocide is used to prevent fungal diseases during its storage. Both these countries have set an MRL. The EU has set an MRL of 0.01 ppm and Japan has set it to 20 ppm. The carrots being exported from *Alpha* have 5 ppm of 2-phenylphenol. In the current scenario, MRL by the EU will act as a barrier whereas, those set by Japan will be NTM for carrots from *Alpha*.

NTMs that are intended or appear to discriminate and restrict free trade are viewed as "barriers" and referred to as "Non-Tariff Barriers" (NTBs). Although there is no written differentiation between the two, the understanding has developed over discussions held at the WTO and other relevant fora. A "measure" may be NTM for one country and NTB for another. It is a matter of perspective.

Notification of NTMs to WTO

Similar to tariff notifications to the WTO, NTMs are also notified to the WTO to ensure transparency among countries. The notification on a commonly accessible WTO platform ensures that member countries are aware of the steps taken by their trading partners to monitor their trade. As per UNCTAD's *International Classification of NTMs* (2019 version), there are 16 different ways in which NTMs can be classified.

How do NTMs affect trade?

NTMs have gained substantial importance in global trade environment with tariffs going down. One of the critical factors to judge the health of the economy is *trade* balance, which is the difference between exports and imports. The greater the 'positive' difference, the more favourable the trade balance is. In an ideal situation, a country will aspire to have more and more exports and less of imports, allowing its domestic industry to support the demand of goods by producing them locally. However, in a real life situation, this is not true, because a country may not have the

Sanitary & phytosanitary measures	Technical barriers to trade	Pre-shipment inspection & other formalities	Contingent trade-protective measures
Non-automatic import licencing, quotas, prohibitions, quantity-control measures and other restrictions	Price-control measures	Finance measures	Measures affecting competition
Trade-related investment measures	Distribution restrictions	Restrictions on post-sales services	Subsidies & other forms of support
Government procurement restrictions	Intellectual property	Rules of origin	Export-related measures

Figure 2: UNCTAD classification of NTMs

resources to produce all goods domestically and have zero imports. There will always be some or the other essential commodity that has to be imported to sustain the economy. It may be in the form of raw material or intermediate good or final good. Thus, imports are a necessary evil. However, much has to be seen by the government to ensure that only required imports take place and that too of atleast a certain quality. One way of doing this is through tariffs. The other is through NTMs.

A true synergy between exports and imports will not only boost the overall trade but also strengthen the economy in enhancing financial stability and manufacturing capabilities.

For example, if a country *Alpha* has a booming industry of toy manufacturing but there is a surge of import of toys from a neighbouring country at almost half the price and of poor quality, it is likely to hit the domestic industry because it will be more viable for a consumer to buy imported toys than those manufactured in *Alpha*. Now, the applicable tariff and the bound tariff are the same in *Alpha*, i.e., *Alpha* cannot increase its tariffs to regulate imports. If bound and applied tariffs would have been different then, *Alpha* would have been in a position to increase tariffs and make imports costly enough to provide a level playing field to its domestic industry. But in the current situation, *Alpha* has no other choice other than to look for imposition of NTMs to monitor imports. *Alpha* can impose an NTM by mandating specific requirements to be adopted by both domestic and imported toys. These requirements may be cumbersome for the imports and thus, will discourage them. On the other hand, as a long term measure, *Alpha* may impose anti-dumping duties on imports.

Thus, where tariffs fail, NTMs can be used by countries to 'monitor' or 'regulate' imports.

Interplay between Tariffs and NTMs

The WTO policy of trade liberalization was supported by lowering of tariffs and the trend has continued since then. There have been times when major trade partners have opted for protecting their economy by resorting to tariffication but after 30 years of the WTO, lot of changes have taken place which are irreversible. International trade today is so deeply integrated that major policy change by one economy is bound to have effect on others.

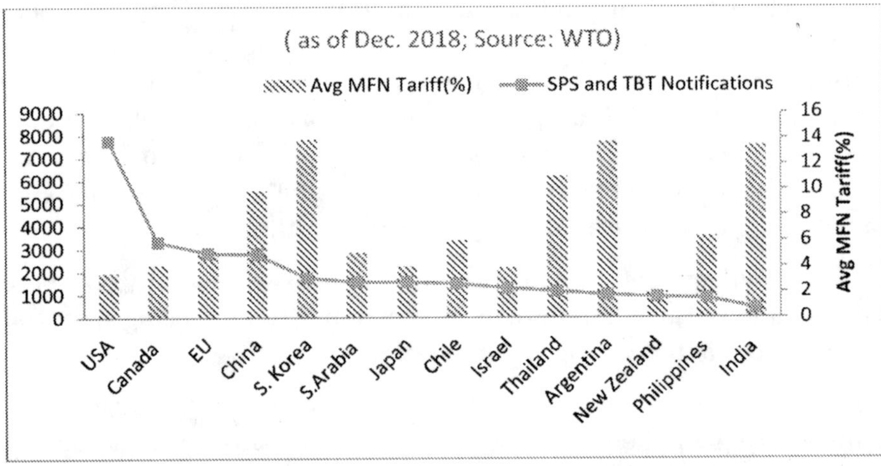

Figure 3: Relation between total no. of notifications & avg. MFN tariff rates

An upward or downward movement of tariffs by a country determines if the country is moving towards protectionism or liberalization. At the inception of the WTO, developed countries had lower average bound tariffs than developing countries. This stifled their regulatory space and thus NTMs gained importance as a policy measure to regulate trade. Since developed countries were forced to explore it early on while developing countries still played on tariffs, the expertise and dominance of developed countries in the sphere of NTMs has grown and matured. Thus, the relation between tariff and NTMs is near substitutionary in nature. The best case scenario is when a country is able to strike a balance between the two.

The numbers also speak about the balance. In an analysis, based on the number of notifications of TBT and SPS measures made by various countries to the WTO as part of their transparency commitments, it can be seen that since 1995, the highest number of notifications have been made by the USA even though its average MFN is low. For countries like China whose average MFN is high, the number of NTMs imposed is also high. For India, average MFN is high but the number of NTMs imposed is on the lower side as compared to similar market economies. More or less, the export aggressive countries such as EU, China, Korea have used a balance of both tariff and non-tariff measures to regulate trade.

NTMs and WTO

While deciding on the WTO commitments in the Uruguay round that lasted for seven-and-a-half years, apart from laying down ground rules for tariff commitments, other areas such as agriculture were hotly contested. What emerged from the discussion was signed and came into effect from 1 January 1995.

The following dedicated agreements were adopted as annexures to the WTO-GATT agreement:

- Agriculture
- Sanitary and Phytosanitary Measures
- Textiles and Clothing
- Technical Barriers to Trade
- Trade-related Investment Measures (TRIMs)
- Anti-dumping
- Customs valuation
- Pre-shipment Inspection
- Rules of Origin
- Import Licensing
- Subsidies and Countervailing Measures
- Safeguards
- Trade facilitation (came into force in 2017)

These agreements laid down basic rights and obligations of WTO members within the scope of goods and services, wherever applicable.

Even though, there are as many ways to classify NTMs as illustrated in Figure 2, more than 84 per cent of NTMs adopted by countries are Sanitary and Phyto-Sanitary (SPS) Measures or Technical Barriers to Trade (TBT). These two measures cover the entire gamut of merchandise goods. Given the importance associated with TBT and SPS measures, the ensuing discussion is focused on TBT and SPS Measures.

Basics of WTO SPS and TBT Agreement and commitments under them

We saw in the last section that the WTO has a number of agreements that set out rights and obligations in various aspects of international trade. These agreements provide framework for countries of what they can do as a right and what they are obligated to do as part of the WTO fraternity in their regulatory space. Some of these rights and obligations are mandatory in nature i.e. a country has to follow them while some are on encouragement basis. This difference in level of rights and duties has been done taking into account the disparity among member countries' economies and their abilities to adhere to them.

Among the agreements, what interests us the most are its two specific agreements on NTMs: Agreement on the Application of Sanitary and Phytosanitary (SPS) and Agreement on Technical Barriers to Trade (TBT).

The rights and obligations under these agreements are intended to ensure that the WTO members do not use policies such as national security, environment protection, or human, animal, or plant health as a disguise to discriminate against imports, favouring domestic goods.

SPS Agreement

The basic objective of the SPS Agreement is to maintain the sovereign right of a country to protect its human health and plant and animal life. A country can do this by taking any policy decision or "measure" such as law, decree, regulation, requirements, and procedures. Under the Agreement, these are called SPS measures.

The SPS Agreement is based on principles of harmonization,

equivalence, appropriate level of protection (ALOP), risk assessment and transparency that are discussed further.

SPS Measure

A country Alpha is free of Avian Influenza (H1N1) in its meat and poultry products. Country Gamma is its major trading partner for import of bovine meat but has the presence of H1N1 in its country.

Country Alpha imposes an SPS Measure (based on scientific justification) requiring "H1N1 free" endorsement on the health certificate that accompanies bovine meat consignment from country Gamma.

This is a valid SPS measure as Alpha has imposed this measure to protect its human health and is substantiated scientifically, as required by the WTO Agreement.

A measure is based on certain requirements such as MRL, presence of aflatoxins, foot and mouth disease, avian influenza etc. These requirements and many more are standardized at the global level by international setting organizations *viz.* International Plant Protection Convention (IPPC) for plant health; World Organization for Animal Health (OIE) for animal health and Codex Alimentarius Commission (Codex) for food safety. They are also called as the Three Sisters in SPS context.

Harmonization

Because an SPS measure is aimed at protection of plant, animal life, and human health, each country can impose stricter regulations than what is proposed globally by the Three Sisters. Although the standards set by these standard-setting organizations is only recommendatory in nature, they are prepared after intense discussion by its members, based on scientific data and justification made available to them. Harmonization as a principle aids countries by providing basis for an SPS measure, i.e., international standards, guidelines, and recommendations (ISGRs) wherever possible. In case a country decides to go beyond ISGRs, a scientific justification has to be provided for doing so.

If an SPS measure is less stringent than the global standards, it might lead to increase in imports from countries where the standards are followed because then the exporter will not have to worry about compliances. Thus, there will be lesser chances of rejection. The challenge arises when a country goes beyond the globally adopted standards. In that case, exporters have to be overly conscious of the products being exported. If they fail to comply, goods will be rejected. This is the real issue in non-harmonization from the export perspective.

The flexibility to be stricter than the standards proposed by the standard setting organizations is given under the SPS Agreement. However, this may also encourage protectionist tendencies among developed countries to discourage trade from developing countries.

> *One of the classic cases of being stricter than international standards that affected the trade globally was the shift in the policy of the EU in 2009 when it adopted regulation EC No. 1107/2009 which introduced changes in the regulatory framework of pesticides. Following the precautionary principle, it adopted the 'Hazard criteria', replacing the 'risk-based assessment approach' in evaluating the effect of pesticides effect on human health, animals, and environment.*
>
> *As per 'Hazard criteria', even a minimal presence of side effects would be treated as unsafe to human health, plant, and wildlife. This approach discarded the 'acceptable daily dosage' of substances. In other words, any inherent presence of risks in the chemical substances would be considered hazardous. This gave leeway to the EU to lower the MRL at the slightest risk to the Level of Detection (OLD).*
>
> *Since none of the countries were following this approach, many imports from developing countries suffered a set-back owing to rejection of their consignments at EU borders. Countries like the USA, Canada, and Australia were also against this approach.*

Equivalence

Equivalence is the acceptance of an SPS measure of one country by another and is more relevant for imports. The initiation for a request for equivalence may be undertaken by the government or by the industry of the exporting country but the process of pursuing equivalence is done at the government level. This is more commonly known as market access for a product. An industry interested in exporting non-processed food such as cereals, fruits, vegetables, meat, poultry, etc., may seek market access from the importing country through their own government.

Risk Assessment

Until now, we have read about an SPS measure, how it needs to be trade facilitative, non-trade restrictive, based on ISGRs and have a scientific justification if not based on one. But how does one arrive at a "scientific justification"? What if the basis of a stringent measure is not acceptable to other countries?

In such cases, the concept of risk assessment comes in. Risk assessment is a scientific process by which evaluation of the likelihood of the spread of a disease or potential for adverse effects on human health is done. In conducting such risk assessments, the WTO members are required to take into account risk assessment techniques developed by relevant international organizations. Risk assessment helps in providing scientific justification for an SPS Measure, which is in deviation from the global standards.

Transparency

Transparency refers to sharing of information of procedures and measures taken by a country with the other WTO members. This will include sharing of information on a draft SPS measure which is a mandatory obligation under the WTO. While notifying an SPS measure, the notifying country has to provide time to other countries to send comments on the draft SPS measure; discuss those comments. All these activities are routed through a designated "Enquiry Point(s)" that is a government agency of the notifying country.

The WTO also indicates that every member country may have a National Notification Authority "to notify" SPS measures of a country.

Enquiry Point

Enquiry Point(s) is responsible for providing information on a draft or a final SPS measure adopted by the country. For India, they are National Plant Protection Organization, Department of Animal Husbandry, and Food Safety and Standards Authority of India (FSSAI).

The National Notifying Authority is responsible for sharing notifications with WTO for disseminating through the designated e-ping portal. For India, it is the Department of Commerce.

Details of Enquiry Points and National Notifying Authority can be checked on SPS-IMS (Information Management System). It is obligated by the WTO that the information on National Notifying Authority and Enquiry Points be kept updated by member-countries on the website.

TBT Agreement

The subject matter covered by SPS Agreement was related to plant health, animal health and food safety. The TBT Agreement, on the other hand, scopes over all products, including industrial and agricultural sans those regulations that are covered under the SPS Agreement. There is a no definite demarcation.

Difference between SPS and TBT Agreements

One of the major differences between the two agreements is of scope. While an SPS Agreement focuses on obligations for protection of plant and animal life and human health, a TBT Agreement focuses more on measures that have legitimate objectives such as national security requirements; prevention of deceptive practices; protection of human health or safety, animal or plant life or health, or the environment. A country is free to bring in any measure based on the above objectives, provided it is able to provide justification for it.

Additionally, the use of scientific justification as a basis for an SPS measure is a must whereas in a TBT Agreement, it is not. Whenever a country brings an SPS measure stricter than those suggested by Three Sisters or where there is no standard at all, the country imposing the measure must base the measure on scientific justification. If it does not, a country whose trade is affected may take the notifying country to dispute at the WTO after exhausting all other means.

Unlike the Three Sister organizations mentioned in the SPS Agreement, there is no acknowledgement (in terms of finding a mention in the Agreements) of a standard setting organization in the TBT Agreement. There is a reference to the ISO/IEC guide in Annex-1 but nothing as a standard setting organization.

A TBT measure is required to be applied on the MFN basis whereas not all SPS measures follow the MFN basis. Some SPS measures are region- or country-specific.

Difference between SPS and TBT with examples:

- *The quality requirements of a packaged jam are governed by the principles in the SPS Agreement whereas the labelling aspect is governed by the TBT Agreement*
- *The content of bottled water is covered by an SPS Measure, whereas the packaging requirement on the bottle is TBT*

Back to TBT Agreement...

There are three major concepts in the TBT Agreement: Standards, Technical Regulations and Conformity Assessment Procedures.

Standards in the TBT Agreement

Standards are one of the building blocks of the TBT Agreement. As per the TBT agreement, standards are defined as *"Document approved by a recognized body that provides, for common and repeated use, rules, guidelines or characteristics for products or related processes and production methods, with which compliance is not mandatory. It may also include or deal exclusively with terminology, symbols, packaging, marking or labelling requirements as they apply to a product, process or production method."* There are no definitions for international standards or a standard setting body.

Thus, the standards are benchmark requirements for a product or a process and are voluntary in nature. It means that it is not necessary to manufacture or follow them for exports or imports. Apart from what is defined in the WTO Agreement, the TBT Committee has also come up with guidelines and recommendations, which are recommendatory in nature. These are called as Committee decisions and are prepared as part of review of the implementation of the TBT Agreement that takes place every five years.

One of the important takeaways from the Committee's decisions is the six principles that serve as guiding principles for recognizing a standard as an international standard as illustrated below:

Transparency	Work programme/proposal accessibility, adequate time and opportunity for comments;
Openness	All Members have the right to participate at all levels of standard setting;
Impartiality and Consensus	No bias against any member, region, supplier & consensus procedures;
Relevance and Effectiveness	Respond to regulatory and market needs, as well as scientific and technological developments in various countries; performance-based;
Coherence	Avoid duplication/overlap with other international standardizing bodies, through co-operation and coordination;
Development Dimension	Promotion of developing countries' participation in international standards; take into account constraints on developing countries.

Figure 4: Six principles to recognize a standard as international standard

The majority of us are aware of ISO 9001:2008 requirements. These are Quality Management System (QMS) requirements defining certain parameters that an organization needs to demonstrate to be continuously certified with ISO 9001:2008. It specifies requirements for a quality management system where an organization

- *needs to demonstrate its ability to consistently provide a product that meets customer and applicable statutory and regulatory requirements, and*
- *aims to enhance customer satisfaction through the effective application of the system, including processes for continual improvement of the system and the assurance of conformity to customer and applicable statutory and regulatory requirements.*

International standard setting

There are specific international standard setting organizations, none of which are recognized by the TBT Agreement, and yet their global popularity gives them the much-needed acceptance. One of the most common international standard setting organizations is the International Organization for Standardization (ISO), which is an independent, non-governmental entity with membership of more than 165 nations.

History of ISO

The term, ISO, has been derived from the Greek word 'isos', meaning equal. It officially came into existence as an organization in 1946 when 25 countries came together to form 67 Technical Committees (TCs). The Technical Committees work in specific areas to form standards.

Today the ISO has 802 TCs with representation from 165 countries that have prepared more than 24,112 standards in various fields, including products and services.

The ISO uses following key principles for standards development:

- *Respond to need in market:* The need to formulate a standard is first felt by the consumer or the industry. The industry group, however, cannot contact the ISO for formulating a standard. It has to go through the concerned member-country to request for formulation of a standard.
- *Based on global export opinion:* The experts who are part of the TCs are from consumer associations, academia, NGOs, and even the government.
- *Developed through a multi-stakeholders process:* Multi-stakeholder consultations are held by experts from across the world that are

part of the larger technical committees. All aspects of standards, including scope, key requirements, and content are developed.
- *Based on consensus:* All decisions are made by consensus.

Another major international standard setting organization is the International Electrotechnical Commission (IEC) that prepares and publishes standards for all electrical, electronic, and related technologies, collectively known as electrotechnology. The IEC is a not-for-profit organization with membership of 170 countries.

An IEC international standard is developed only when several IEC member-countries are willing to send experts to work together on a standard to increase the safety, efficiency, or reliability of a given electrical/electronic product or system.

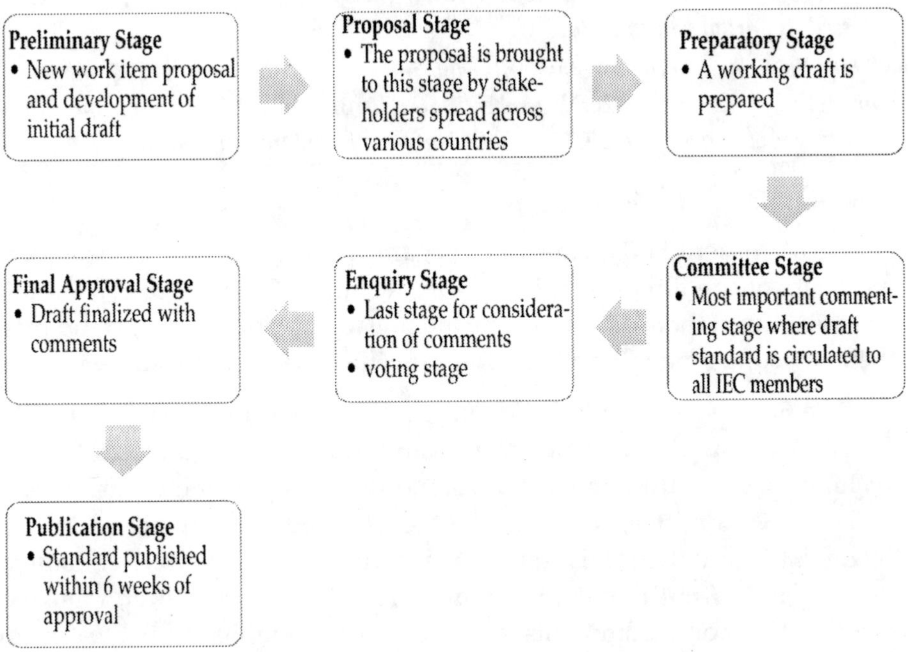

Figure 5: Stages of development of standards by IEC

From India, the Bureau of India Standards (BIS) is the representative organization at the ISO and the IEC.

National standard setting process in India

The Bureau of India Standards (BIS) is the national standard setting body for India under the BIS Act, 2016. However, the BIS is not the only standard setting organization in India. There are other standard setting organizations that set standards in their specific areas of expertise such as the Research and Design Standards Organization, Food Safety and Standards Authority of India (FSSAI), Central Drugs Standards Control Organization, Petroleum and Explosives Safety Organization, etc.

Bureau of India Standards

The BIS was formed as the Indian Standards Institution (ISI) in 1947. In the initial years, the organization focused on standardization activities but moved on to include certification activities under its umbrella in 1952 to give benefit to consumers using the ISI mark. Since there was no legislation governing such activities, a bill was passed in Parliament in 1986.

Thus, the Bureau of Indian Standards came into existence on 1 April 1987, through an Act of Parliament on 26 November 1986. The BIS Act, 2016 later amended the existing Act to designate the BIS as the National Standardizing Body.

How are standards made in India?

Any government body, consumer organizations, industry associations, members of the BIS or members of its Technical Committee can submit proposals for standards. These may include formulation of new standards, their revision, amendment, or even cancellation of an old standard.

The BIS has 15 Technical Committees that report to Division Councils. These Division Councils are responsible for setting mandates for the Technical Committees to work on standards. They may establish a new Technical Committee, if required. Once a standard is finalized by the Technical Committee, it is issued in a draft form and widely circulated for a period of not less than a month. The draft is thereafter, finalized taking into account comments received and then published in the official gazette.

To take up standards formulation on a priority basis, the Standards National Action Plan (SNAP) was prepared by the BIS and inaugurated during the Special Standards Conclave organized by the Department of Commerce, Government of India in 2019. The SNAP proposed a set of actions that would enable the BIS to fulfil the specified objectives, drive the national standardization work and participation in international standardization activities.

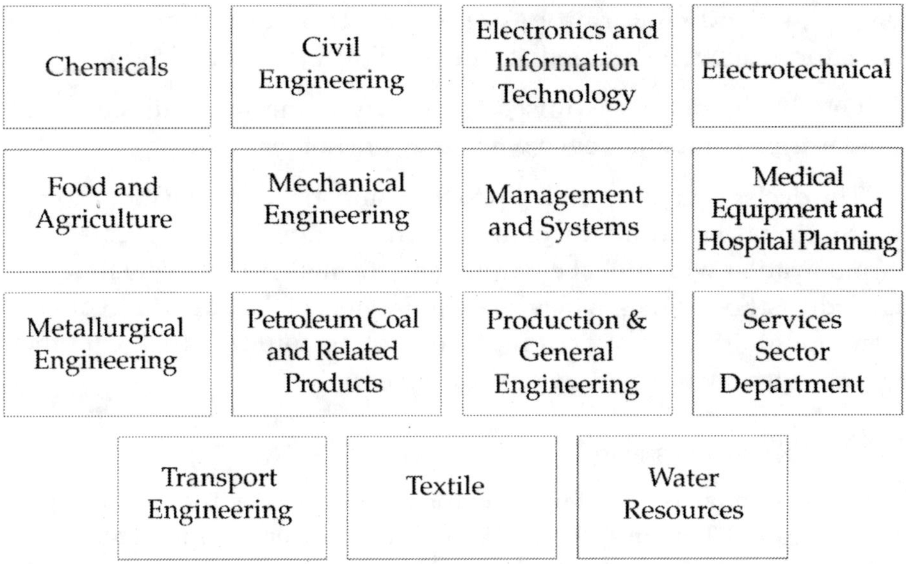

Figure 6: Technical Committees (15)

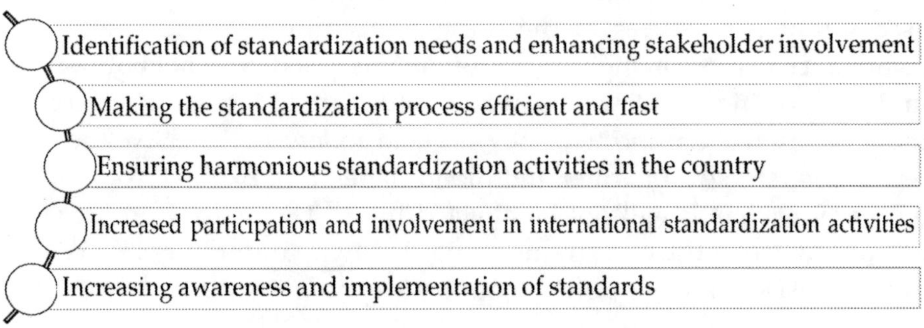

Figure 7: Objectives of SNAP

There are more than 20,000 standards of the BIS relating to products, services, and quality management. Of these, only about 10,000 standards relate to products; 85 per cent of which are harmonized to international standards.

How can standards support regulators?

Standards form a basis for deeper cooperation between regulators of various countries, by providing an opportunity to understand each other's regimes. Standards are stepping stones for formulation of technical regulations and conformity assessment procedures. They promote regulatory alignment and reduce the possibility of trade friction.

One of the questions raised frequently is the necessity of use of standards by companies even when they are not mandatory.

The decision is completely up to the company to use a national or an international standard to manufacture its goods. The greater the harmonization with global environment, the higher the acceptability of its products. Sometimes, it may be a requirement of the importing country even though it may not exist in the exporting country at all. On other instances, it may be requirement of a buyer only.

Technical Regulations (TRs)

Once the standards are mandated for compliance by the government, they are called Technical Regulations (TRs). As per requirements of the TBT Agreement, these TRs are prepared keeping legitimate objectives[1] in mind. They must not be trade restrictive.

The exporters have to be aware of TRs along with the conformity assessment procedures of the importing country because without compliance to these mandatory requirements, goods will not be allowed in the importing country. So if, water bottles are to be manufactured in India or are to be imported, they need to follow both FSSAI and BIS regulations (FSSAI for water and BIS for labelling). Exports from India, on the other hand, will not be affected by its TRs as they are usually exempted from the requirements laid down under the TR. While exporting, TRs of the importing country are more relevant.

TRs in the TBT Agreement

A TBT Agreement defines 'Technical Regulation' as a "*Document which lays down product characteristics or their related processes and production methods, including the applicable administrative provisions, with which compliance is mandatory. It may also include or deal exclusively with terminology, symbols, packaging, marking, or labelling requirements as they apply to a product, process, or production method*".

There are two main heads (or articles as they are called) under which

1. Includes national security requirements; prevention of deceptive practices; protection of human health or safety, animal or plant life or health, or the environment.

the WTO members have to operate while making a TR: one relates to what the central government is supposed to do and the second relates to the state/local and non-governmental bodies. The TBT agreement specifies obligations for central government bodies and local government bodies. Both of them are defined in the agreement itself. The central government, as we know it, includes ministries and departments or anybody under the control of the central government. The local government bodies' framework are other than central government bodies and includes states, provinces, municipalities, etc.

The majority of the obligations under the TBT agreement are for central government bodies. They have to ensure that they do not discriminate among like products that are being imported from other countries. The TRs so formulated shall not create unnecessary requirements that may hinder trade.

For example, a country has specified testing requirements for a product without clarifying if the test has to be in-house i.e. in importing country alone or, to be done in the exporter's country. The exporter gets the test done in his own country and exports the product. The importing country then insists on doing the test again in their country and does not accept the test report provided by the exporter, although there is no such mention of testing requirement at the borders of the importing country. This leads to dual testing of the same product for the same criteria, thereby increasing the burden of cost and compliance on the exporter.

The TRs formulated must be based on risk assessment: Although this is a requirement more suited for agricultural products under the SPS Agreement, products under the ambit of a TBT agreement are also regulated by countries on the basis of risk assessment fulfilling the requirements of national security; the prevention of deceptive practices; protection of human health or safety, animal or plant life or health, or the environment. These are the broad objectives with which the countries can make a TR. This list of objectives is non-exhaustive.

More and more countries are formalizing ways to associate risk with products to make TRs more meaningful. For example, products such as toys are classified as high-risk products because they come in contact with children and can lead to mechanical shocks, migration of harmful chemicals from toys to children, be flammable, etc. Chairs on the other hand may be classified as low-risk products as they may not pose health risks to its users as much as toys. Therefore, the requirements in a TR for toys will be more stringent compared to requirements in a TR on chairs.

These requirements may be laid down by a country either specifically mentioning them in the regulation itself or by referring to relevant standards that contain such requirements. These standards may be international, regional, or national.

The next most important obligation on central governments is of notification as a transparency measure under the Agreement. When a TR is not based on an international standard or deviates from it, the country has to notify the TR in the draft formulation stage to the WTO giving sufficient time to other countries and its stakeholders to comment on it. However, it is up to the country to consider such comments and amend the regulation while finalizing it. At the WTO, there is no obligation to notify the final regulation.

In case of an emergency situation, when a country does not have sufficient time to notify the draft TR or seek comments on it, it can notify the final TR directly. The reasons for adopting an emergency TR have to be shared later and a due period for comments has to be given.

TR setting in India

In India, there is no one ministry/department/regulator for preparing a TR. There are different regulators for different products because each ministry/department has its own allocated products for which it is responsible. However, many may not have the power to formulate regulations under their governing legislation.

There is also a manpower constraint and administrative limitations of implementing the regulation and monitoring it across the country. To take care of such issues, most ministries/departments prefer using the alternative route of the BIS by preparing and implementing TR under the BIS Act, 2016. We will discuss these details in subsequent sections.

The TRs prepared under the BIS Act, 2016 are called as Quality Control Orders (QCOs) or Compulsory Registration Scheme (CRS). These are defined on the basis of the conformity assessment procedures used to implement a TR under the BIS (Conformity Assessment) Regulations, 2018.

As on 1 December 2021, there were 458 product categories under regulation with the BIS Act, 2016. The following steps are taken while formulating a TR in India:

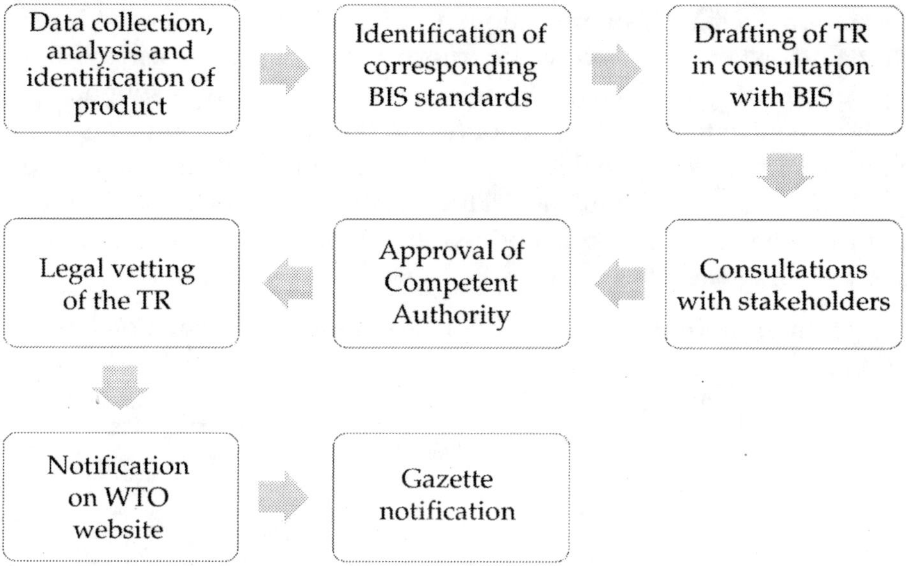

Figure 8: Process flow of formulation of a TR

TR formulation process under BIS Act, 2016

The formulation process is more or less the same across all the ministries/ departments formulating TRs under their own regulations.

First, the need to formulate a TR is to be identified. This may include requests from stakeholders, assessment of risk for the product, supply-demand in the market, manufacturing capacities, etc. Once the need is identified, the BIS then identifies the standard, if it already exists. If there is only one standard, it is an easy task to just mandate that standard with relevant conformity assessment requirements. If there are no standards, it takes time to prepare it. If there are multiple standards, then stakeholders need to be consulted to understand which standard needs to be mandated, and whether the industry has the capability to comply with it. An old standard has to be updated to its current requirements. This may mean alignment of the national standard with international standards such as the ISO/IEC standards. Once the standard is ready, the process of TR formulation moves to the next step.

A draft TR is prepared in consultation with the BIS, including what conformity assessment is to be followed. Thereafter, the draft TR is shared with stakeholders and their inputs are sought. The stakeholders include industry, associations, organizations, testing labs, consumers, producers etc. Based on the inputs received, necessary changes are made in the draft regulation and the approval of the competent authority is sought. The draft is then vetted legally and notified to the WTO for comments from other countries. A reasonable period of time is given for the comments. Based on these comments, the draft regulation is modified, if required, and then the final version is notified in the official gazette in Hindi as well as in English.

As on 15 December 2021, India had notified 300 regulations to the WTO since 1995.

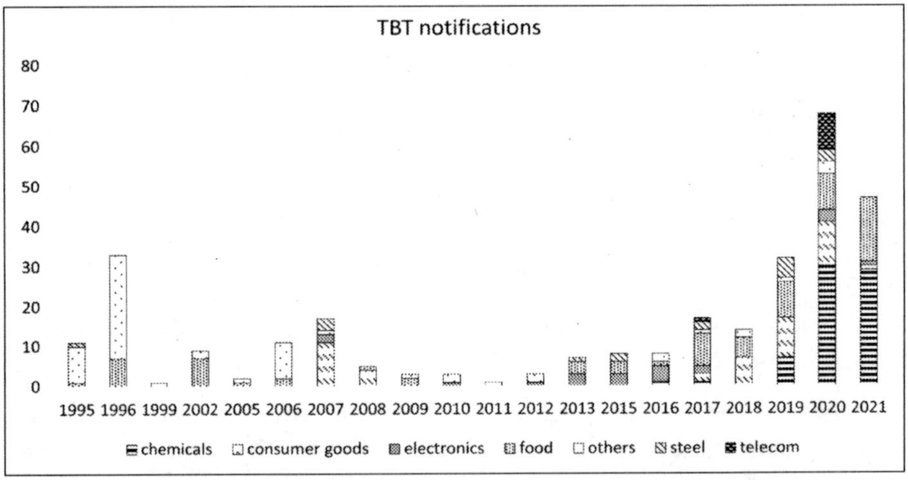

Figure 9: TBT notifications by India as on 15.12.2021

From Figure 9, it can be seen that, of late, India has renewed its focus on the chemicals sector with increase in number of TRs being made to regulate it. Food has been an all-time favourite, as it requires constant monitoring.

Conformity Assessment Procedures (CAPs)

The core of compliance of a technical regulation lies in its enforcement. This is done through conformity assessment procedures. These may include procedures for sampling, testing and inspection, evaluation, verification and assurance of conformity, registration, accreditation or a combination of the above procedures.

Each country has a different set of requirements for different sectors, different products. Depending on the risk associated with the product, sampling and testing requirements are ascertained. In certain cases, there may be a pre-registration requirement before placing the goods in the market or a requirement for factory inspection before grant of licence by the importing country.

There are four main pillars of conformity assessment that need to be understood clearly. If used interchangeably, they may create confusion.

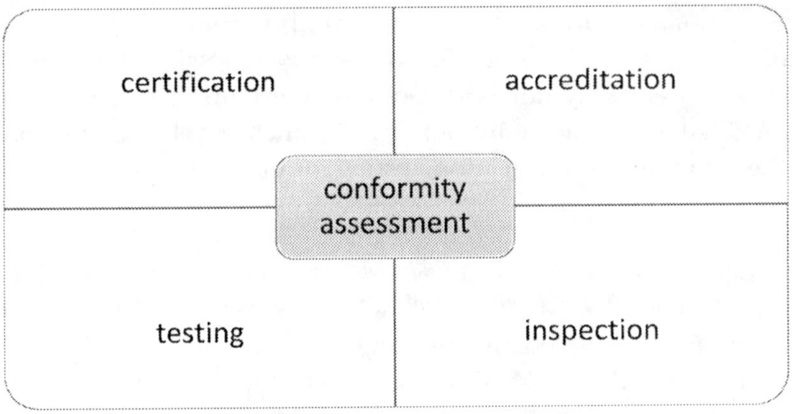

Figure 10: Pillars of CAPs

Usage of these concepts rests with the risk associated with the product. Conformity assessment can be performed by organizations or individuals as a first party (generally a supplier or a manufacturer), second party (purchaser or user of the product), third party (independent entity having no linkage to first or second party) or by a government entity. Let us start with getting to know the pillars.

Accreditation

To understand accreditation, we first need to understand what conformity assessment is. Conformity assessment is a demonstration of fulfilment of specific requirements. This demonstration is through specific procedures. Together, they are called conformity assessment procedures. The bodies that carry them out are called conformity assessment bodies (CABs). They can either be first, second or third party CABs as explained previously. These CABs can perform conformity by either certification, testing, or inspection. If they do certification, they are called certification bodies. If they conduct inspections, they are called inspection bodies and if they carryout testing, they are called testing bodies or testing labs.

The next question arises as to how does one establish the authenticity of these CABs and the genuineness of the documents or certificates or reports issued by them.

This is where accreditation comes in. As per ISO/IEC 17000:2020 (Conformity assessment: vocabulary, and general principles), accreditation is a third-party attestation related to a CAB, conveying formal demonstration of its competence, impartiality, and consistent operation in performing specific conformity assessment activities. In simpler terms, accreditation is a process that recognizes these CABs to be genuine. That is why accreditation is not something that CABs do. This limit their domain to certification, testing, or inspection.

Role of IAF

- *Ensuring that its Accreditation Body Members only accredit bodies that are competent to do the work they undertake and are not subject to conflicts of interest*
- *Maintaining the IAF Multilateral Recognition Arrangement (MLA) among Accreditation Body Member signatories, which reduces risk to businesses and their customers by ensuring that an accredited certificate or validation/verification statement may be relied upon anywhere in the world*
- *Working to find the most effective way of achieving a single system that will allow companies with an accredited conformity assessment certificate or validation/ verification statement in one part of the world to have that certificate or validation/ verification statement recognized elsewhere in the world*
- *Eliminating the need for suppliers of products or services to be certified in each country where they sell their products or services. Certified once—accepted everywhere*
- *Promoting accreditation as an effective mechanism for providing confidence in goods and services, which is essential to global trade facilitation*

At the global level, the International Accreditation Forum (IAF) is a worldwide association of accreditation bodies and other bodies interested in conformity assessment in the fields of management systems, products, processes, services, personnel, validation and verification and other similar programs of conformity assessment. As per their website, they have 87 accreditation bodies, 24 associate members and 6 regional accreditation groups as members. The accreditation bodies that are its members are generally the national accreditation bodies of various countries.

But how does this benefit exporters?

It is not just about having a membership of an international organization but about how it facilitates trade across borders. A national accreditation body becomes a member of Multilateral Recognition Arrangement (IAF MLA) after an evaluation of its operations by a peer evaluation team that checks for full compliance with both international standards and IAF requirements. Once an accreditation body of a country is a member of the IAF MLA, it is required to recognize certificates and other documents issued by CABs accredited by all other signatories of the IAF MLA.

This means that a certificate issued by a CAB, accredited by the national accreditation body, which is a member of the IAF MLA, will have to be recognized by other countries. For an exporter, this translates into recognition of their testing reports issued by a testing body accredited by the national accreditation body signatory of the IAF MLA by an importing country.

However, there is many a slip twixt cup and the lip. This would have made trade all the more easier, but countries maintain their policy space by bringing in regulations that can, in a way, circumvent this arrangement and put the regulating country back in the driving seat to regulate trade.

Certification

Once accreditation is clear, certification becomes obvious. Certificates are given by CABs as third-party attestations specifying that organization/ individual/product/services conform to a norm. It is not a blanket certificate for all activities. Certification is specific. It assesses the product as well as the production process to ensure that quality is maintained during manufacturing. It is reflected in the form of a certification mark and a certificate of conformity. For example, an ISI mark on specific products or a CE marking on electronic goods is an indication that the manufacturer's products and processes have been assessed by a certification body.

Testing

Testing is another important pillar of conformity assessment procedure that allows for determination of specific requirements. Typically, a certification body may require samples of products to be tested to certain parameters, to judge compliance to a standard, before issuing a certificate or a mark. Testing is limited to products only. No processes are tested. It is a one-off process with no follow-up. Testing is carried out by testing labs, the efficacy of which can be established by accreditation.

Similar to association of accreditation bodies, the accreditation system for labs for specific testing also exists. It works in a similar fashion as an accreditation body for CABs. The body is called International Laboratories Accreditation Cooperation (ILAC). The primary purpose of the ILAC is to establish an international arrangement between member accreditation bodies based on peer evaluation and mutual acceptance.

Developing and harmonising laboratory, inspection body, proficiency testing provider and reference material producer accreditation practices	104 accreditation bodies from over 105 economies have signed the ILAC
Recognising accredited calibration laboratories, testing laboratories, medical testing laboratories, inspection bodies, proficiency testing providers and reference material producers internationally under the ILAC MRA	The ILAC MRA signatory accreditation bodies assess and accredit conformity assessment bodies against the relevant international standards, including calibration laboratories, testing laboratories, medical testing laboratories, inspection bodies, proficiency testing providers and reference material producers
Promoting laboratory, inspection body, proficiency testing provider and reference material producer accreditation to industry, governments, regulators and consumers	Industry, governments, regulators, and consumers are encouraged to use and accept results from accredited conformity assessment bodies, including in other economies in order to avoid duplication of testing
Assisting and supporting developing accreditation systems	For developing countries

Figure 11: International cooperation activities of ILAC

Inspection

As per ISO/IEC 17000:2020, inspection is "examination of an object of conformity assessment and determination of its conformity with detailed requirements or, on the basis of professional judgement, with general requirements". In other words, inspection can be of a product or of a process as a sub-part of the certification process. A certification body can choose to either carry out the inspection itself or choose to outsource it to inspection bodies. Inspection as a conformity assessment technique can include:

- visual examination of physical items
- measuring or testing of physical items
- examination of specification documents such as design drawings
- comparison of the findings with the requirements of specification documents or with generally accepted good practice in the field; and
- drawing up a report on the results of the inspection.

Conformity assessment in India

Conformity assessment in India is done by bodies that are administratively controlled by the government. Accreditation is managed by the National Accreditation Board for Certification Bodies (NABCB). It provides accreditation to certification bodies (for product and system certification) and inspection bodies. The NABCB has been certifying inspection bodies as per ISO/IEC 17020 since 2013.

Table 1: List of certification bodies in various fields as on 27 December 2021

S. No.	*Certification bodies for*	*No. of certification bodies*
1.	Environmental Management Systems	15
2.	Energy Management Systems	5
3.	Food Safety Management Systems	20
4.	Information Security Management Systems	8
5.	Information Technology Service Management Systems	2
6.	Occupational Health and Safety Management Systems	11
7.	Product Certification Body	23
8.	Certification of Persons	7
9.	Quality Management Systems	41
10.	Medical Devices Quality Management Systems	14
11.	Trustworthy Digital Repositories Management System	1
12.	Greenhouse Gas Validation and Verification Bodies	3
13.	Indian Certification of Medical Devices (ICMED)	7

There are 83 inspection bodies, the list of which is available on the NBACB website.

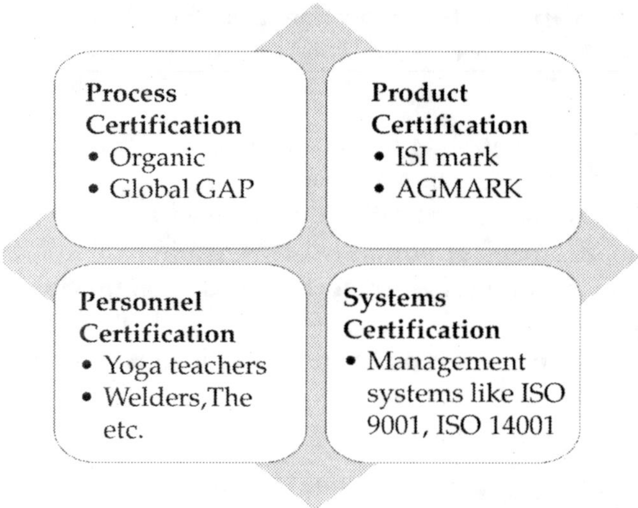

Figure 12: Kinds of Certifications by NABCB

The National Accreditation Board for Testing & Calibration Laboratories (NABL), on the other hand, accredits labs for testing and calibration as per ISO/IEC 17011. "Conformity Assessment—Requirements for Accreditation bodies" accrediting conformity assessment bodies. It also provides voluntary accreditation services to:

- Testing laboratories in accordance with ISO/IEC 17025 'General Requirements for the Competence of Testing and Calibration Laboratories'
- Calibration laboratories in accordance with ISO/IEC 17025 'General Requirements for the Competence of Testing and Calibration Laboratories'
- Medical testing laboratories in accordance with ISO 15189 'Medical laboratories—Requirements for quality and competence'
- Proficiency Testing Providers (PTP) in accordance with ISO/IEC 17043 "Conformity assessment—General requirements for proficiency testing", and
- Reference material producers (RMP) in accordance with ISO 17034 "General requirements for the competence of reference material producers".

The NABL is a signatory to ILAC as well as to APAC for the accreditation of Testing and Calibration Laboratories (ISO/IEC 17025), Medical Testing Laboratories (ISO 15189), Proficiency Testing Providers (PTP) (ISO/IEC 17043) and Reference Materials Producers (RMP). The following is the scope of accreditation by the NABL. Depending on the expertise of the labs, they may have to apply separately for separate disciplines.

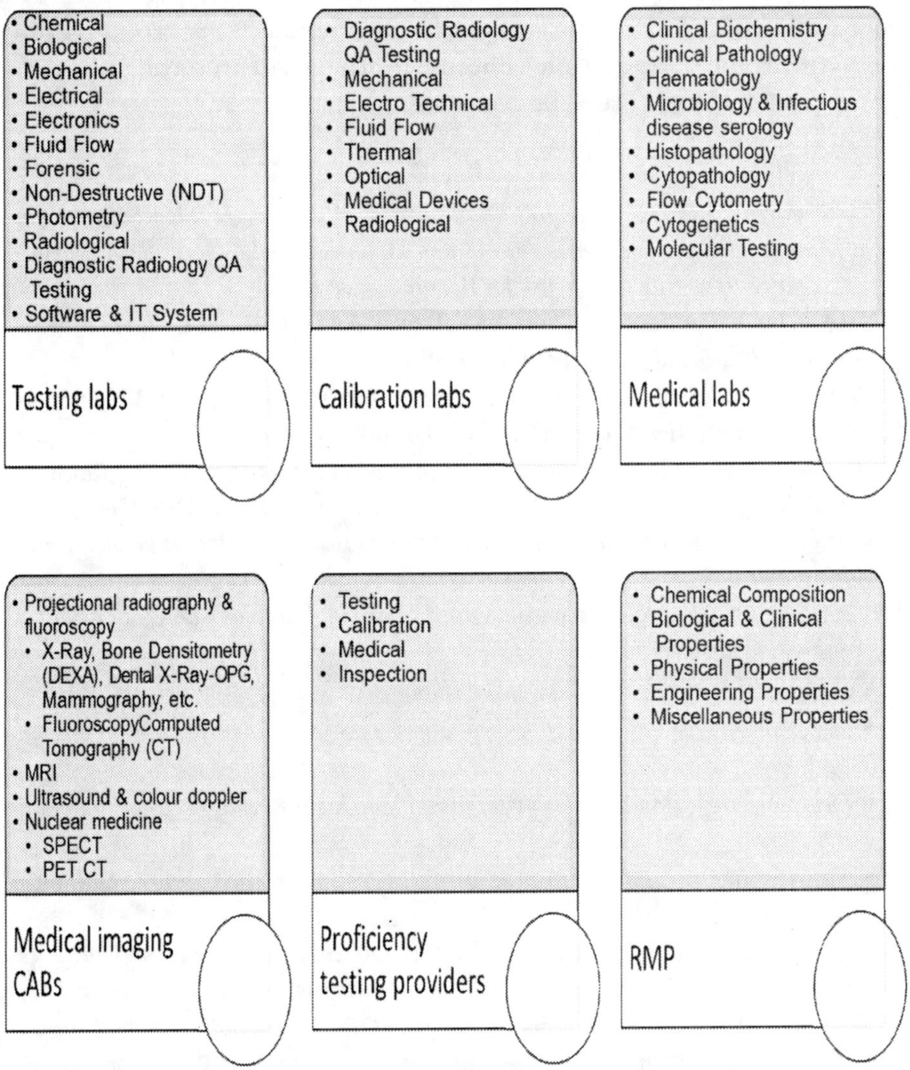

Figure 13: Voluntary accreditation services by the NABCB

BIS Standards Developing Organization (SDO) recognition scheme

The BIS has a parallel Standards Developing Organization (SDO) recognition scheme. The scheme has statutory backing of the BIS Act, 2016 and BIS Rules, 2018 and has its origin in the Standards Conclave document, the Indian National Strategy for Standardization (INSS). As part of the first goal of standards development, it was suggested that a recognition scheme of SDOs be developed, so that SDOs working in specific sectors and looking for validation of their processes and recognition of their standards as per Indian Standards are brought under one umbrella. Under this scheme, both governmental and non-governmental SDOs are to be covered.

RDSO

The Research Designs & Standards Organization (RDSO) is the sole R&D Wing of the Ministry of Railways, and is one of India's leading Standard formulating bodies undertaking standardization work for the railway sector.

In 1903, the Indian Railway Conference Association (IRCA) was set up to provide for standardization and coordination amongst various Railway systems.

This was followed by the Central Standards Office (CSO) established in 1930 at Shimla for preparation of designs, standards, and specifications.

The Research Section of the CSO was reorganized as the Railway Testing Research Centre (RTRC) and established on 1 September 1952 as a separate Directorate of the Railway Board with headquarters at Lucknow and two sub-centres at Lonavala and Chittaranjan.

In 1957, the CSO and RTRC were integrated into a single unit as RDSO at Lucknow. Its functions include:

- *Development of new and improved designs*
- *Development, adoption, and absorption of new technology for use on Indian Railways*
- *Development of standards for materials and products specially needed by Indian Railways*
- *Technical investigation, statutory clearances, testing and providing consultancy services*
- *Inspection of critical and safety items of rolling stock, locomotives, signalling & telecommunication equipment and track components*

The scope of the RDSO's recognition as SDO, is "Standards Developing Organization for products, processes and services the for railway transportation sector in India".

This scheme is aimed to strengthen the 'One Nation One Standard' vision. Through this scheme, the BIS aims at aggregating and integrating the existing capabilities and dedicated domain-specific expertise available with various organizations in the country engaged in standards development in their specific sectors. The Research Design & Standards Organization (RDSO) of Indian Railways has become the first institution to be declared an SDO under the "One Nation One Standard" mission by the BIS.

Conformity assessment by BIS

BIS carries out conformity assessment under four different heads:

I. Product certification

Under the new BIS (Conformity Assessment) Regulations, 2018, the BIS has nine conformity assessment schemes for regulators to choose from for mandating conformity assessment procedure for their products. Most of the ministries/departments opt for Scheme-I of Schedule-II of the BIS (Conformity Assessment) Regulations, 2018. Under this scheme, a licence to use the Standard Mark (ISI Mark) on a product is granted to a manufacturer after assessing the manufacturing and testing capabilities of the manufacturer as well as ensuring conformity of the product with the requirements of the relevant Indian Standard(s) through testing. The TRs issued with this CAP are called QCOs. As on 20 July 2022, there are 379 product categories that are under compulsory certification under Scheme-I of Schedule-II of the BIS (Conformity Assessment) Regulations, 2018, such as iron and steel products, chemicals, consumer goods, etc. Details of schemes, products, fees, testing facilities, etc., are mentioned on the BIS website.

This scheme has proved to be burdensome for exporters from other countries during the pandemic period as foreign travel (for inspection pf manufacturing facilities) was restricted. This limited opportunities for grant of licence. However, with the restriction now removed, the BIS is working towards clearing the backlog of applications from foreign manufacturers.

II. System certification

The Management Systems Certification Scheme by the BIS has been operational since 1991. Initially, the BIS started the scheme with Quality Management System Certification (IS/ISO 9001) and, over the years, it has gradually expanded its activities to various other management systems. The NABCB has accredited the Quality Management System, Food Safety Management System, and Environmental Management System Certification Schemes of the BIS.

III. Foreign Manufacturers Certification Scheme (FMCS)

The BIS has been operating this scheme since 2000. Under it, a licence is granted to a foreign manufacturer for use of the standard mark of the BIS on a product that conforms to an Indian Standard. The scheme is applicable for grant of licence for all products in Scheme-I of Schedule-II of the BIS (Conformity Assessment) Regulations, 2018 (except Electronics & IT Goods notified by MeitY).

IV. Registration scheme

This scheme uses CAPs mentioned in Scheme-II of Schedule-II of the BIS (Conformity Assessment) Regulations, 2018. As per this scheme, no factory inspection is required as the time of grant of a licence. It is granted based on registration based on self-declaration of conformity for goods and articles as per Indian Standards.

MeitY, using this scheme, has notified "Electronics and Information Technology Goods (Requirement for Compulsory Registration) Order, 2012" on 3 October 2012 for fifteen categories of electronics items. Fifteen more product categories were added by MeitY under this order in 2014. Another thirteen product categories were added under this order in 2017. Thus, most of the products notified under this scheme are electronic & IT goods. Regulations under this scheme are called Compulsory Registration Order.

In addition to these certification schemes, ministries/departments can choose any scheme from the BIS (Conformity Assessment) Regulations, 2018, for regulating their products under the BIS Act, 2016.

REFERENCES

- https://www.iso.org/developing-standards.html
- https://www.iec.ch/who-we-are

- https://www.bis.gov.in/index.php/standards/standard-formulation/process-of-setting-standards/
- https://iaf.nu/en/home/
- https://solar-rating.org/faq/whats-the-difference-between-testing-and-certification/
- https://www.linkedin.com/pulse/testing-evaluation-certification-why-difference-should-beauchamp?articleId=6541282187126337536
- https://casco.iso.org/techniques-and-schemes.html
- https://www.services.bis.gov.in:8071/php/BIS_2.0/sdo/sdonew/SDO-recognition-scheme-document.pdf
- https://journalsofindia.com/one-nation-one-standard-mission/?print=pdf
- https://www.bis.gov.in/index.php/system-certification-overview/systems-certification/
- https://www.bis.gov.in/index.php/fmcs/fmcs-overview/
- https://www.intechopen.com/chapters/71866

CHAPTER TWO

REGULATIONS IN DIFFERENT SECTORS

After elaboration of concepts, this section presents regulatory regimes in developed and developing countries, that are major trade partners in that sector. Based on the discussion, the challenges faced by exporters of developing countries, like India, are elaborated and how one can overcome such challenges posed in the form of NTBs or other regulatory difficulties.

AUTOMOBILES

The automobile sector is at the core of any manufacturing economy. It not only caters to the transportation requirements, technology, and brand of a nation but also serves as an important link among various sectors. It has a multiplier effect on other industries like steel, chemicals, textiles, etc. and is a major source of employment generation. Globally, in 2020, the automobile sector accounted for an export of USD 1.26 trillion. This is about 7 per cent of global exports. The largest importer is the USA, followed by Germany, China, France, and the UK. Together, these countries account for 45 per cent of the total import basket of the world.

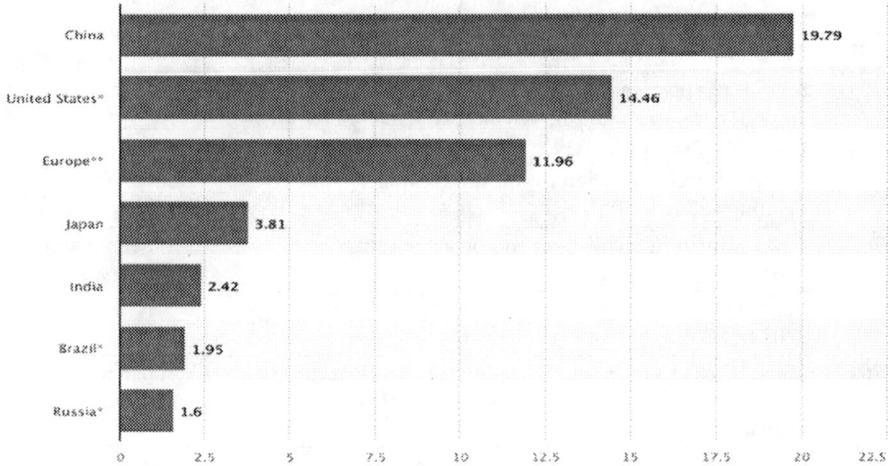

Figure 14: New car registration in million units

Based on new car registrations data, China is the largest market followed by the USA, EU, Japan, and India. China's motorization rate indicates that there is less than one car for every five individuals. In the USA, there are in excess of 800 motor vehicles per 1,000 inhabitants. In terms of brands, Toyota was ranked as the automobile brand with the highest brand value.

In 2019, the world's most traded cars, disaggregated at HS 6-digit level were medium sized cars (USD 281 billion), small sized cars (USD 119 billion), medium diesel engine cars (USD 105 billion), large sized cars (USD 90.9 billion), and other vehicles including gas turbine powered (USD 84.2 billion).

Automobile goods are exported and imported under chapter 87 of HS Code classification of 2017. At the 4-digit level, there are 16 sub-tariff classifications, from 8701 to 8716. HS code-wise break-up of the sector in four major segments (two-wheelers, three-wheelers, passenger vehicles, and commercial vehicles) is as follows:

Table 2: 4 digit level HS codes for chapter 87

HS code	*Description*	*Segment*
8701	Tractors (other than tractors of heading 8709)	—
8702	Public-transport type passenger motor vehicles	Passenger vehicles/ three-wheelers
8703	Motor cars and other motor vehicles for transport of persons(excluding 8702) including racing cars, etc.	Passenger vehicles
8704	Motor vehicles for the transport of goods	Commercial vehicles
8705	Special purpose motor vehicles (e.g., breakdown lorries, crane lorries, fire-fighting vehicles, concrete mixer lorries, road sweepers, etc.	Commercial vehicles
8706	Chassis fitted with engines, for motor vehicles under headings 8701 to 8705	Commercial and passenger vehicles
8707	Bodies (including cabs), for motor vehicles under headings 8701 to 8705	Commercial and passenger vehicles
8708	Parts and accessories of motor vehicles under headings 8701 to 8705	Parts
8709	Work trucks used in factories, dock areas/airports, etc., for short-distance transport of goods; tractors used on railway platforms	Commercial vehicles
8710	Tanks and other armoured fighting vehicles, motorized, whether or not fitted with weapons, and parts of such vehicles	—
8711	Motorcycles (including mopeds) and cycles fitted with an auxiliary motor, with or without side-cars;	Two-wheelers
8712	Bicycles and other cycles (including delivery tricycles), not motorised	—
8713	Invalid carriages, w/n motorised/otherwise mechanically propelled	—
8714	Parts and accessories of vehicles under headings 8711-8713	Parts
8715	Baby carriages and parts thereof	—
8716	Trailers and semi-trailers; other vehicles, not mechanically propelled; parts thereof	Commercial vehicles

India

India is the world's fourth-largest vehicle market[2] and is expected to be the world's third-largest automotive market in terms of volume by 2026. Currently, India manufactures USD 26 million of vehicles in all categories. Two-wheelers and passenger cars accounted for 80.8 per cent and 12.9 per cent market share, respectively. Passenger car sales are dominated by small and mid-sized cars. It is the largest tractor manufacturer, second-largest bus manufacturer and third largest heavy trucks manufacturer in the world. India is fast catching up in the new segment of Electric Vehicles (EVs) which is expected to create five crore jobs, directly and indirectly.

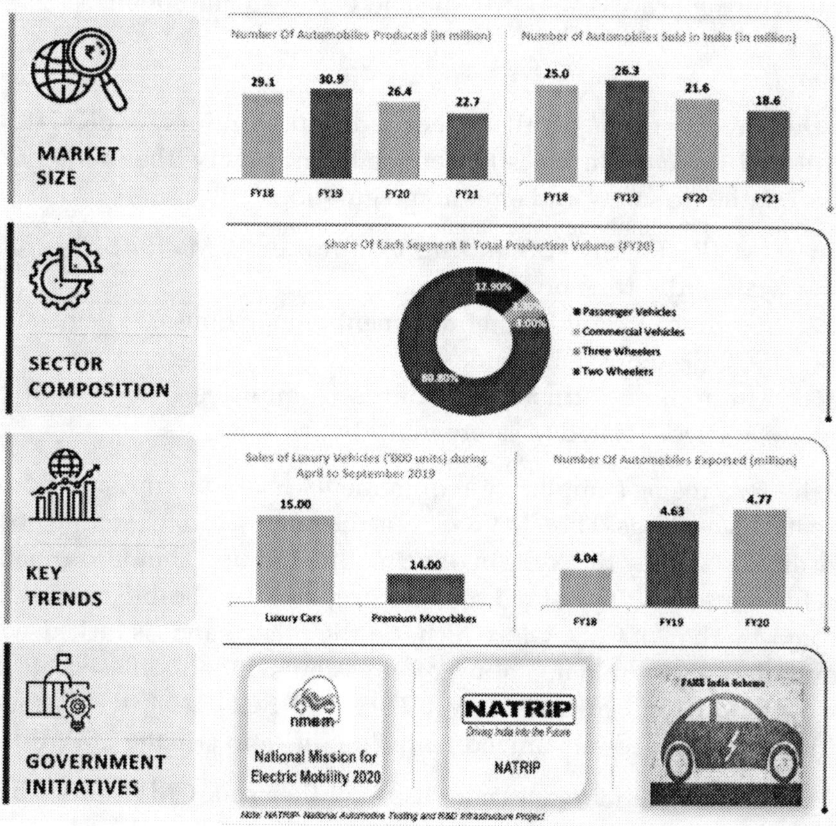

Figure 15: IBEF snapshot-automobiles

2. Excluding the European Union.

Regulatory regime

Regulators

The Ministry of Road Transport and Highways (MoRTH) is the regulating ministry that regulates the sector through the Motor Vehicles Act, 1988 (MVA) read with the Central Motor Vehicles Rules, 1989 (CMV Rules). The MVA regulates construction equipment, and maintenance of automobiles with respect to various parameters such as dimensions, emission norms, automobile parts (e.g., brakes, steering gears, safety devices). The checks and controls are formulated at the stages of (i) proposal to manufacture or import a new automobile; (ii) during the manufacturing process; and (iii) sale and use of an automobile.

Standards

For the involvement of all concerned stakeholders, MoRTH has constituted three committees to deliberate and advise the ministry on issues relating to safety and emission regulations:

1. CMVR: Technical Standing Committee (CMVR-TSC)—main standard setting body
2. Standing Committee on Implementation of Emission Legislation (SCOE)—emission standards
3. Automotive Industry Standards Committee (AISC)—adopts standards related to safety made by the BIS

The two major compliance requirements relate to emission norms and safety standards. The CMVR-TSC is the main standard setting body. They are assisted by the AISC in drafting the technical standards related to vehicular safety. The standards are prepared by the BIS, which are adopted by the AISC. SCOE, which, on the other hand, is tasked with formulation and implementation of emission standards. Based on the recommendations of the CMVR-TSC and SCOE, MoRTH issues notifications for necessary amendments/modifications in the CMV Rules.

Additionally, certain states may also have their state CMV Rules. These are mostly related to seating arrangement in transport vehicles.

Regulation

Under Rule 126 of the CMVR, various test agencies have been established to test and certify vehicles based on the safety standards and emission norms prescribed by the ministry. Every manufacturer of a motor vehicle has to submit a prototype of the vehicle to be manufactured to any of the test agencies mentioned below. After testing the vehicle for compliance of all standards and norms, the test agency shall grant a certificate to the manufacturer.

The test agencies are:

- Automotive Research Association of India (ARAI), Pune
- Vehicle Research and Development Establishment, Ahmednagar
- Central Farm Machinery Testing and Training Institute, Budni
- Indian Institute of Petroleum, Dehradun
- Central Institute of Road Transport, Pune
- International Centre for Automotive Technology, Manesar

ARAI

The Automotive Research Association of India (ARAI), established in 1966, is the leading automotive R&D organization of the country set up by the automotive industry with the Government of India. It is an autonomous body affiliated to the Ministry of Heavy Industries. It is one of the prime testing and certification agencies notified by the Government of India under Rule 126 of the Central Motor Vehicle Rules, 1989.

The ARAI is certified to ISO 9001, ISO 14001, ISO 27001 and ISO 45001; and is also accredited for its testing and calibration scope as per ISO/IEC 17025 by the NABL.

United States of America

Major imports by the USA are from Mexico, Japan, Canada, Korea, and Germany. Historically, the USA imported its major requirements from Mexico and Canada under the North American Free Trade Agreement (NAFTA). However, after the enforcement of the United States-Mexico-Canada Agreement (USMCA) in July 2020, exports to the USA from Mexico and Canada have dipped. This is due to the changed provisions in the USMCA. Under NAFTA, the only requirement was to manufacture 62.5 per cent of the vehicle components in North America. In the revised USMCA, the requirement has been upped to 75 per cent. A new requirement was also added that 40 to 45 per cent of the parts must be from a factory paying USD 16/hour. For a developing country like Mexico, the latter is a difficult condition to fulfil as wages in Mexico (USD 3.14/hour) are lower than those in the USA.

The major American brands are Buick, Cadillac, Chevrolet, GMC, Chrysler, Dodge, Jeep, Ram, Ford, Lincoln, and Tesla. The major manufacturing units are located on the eastern side of the USA. What is unique about the automobile sector is that while setting up a manufacturing unit, it is not just the unit that needs to be set up but the entire supply chain needs to be integrated. That includes iron and steel, plastics, chemicals, auto components, etc.

Regulatory regime

Regulators

The Department of Transportation (DOT) and Environment Protection Agency (EPA) are the two major regulators in the auto segment. The DOT regulates the safety and performance parameters of the vehicle whereas the EPA regulates the emission norms. Other concerned agencies are the Federal Trade Commission and US customs.

Table 3: Regulators in USA for automobiles

Agency	*Scope*
Customs and Border Protection (CBP)	Country of origin
Department of Transportation (DOT)-National Highway Traffic Safety Administration (NHTSA)	Federal motor vehicle safety standards (FMVSS)
Environment Protection Agency (EPA)	Emissions from engines
Federal Trade Commission (FTC)	Packaging, labelling, and advertising

The National Highway Transport Safety Administration (NHTSA) notifies Federal Motor Vehicle Safety Standards (FMVSS) that lays down minimum safety performance requirements for vehicles and 13 equipment items. These include tyres, rims, brake hoses, brake fluid, seat belt assemblies, lighting equipment, glazing, motorcycle helmets, child restraints, compressed natural gas containers, rear impact guards for trailers, platform lift systems for the mobility-impaired, and triangular reflective warning devices.

Interestingly, the NHTSA does not issue type-approval certificates nor does it certify any motor vehicle or equipment as complying to the FMVSS. Instead, under the Vehicles Safety Act, there is a "self-certification" process, which puts the responsibility on the manufacturer to certify its vehicle or equipment items are compliant to FMVSS. The NHTSA only encourages manufacturers to conduct tests for compliance as per the FMVSS.

Standards

In the USA, standards are developed by the private sector. The most common SDO is the American National Standards Institute (ANSI) which is a non-governmental, not-for-profit organization. In the automobile sector, standards are primarily developed by the SAE International and Auto Glass Safety Council. Safety requirements for air bags, child passenger safety, seat belts, and tyres are mentioned separately.

Regulation

The USA market has either the U.S. version of vehicles or non-U.S. version. The U.S. version complies with 'federal emission requirements'. Such vehicles carry an "EPA emission compliance" label or need a written statement from the manufacturer's U.S. representative. Canadian vehicles can be imported into the USA as "Canada version vehicles". The "Transport Canada label" is considered equivalent to the American EPA label.

For all imports, a permanent resident of the USA needs to be designated as an agent for service of process. Non-conforming vehicles can be imported either by certification or by exemption:

(i) The *certification* will have to be done by an Independent Commercial Importer. This is a requirement under the Clean Air Act.

(ii) The *exemption* criterion are for testing, repair, display, and racing. Additionally, the U.S. Department of Agriculture (USDA) requires that the undercarriage of the imported vehicle be free of foreign soil to safeguard against importation of dangerous pests.

In the USA, apart from the federal TRs, some state-level regulations are also applicable that are more stringent than the federal laws. These include regulations in the field of labelling, packaging, and toxic chemicals. For example, in California, all vehicles need to carry the following:

WARNING: This product contains chemicals known to the State of California to cause cancer and birth defects or other reproductive harm.

Similarly, in the State of Illinois, if lead-based paint or a lead-bearing substance is used, the following is required:

WARNING: Contains lead. May be harmful if eaten or chewed. May generate dust containing lead. keep out of reach of children.

European Union

The European Union (EU) is one of the biggest markets and an exporter of automobiles. Germany is the biggest importer as well as the biggest exporter in the EU. Some of the well-known brands like Volkswagen, Mercedes-Benz, Audi, BMW, and Porsche have their origin in Germany.

Table 4: Popular brands of EU (automobiles)

Brand	*Founding year*	*Founded by*
Volkswagen	1937	Government agency in Berlin
Mercedes-Benz	1926	Karl Benz & Gottlieb Daimler in Stuttgart
Audi	1910	August Horch in Zwickau
BMW	1916	Karl Rapp in Munich
Porsche	1931	Ferdinand Porsche in Stuttgart

There are no country-specific regulations in this sector. All the TRs are harmonized across the borders within the Union.

The EU had actively participated in the formation of a global forum for TRs in the automobile sector, i.e., the United Nations Economic Commission for Europe (UNECE). It was formed as one of the five regional commissions under the UNECOSOC[3] to promote economic cooperation and integration among its member-states. The regulations provide rules for safety and environment protection.

Under its aegis, a World Forum for Harmonization of Vehicle Regulations (WP.29) has been actively working towards creation of a harmonized set of regulations. There are two major agreements—the 1958 and 1998 agreements.

The 1958 Agreement provides a legal and administrative context for harmonization with performance tests, conformity of production, mutual recognition of type approvals and administrative procedures to grant them. The 1958 Agreement has 56 contracting parties. The 1998 Agreement

3. United Nations Economic and Social Council

runs parallel to the 1958 Agreement and builds on it by the development of Global Prescription Regulations (GTR) for wheeled vehicles, equipment and parts which can be fitted and/or be used on wheeled vehicles. However, this Agreement does not provide for mutual recognition of GTRs.

India signed the 1998 Agreement in February 2006. It has currently more than 70 per cent safety regulations, which are either partially or fully technically aligned with UN Regulations while retaining India-specific driving and environmental conditions.

Regulatory regime

Regulation

The EU recognizes the Whole Vehicle Type-Approval system under which a manufacturer can obtain certification for a vehicle type in one EU country and then use that certification to sell its cars across other EU member-states. Tests on prototypes of vehicles are done for installation of lights, braking performance, stability control, crash tests with dummies, noise and emissions limits as well as production requirements (of individual parts and components, such as seats or steering wheel airbags). Each EU member-state has a designated National Type Approval Authority (TAA) (e.g., RDW in the Netherlands, KBA in Germany) that ensures that the tests on the vehicles have been done appropriately.

Emission

It is not just the pre-certificate emission norms that are tested by EU authorities but on-road vehicles are also tested to see if they still follow emission norms during use. This is done through market surveillance with the right to impose penalties in case of non-compliance.

Safety

Safety is one of the important parameters for vehicles in the EU. Norms for safety of vehicle occupants such as children and road users—pedestrians and cyclists—are primary. Table 5 mentions requirements that are mandatory from 2022:

Table 5: Mandatory requirements from 2022

For cars, vans, trucks, and buses	Warning of driver drowsiness and distraction—use of mobile phone while driving—reversing safety with camera/sensors, data recorder
For cars and vans	Lane-keeping assistance, emergency braking and crash test, improved safety belts
For trucks and buses	Specific requirements to improve the direct vision of bus and truck drivers and remove blind spots, and systems at the front and sides of the vehicle to detect and warn of vulnerable road users, especially when making turns

Other requirements

The compliance requirement for automobiles includes compliance to other indirect legislations of the EU. One such regulation is REACH, to which the manufacturer and all those involved in the supply chain have to abide by. This includes providing safety data of chemicals for registration, evaluation and use, etc.

In the new set of regulations, the Original Equipment Manufacturers (OEMs) are required to provide technical information captured by onboard devices (OBDs) and other vehicle components to independent vehicle repair operators so that they have an equal ability to compete with authorized dealers. The regulation furthers the concept of an "extended vehicle" which includes not just the physical form of the vehicle but also the data it creates.

China

China has emerged as a major manufacturing hub of automobiles in recent decades. Not only has it aced the competition of attracting foreign investment in the sector, but has also built up its industry and its own brand. Its company, BYD, has become a leader in the electric vehicle segment across the globe. China imported about USD 63.9 billion of automobiles and auto parts in 2020 and exported about USD 76.2 billion vehicles during the same period. The USA is its largest market with exports of USD 14 billion. The largest exported product to the USA by China are parts and components for tractors and larger vehicles. The major Chinese brands are BYD, SAIC Motor, NIO, Geely, Great Wall Motor, Xpeng Motors, GAC Group, Li Auto, FAW Group, and Changan Automobiles.

Regulatory regime

Just like the markets of developed countries, China's auto sector is also heavily regulated.

Regulator

The concerned ministry in China is the Ministry of Industry and Information Technology (MIIT) that oversees a wide variety of technology fields and institutions, including basic and applied scientific research, industrial policy, China's telecommunications industry, internet regulation, cyber security, radio frequency regulation, emergency broadcasting, etc. The MIIT is supported by the State Administration for Market Regulation (SAMR) for licensing processes and China's Certification & Accreditation Administration (CNCA) for certification.

Standards

The national standards followed in China are commonly known as GB standards.

GB standards

GB standards are China's national standards, also called Guobiao Standards. They are classified under two types: mandatory and recommended. Mandatory standards have the force of law as do other technical regulations in China. They are enforced by laws and administrative regulations and concern the protection of human health, personal property, and safety. All standards that fall outside these characteristics are considered recommended standards.

China's GB standards can be identified as mandatory or recommended by their prefix code. The prefix code GB is used to denote mandatory standards, whereas GB/T are recommended standards (Quasi-mandatory standards).

Regulation

(A) PERFORMANCE

A manufacturer must meet the relevant mandatory standards, obtain a China Compulsory Certification (CCC) and pass inspection by a quality inspection institution. Each vehicle model is subject to an "access permit for automobile manufacturers and their products" granted by the MIIT.

Apart from performance requirements, there are other conditions for manufacturing in China such as venue for manufacturing, capital, workforce, etc.

(B) ENVIRONMENT/EMISSION

Environment-related norms are implemented under the National Environmental Protection Catalogue that are to be complied with by the manufacturer.

For manufacturing of automobile parts, the regulatory system is slightly different. A production licence is to be obtained from the SAMR, in addition to following GB standards and obtaining a CCC from CNCA for tyres, vehicle windows, rear-view mirrors, safety belts, seats, and door locks. Follow-up factory inspections are to be done to maintain the validity of the CCC.

China has introduced a cyber security law that is applicable to manufacturers, dealers, and online ride-hailing services operating through mobile applications. As per the regulation, personal information should be stored in China only.

Japan

Vehicle manufacturing is an important pillar of the Japanese economy, the common brands being Honda, Nissan, and Toyota. Japan's automobile market has matured and there is very limited space for growth in the traditional segment. It imported USD 19.78 million worth of vehicles and its parts in 2020 and exported USD 122.47 million during the same period. Japan imported about 39 per cent of its requirements from Germany and China. Its major imports from Germany are passenger vehicles with a capacity of more than 1500 cm^3 but less than 3000 cm^3, whereas its imports from China are parts and accessories of vehicles and bicycles. It is evident that China is an important link in Japan's supply chain for manufacturing.

Being an island country, space is valuable in Japan. Maximum benefits are drawn out of limited spaces. To take care of space, ageing population, and single households, Japanese have opted for Kei cars. These are box cars with length less than 3.4 metres and a maximum width of 1.48 metres. The engine capacity is restricted to 0.66 litres. They are specific to Japan.

Regulatory regime

Regulator

The agency that handles vehicle certification and homologation is the Ministry of Land, Industry, Transport and Tourism (MLITT). The testing is done by the National Agency for Automobile and Land Transport Technology (NALTEC).

Regulation

The governing regulation is the Road Transport Vehicle Act (Act No. 185 of 1951). Every vehicle is required to have a type approval certificate for safety and environmental standards.

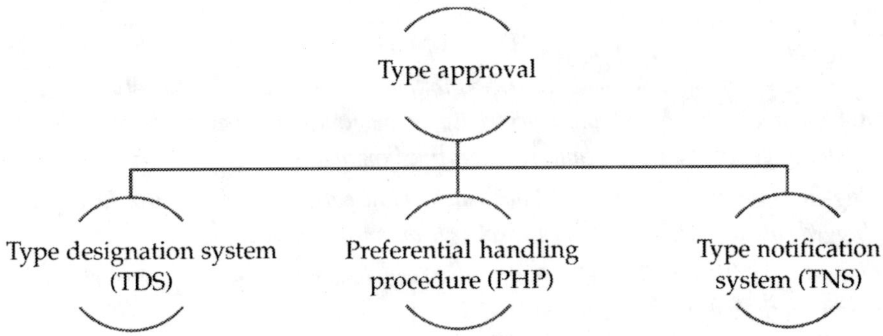

Figure 16: Frameworks for type approval in Japan for automobiles

Type designation system (TDS): This is the most common framework for type approval for passenger cars that includes inspection of sample vehicles and quality control systems. It is to be done at the factory. For overseas manufacturers, NALTEC sends officials for inspection.

Type notification system (TNS): This kind of type approval is suitable for heavy duty vehicles. A sample of vehicles is inspected. The inspection of quality control systems is omitted.

Preferential handling procedure for imported motor vehicles (PHP): This is specific to imported vehicles of less than 5,000 in number. The vehicle is sent to NALTEC. No sample testing is done but one in every fifty vehicles are tested for emission standards by NALTEC.

Japan is a member of UNECE. The UNECE World Forum for Harmonization of Vehicle Regulations held in November 2017 (WP.29) adopted the International Whole Vehicle Type Approval (IWVTA) together with UN Regulation No. R0 (UNR0). This came into effect in 2018. As a member that ratifies UNR0, Japan will reciprocally accept vehicle inspection certificates issued by other countries.

Looking ahead

The automobile sector is undergoing a drastic change with the increasing acceptability of electric vehicles (EVs). Technologically-advanced countries and those countries that either have natural resources for EVs or are able to gather such resources are becoming pioneers in this evolving segment. Hybrid EVs (HEVs), Plug-in hybrid EVs (PHEVs), Battery EVs (BEVs) and Fuel Cell EVs (FCEVs) are the major categories of EVs. They are differentiated by technologies.

Types of EVs

Hybrid EVs (HEVs): A small electric motor assists the internal combustion engine (ICE). Under a light load, only electricity is consumed. The battery is replenished by energy generated by ICE and regenerative braking.

Plug-in hybrid EVs (PHEVs): Powered by both petrol and electricity. It may be plugged into a charging station to recharge an on-board battery.

Battery EVs (BEVs): No ICE, fuel tank or exhaust pipe. Uses only electricity to power up the battery.

Fuel Cell EVs (FCEVs): Run on compressed liquid hydrogen, which is combined with air inside fuel stack to produce electricity and water.

One of the key components of EVs, is the battery. Lithium is its basis. Latin American and African countries are rich in lithium reserves. However, since, these countries have not evolved their own automobile manufacturing industry, they make most of it by outsourcing mining of resources to countries such as China and the USA. For countries like India, this luxury is unavailable. Even though there are initiatives to promote manufacturing of EVs, the battery is the major stumbling block, which limits the ability of manufacturers.

In EVs, the battery is the soul of the vehicle. They are lithium based that circulate electrons from negative to positive electrodes when in use and vice versa when charging. Recent accidents related to batteries have questioned the safety of EVs. A sodium ion-based battery is being considered as an alternative to a lithium ion one. This is a relatively new concept and will bring in first mover advantage because sodium is more abundant than lithium. The one that moves first to capitalize it is likely to capture the market. The larger companies operating in the battery segment should consider investing in R&D in this segment. This will help in gaining markets.

"Future mobility" is key to the change leading to environment-friendly, integrated, automated, and personalized travel. Countries having a large focus on R&D will have a head start in the dynamic market. To promote EVs and protect the environment, countries are providing tax exemption on purchase of vehicles and subsidies for manufacturing them. For example, China has set up "green channels" for grant of licence plates in major cities where its issuance is under a quota system.

In the traditional automobile sector, exporters have a very different set of challenges than from an evolving market. Type approval is a common feature across countries. The liability for the approval lies with the manufacturer in some countries. Up to now, emission and safety standards were the deciding factors for promoting or prohibiting trade. However, with the new performance standards, the level of barriers has changed.

Since setting up of an automotive sector is a huge investment (which includes setting up of ancillary industries and a supply chain), stability in policy and willingness of the manufacturer are crucial elements to the success of the sector. The volume of domestic production has to meet the demand for vehicles in a country despite imports. Separate assembly lines may also be required for complying with varied norms by various countries. The sector is important to economies as it generates employment and investments. No wonder it is a closely regulated sector.

The exporter, thus, has to be an established brand to be able to meet the import requirements of other countries. There is limited space for small and new players in vehicle manufacturing. However, in the ancillary production of parts and accessories, small industries may co-exist but the competition is heightened due to patents on technologies.

Every new requirement is burdensome on the exporter who has to comply to import requirements or lose a share to its competitors. If today an exporter is exporting a passenger vehicle with two seat belts for the rear passengers to a country *Alpha*, and *Alpha* changes its norms to mandate import of three seat belts for rear passengers, the exporter will have to amend the design, supply chain, and assembly line to adhere to the revised norms. The same holds good for emission norms. Any change that disturbs the existing set-up is a barrier as it amounts to additional costs for the exporter.

Internal combustion engine vehicles are expected to taper in demand in major markets because of evolution of EVs and support by various governments to encourage domestic manufacturing. Since vehicular emission is one of the major sources of pollution, countries are cutting down on emission norms to meet climate change goals. Promotion and adoption of EVs is the quickest method to do so. EVs have zero emission. Hence, a country acing this segment will not only dominate the future mobility market but also earn parallel gains in achieving climate change goals.

The COVID-19 pandemic affected the industry holistically and reduced the purchasing power of consumers. With people losing jobs, even automotive manufacturers had to lay off workers as supply was exceeding demand. This has given an opportunity to the use of online platforms for sales. Many consumers now prefer to experience the vehicle online through simulation modules before deciding on the final purchase.

The challenges of the slowdown in demand and the COVID-19 pandemic after-effects appear to be short lived. However, the shift in the form of EVs, online sales and downstream value chain needs to be factored into the long-term strategy of exporters. This may also include exploring avenues of ancilliary services such as fuel, service, financial transactions, resale value, etc.

The automobile sector is a sensitive sector for opening up of trade. Even if tariff reduction or elimination obligations are taken by countries in their FTAs, the NTMs ensure that no unregulated imports can take place. For developed countries like the EU that have annexures on automobiles in their FTAs to gain greater market access for their products by way of harmonizing technical regulations and mutual acceptance of test certificates, this is a new and a faster channel to aid their industry to enter and capture markets. However, for countries like India that have both demand and supply markets, opening up of the sector to other countries needs to be done cautiously through FTAs, mutual agreements, and other means of cooperation with manufacturing countries.

Developing countries have an advantage of a cheaper workforce but the skill part needs to be emphasized. Countries that are looking to establish themselves as exporting hubs have to focus on the training of the workforce. This should include rolling out specific courses and diplomas in specialized areas, assistive schemes to start businesses in ancillary sectors of automobiles, etc.

In terms of opportunities, there is little possibility of penetration of EVs in developing countries because for the functioning of EVs, the entire infrastructure has to be set up. This will require a greater involvement of the governments and incentives by them for purchase of vehicles. Additional efforts have to be made by the government to promote acceptance of EVs by consumers. India has realized this and is taking measures to promote manufacture, sale, and purchase of EVs.

Developing countries and LDCs are more prone to becoming dumping grounds by developed countries for second-hand vehicles, which no longer meet safety, performance or emission norms in the countries of origin. This market is unregulated and growing fast. Between 2015 and 2018, as per a UNEP report, developed countries such as the USA, the EU and Japan exported 14 million used passenger cars abroad, with 70 per cent ending up in low-income developing countries in Africa, Eastern Europe, Asia, Latin America and the Middle East. If this trade is left unregulated, it may have an effect on climate change and public health in the decades to come. A few countries have started taking steps to crack down on the oldest and dirtiest used cars: Kenya now accepts only imports of vehicles less than eight years old, mainly from Japan. As a result, its vehicle fleet is about one-third more fuel-efficient than that of neighbouring Uganda, which only last year set an age limit of 15 years for its imported cars.

For India, that has an established name in this sector, we need to divest exports in newer segments that should not be limited to goods but also extend to services. This is an opportunity for small companies and start-ups to bring out innovative services such as software development, interior and exterior designing, simulations, etc.

With growing population and increasing density in cities, mobility options are never going to die. A smarter way is to live in the future and plan for it today.

REFERENCES

- ITC TradeMap as on 6.6.2021
- https://www.investindia.gov.in/sector/automobile
- https://www.ibef.org/industry/india-automobiles/infographic
- https://edition.cnn.com/2019/05/31/business/mexico-tariffs-auto-industry/index.html
- https://www.investopedia.com/terms/n/nafta.asp

- https://www.caranddriver.com/features/g25062312/american-car-brands/
- Overview of EPA Import Requirements for Vehicles and Engines, United States, Environment Protection Agency, - March 2011
- A Guide to United States Imported Motor Vehicle Equipment and Parts Compliance Requirements, Lisa M. Benson, Karen Reczek; National Institute of Standards and Technology, U.S. Department of Commerce, revised August 2016
- https://www.statista.com/statistics/269872/largest-automobile-markets-worldwide-based-on-new-car-registrations/
- https://www.pcbusa.com/post/3-steps-to-import-vehicle-to-us-8281
- https://carleasespecialoffers.co.uk/blog/top-5-german-car-brands/
- https://ec.europa.eu/growth/sectors/automotive_en
- https://ec.europa.eu/growth/sectors/automotive/technical-harmonisation/faq-auto_en
- https://gowlingwlg.com/en/insights-resources/articles/2018/how-will-brexit-affect-automotive-regulation/?utm_source=Mondaq&utm_medium=syndication&utm_campaign=LinkedIn-integration
- https://otonomo.io/blog/extended-vehicles-a-new-eu-regulation-based-framework-for-car-data-access/
- https://www.lexology.com/library/detail.aspx?g=41615083-c7f9-444b-800d-2dc9672a5f0f
- https://www.jtnfa.com/en/booksdetail.aspx?type=06001&keyid= 00000000000000003022&PageUrl=majorbook&Lan=EN
- https://incompliancemag.com/article/an-overview-of-automotive-vehicle-and-component-regulations-in-china-2/
- https://www.jdsupra.com/legalnews/china-publishes-new-draft-regulations-5022773/
- https://pandaily.com/the-10-most-valuable-automobile-companies-in-china-2020/
- https://www.statista.com/topics/6560/mini-cars-in-japan/
- https://www.lexology.com/library/detail.aspx?g=34c0c790-e3b0-49f8-8e0e-5f4ca3a5b22d
- https://www.lexology.com/library/detail.aspx?g=96fe928c-a7ac-4ddc-828f-a04c09d80ca9
- https://www.siam.in/technical-regulation.aspx?mpgid=31&pgidtrail=34
- https://oec.world/en/profile/hs92/cars?disaggregationValue=value0
- https://www.automotiveworld.com/articles/what-is-the-future-of-mobility/
- An Assessment of Japanese Automakers' Impact & Activity in the United States, Centre for Automotive Research: Bernard Swiecki, Michael Schultz, Terni Fiorelli, Edgar Faler, and Yen Chen—July 2020.
- https://www.mckinsey.com/industries/automotive-and-assembly/our-insights/reimagining-the-auto-industrys-future-its-now-or-never
- https://home.kpmg/xx/en/home/insights/2019/01/global-automotive-executive-survey-2019.html
- https://www.npr.org/2018/10/17/657806248/will-nafta-2-0-really-boost-mexican-wages
- https://openroadautogroup.com/blog/bev-phev-hev-fcev-key-differences-between-electric-car-options
- https://www.mckinsey.com/industries/automotive-and-assembly/our-insights/

reimagining-the-auto-industrys-future-its-now-or-never
- https://www.mckinsey.com/industries/automotive-and-assembly/our-insights/the-indian-automotive-industry-from-resilience-to-resurgence
- Global trade in used vehicles report—UNEP.
- https://www.nytimes.com/2020/10/26/climate/used-car-export-pollution.html
- https://cset.georgetown.edu/publication/ministry-of-industry-and-information-technology-2022-annual-budget/
- https://www.gbstandards.org/
- https://www.pv-magazine.com/2022/03/26/the-weekend-read-sodium-ion-batteries-go-mainstream/#:~:text=Sodium%2Dion%20(Na%2Dion, making%20the%20chemistry%20particularly%20exciting
- https://timesofindia.indiatimes.com/blogs/voices/why-are-evs-catching-fire-in-india-solution-to-avoid-such-incidents/

CAPITAL GOODS

Capital goods are items used by businesses to produce goods and services such as buildings, machinery, vehicles, tools, etc. However, the focus of this segment is on the machinery sector used for manufacturing goods. This is an important sector for the economy as the output is used in sectors such as engineering, construction, infrastructure, consumer goods, etc.

There is no fixed classification for the machinery sector that is accepted and used globally. They can either be divided using Standard International Trade Classification (SITC) or Standard Industrial Classification (SIC). The SIC classification has been prepared by the USA and is used more prominently. The SITC is a standardized way of classifying goods that are used in statistics on imports and exports. There are other country-specific classifications also. For example, in India, the National Capital Goods Policy (2016) lays down the policy for ten sectors, namely, heavy electrical equipment, process plant equipment, earthmoving and mining machinery, printing machinery, food processing machinery, dies, moulds and press tools, textile machinery, machine tools, plastic machinery, and metallurgical machinery.

Machines are generally traded under Chapter 84 (Machinery, mechanical appliances, nuclear reactors, boilers; parts thereof) of the ITC-HS classification. The variety of machines traded under this HS code can be ascertained from the fact that there are 86 HS codes at the 4-digit level itself, which increase as we move from 4-digit to 6-digit to 8-digit level HS codes.

The total trade under chapter 84 was USD 2.16 trillion in 2020 with the major players being the USA (USD 361 billion), China (USD 191 billion), Germany (USD 150 billion), France (USD 71 billion), and the UK (USD 70 billion). India is the 16th largest trading partner in this segment. The largest segment under which trade of USD 408 billion took place was under HS code 8471 (automatic data processing machines).

One of the important things to understand is that given the wide application of the machinery, it is very difficult to have a single regulation governing numerous requirements in different sectors. E.g. safety requirements while operating construction machinery will be different from that being operated in the printing sector. These requirements are based on the risks involved while operating the machine. Therefore, having separate regulations will be cumbersome. Since the underlying requirement is that of safety and associated emission norms during their operation, the machinery sector has been regulated by various countries based on safety standards. This includes the safety of both mechanical and electrical/electronic components.

India

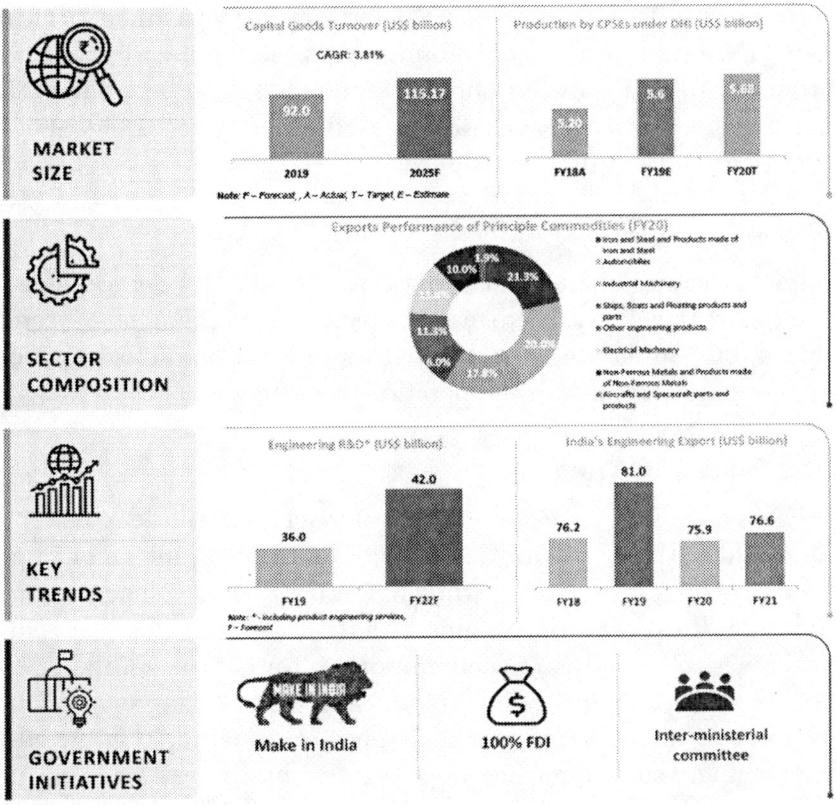

Figure 17: IBEF snapshot: engineering & capital goods

The Capital Goods in India has a market size of USD 43.2 billion. If we look at the export basket of India, chapter 84 accounted for USD 25.4 billion in 2021-22, which is the third largest, with fuel and precious metal, topping the list. India had a trade deficit in this segment by 100 per cent, as imports were USD 50.8 during the same period.

The leading export subsectors in the capital goods sector are heavy electrical and power equipment, earthmoving and mining machinery, and process plant equipment, together accounting for 85 per cent of India's total capital goods exports. The sector also provides approximately 1.4 million direct and 7 million indirect jobs.

Regulatory regime

Regulator

The primary regulator for machinery in India is the Department of Heavy Industry. Depending on sectoral requirements, other ministries may have additional regulatory powers such as for textile-related machinery. The Ministry of Textiles may have additional compliance requirements. The same goes for agricultural machinery.

Regulation

However, it is surprising that India does not have a comprehensive regulation for machinery. There may be piecemeal requirements for certain machines, but unlike the global trend, there is no omnibus regulation based on risks associated with operation of the machinery.

United States of America

The USA is one of the largest importers of machinery (under chapter 84) in the world with imports of USD 361 billion in 2020. Its major import destinations are China, Mexico, Japan, Germany, and Canada. India is the 16th largest exporter of machinery to the USA. About 27 per cent of the machines to the USA are being imported from China. Of these, USD 47.7 billion of imports are under HS code 847130 (mostly laptops). Around 25 per cent of imports under this chapter are of laptops, followed by other machinery such as refrigerators, printing machinery, air or vacuum pumps, spark ignition engines, etc. The major players are Caterpillar, Deere & Co., Parker Hannifin, Xerox Corp., etc.

Similar to the global trend, the USA also has an umbrella regulation implemented by the United States Occupational Health and Safety Administration. One of the most strictly regulated sectors for machinery is the construction sector where the majority of fatalities take place. Details of how the regulation works are mentioned in the following section.

Regulatory regime

Regulator

The regulation is operated by the Department of Labour. It covers both the private and public sectors.

All general and permanent rules by departments and agencies of the US government are published in a Code of Federal Regulations (CFR). It is divided into fifty titles that represent broad subject areas. The subject matter related to labour is mentioned under title 29. The specific part relevant to machinery is mentioned from 1900 to 1910 of this title.

Regulation

The regulation of the Occupational Safety and Health Act (OSHA Act) was passed in 1970 to provide safe and healthy working conditions for workers. Part 1910 of the 29th Code of Federal Regulations (CFR) gives specific standards for machinery operating in various sectors. For example, subpart O of Part 1910 sets standards for machinery and machine guarding, and is divided into Part 1910.211 to Part 1910.219 stating machinery requirements for forging machines, abrasive wheel machinery, mechanical power presses, etc.

OSHA statistics

The United States OSHA cites the construction industry as one of the most dangerous occupations in America. OSHA statistics report that 5,333 workers were fatally injured on the job in 2019. Of those, 20.4 per cent, or 976 workers, were killed on construction projects. That is one in five American workers died due to accidental injuries while working around construction equipment.

According to OSHA, there are four main causes of death and injury to construction workers. OSHA refers to these as the "fatal four" that account for two-thirds of all fatal accidents. The fatal four accident causes (2016 report) are:

1. *Falls: Falling from a height or off-construction equipment accounted for 38.7 per cent of worker deaths.*
2. *Struck by an Object: There were 9.4 per cent of workers who suffered fatal injuries after being hit by an object on a construction site.*
3. *Electrocutions: Being accidentally energized by electricity accounted for 8.3 per cent of construction worker deaths.*

Caught In-Between: The percentage of American construction workers who died after being caught in-between components of construction machinery or materials was 7.3 per cent.

In the USA, applicable safety standards depend on the location of the installed machine. OSHA enforces its standards and may also reference National Consensus standards, such as NFPA, ANSI, etc., as and when needed. In section 1910.132(d)(2), OSHA requires a workplace hazard analysis to be performed. In addition, risk assessment forms the basis of design for machine safeguarding systems. Here, the risk assessment indicates a process by which a team evaluates risk, risk-reduction methods, and team acceptance of the solution. This risk reduction is key in determining the residual risks to which personnel are exposed. Without a risk assessment in place, US safety standards stand violated. A risk assessment is required by the following US standards:

- ANSI[4] B11.0 (Safety of machinery)
- ANSI Z244.1 (Control of hazardous energy lockout/tag out and alternative methods)
- ANSI B11.19 (Performance requirements for risk reduction measures: safeguarding and other means to reduce risk)
- ANSI B155.1 (Safety requirements for the packaging and processing industry)
- ANSI/RIA R15.06 (American national standard for industrial robots and robots systems-safety requirements)
- NFPA[5] 79 (Electrical standard for industrial machinery)

Any manufacturer found using unlabelled equipment may be fined, or closed down by OSHA or simply be banned by local inspectors from switching on such equipment. Also, users of non-compliant machinery put themselves at risk of liability-related lawsuits. The labelling of machines is done by a Nationally Recognized Testing Laboratory (NRTL) under OSHA. These requirements apply to both domestic and imported machinery.

NRTLs are private, third-party organisations recognised by OSHA as meeting the legal requirements in the 29 CFR 1910.7 standard, when providing product safety testing and certification services.

In brief, these requirements cover the capability, control programmes, complete independence, and reporting and complaint-handling procedures to test and certify specific types of products for workplace

4. American National Standards Institute
5. National Fire Protection Association

safety. This means that an NRTL organization must have the necessary capability, both as a product safety testing laboratory and as a product certification body to ensure that the machinery meets relevant safety standards and is safe for use in commercial environments.

The equipment being exported to the USA can be certified in two ways: Field labelling, and certification by an NRTL.

(A) *Field Labelling*

Field labelling is a system that requires an approved NRTL to evaluate and certify machinery on-site, and is a more effective approach for customized or low volume machine production. It is an essential requirement and usually takes three or four days. It is done in two parts—firstly at the OEM's site in the exporting country, and secondly in the USA when the equipment has been installed. If it meets all the requirements, the NRTL engineer will then affix the 'Field Label'.

(B) *NRTL Certification*

NRTL certification is a more in-depth process, which tests and certifies specific types of products. It ensures that they comply with relevant safety standards and are safe for operation in the workplace. The testing includes the capabilities of the equipment, its complete independence, control programmes and procedures for reporting and complaint handling. This is more applicable if bulk machinery is being exported to the USA.

OSHA accepts products 'properly certified' by a NRTL. By 'properly certified', it generally means the following:

(i) the product is labelled or marked with the registered certification mark of the NRTL
(ii) the NRTL issues the certification for a product covered within the scope of a test standard for which OSHA has recognized it
(iii) the NRTL issues the certification from one of its sites (i.e., locations) that OSHA has recognized

OSHA's Nationally Recognized Testing Laboratory (NRTL) Program

Under this program, OSHA recognizes private sector organizations to perform certification for certain products to ensure that they meet the requirements of both the construction and general industry OSHA electrical standards. Each NRTL has a scope of test standards that they are recognized for, and each NRTL uses its own unique registered certification mark(s) to designate product conformance to the applicable product safety test standards. After certifying a product, the NRTL authorizes the manufacturer to apply a registered certification mark to the product. If the certification is done under the NRTL program, this mark signifies it has been NRTL tested and certified, and that the product complies with the requirements of one or more appropriate product safety test standards.

(C) Enforcement

OSHA requires that all machinery is approved before it can be used in places of work that fall within the jurisdiction of municipal, county, and state OSHA authorities. These Authorities Having Jurisdiction (AHJs) enforce the safety requirements for their own particular locations, and are responsible for the approval of the equipment, its installation and operating procedures. AHJs also recognize lists of approved products that are published by OSHA-approved organizations. All OEMs and end-users of machinery in the USA must review them periodically for any amendments to the listed equipment.

Periodic ad-hoc inspections are also carried out by AHJs on listed equipment. These ensure that it is still in compliance with local safety requirements, and is being used for its designated purpose. During such inspections, this mandatory label is required to prove that the equipment meets local regulations and standards.

European Union

The EU imported USD 672 billion of machinery in 2020 with nearly USD 121 billion in the same category as the USA at the 4-digit level. This was followed by turbojets and propellers in the second place.

One of the key factors affecting the industry is the New Industrial Strategy for Europe that lays down a vision for the manufacturing sector by 2030 and beyond. The vision leads with a twin transition of green and digital technology. The digital components are an integral part of European machinery. The strategy comes in the wake of the COVID-19 crisis that has strongly affected the EU economy exposing the inter-dependence of global value chains.

Regulatory regime

Regulation

Similar to the USA, EU regulation for machinery is an omnibus one based on risk assessment for health and safety requirements. The main legislation governing machinery at the EU level is the Machinery Directive 2006/42/EC, which was put in place in 2006 and has been amended a number of times since then.

The directive is intended to:

- promote free movement of machinery within a single market
- guarantee a high level of protection for EU workers and citizens

The machinery directive is a 'new approach' directive. This approach includes those directives for which the principle of self-certification is relied upon through CE-marking.

The directive is a harmonisation of mandatory health and safety requirements and voluntary harmonised standards. It only applies to products that are to be placed on the EU market for the first time.

Definitions of machinery as per the EC directive

Machinery: An assembly consisting of linked parts, at least one of which moves (and also machine systems, i.e., assemblies of machinery, which are arranged and controlled so that they function as an integral whole).

Partly completed machinery (formerly part-machines):...cannot in itself perform a specific function, and will only be complete once incorporated into a complete machine including all necessary protective measures.

Safety components (Art. 2, c and Ann. V–non-exhaustive list): Components, which fulfil a safety, function, e. g., light barriers, safety mats, automatic mobile protective devices.

Interchangeable equipment: changes the function of machinery, e.g., accessories or attachments (swivel, turning, tipping devices) for a basic machine, etc.

The manufacturer has a number of documentary requirements to fulfil. Either he or his representative (resident in the EU) is responsible for carrying out the following activities for approval of machinery:

- Carry out a hazard assessment to analyze all of the risks related to the machinery and, if required, apply measures to reduce them
- Ensure that the machinery conforms to the relevant essential health and safety requirements
- Draw up an EU declaration of conformity/incorporation and affix a CE mark
- Draw up a technical file[6] (The documentation has to be retained and kept available for up to ten years from the time of last manufacture of the machinery)

After performing a critical design review during hazard assessment, making changes to the product design that will minimize risks of harm, and compiling the "Technical file", the manufacturer can affix the CE mark and prepare a "Declaration of conformity". The Declaration must identify:

- Who the manufacturer is
- What product it refers to
- What directives are involved
- What standards are applicable
- Where test results can be found
- Who is responsible in the company

Standards

The directive does not mandate standards. However, to comply with the machinery directive and reduce unnecessary risks, compliance to 'harmonized' standards may be done. The use of these standards, is, in a

---

6. An overall drawing of the machinery together with drawings of the control circuits, full detailed drawings, accompanied by any calculation notes, test results, etc., required to check the conformity of the machinery with the essential safety requirements.
    - A list of the EHSRs (Essential health & Safety Requirements):
        - o Applicable harmonized standards, other standards used
        - o Other technical specifications
        - o that were used when the machinery was designed
    - A description of methods adopted to eliminate hazards presented by the machinery
    - Any technical report or certificate obtained from a competent body or laboratory (optional)
    - A copy of the instruction for the machinery
    - For series manufacture, the internal measures that will be implemented to ensure that the machinery remains in conformity with the provisions of the directive

way, obligatory for manufacturers to reduce risks. These standards are divided into three categories:

- Basic safety standards (type A): These are fundamental standards and give basic concepts, principles for design, and general aspects that can be applied to machinery

  e.g., EN 292 (Basic machine safety issues), EN 1050 (Risk analysis)

- Generic safety standards (type B): These standards deal with one safety aspect or one type of safeguard that can be used across a wide range of machinery. These standards help determine whether a hazard exists and provide concrete information/ measures to perform its risk reduction. This standard is further classified into two sub-standards:
  - B1 standards: They deal with particular safety aspects such as safety distances, surface, temperature, noise, etc., and define by data and/or methodology how they can be addressed. They can be used directly by the designer/ manufacturer or by reference

    e.g., EN 294 (Safety distances to avoid parts of the human body from being endangered)

  - B2 standards: These standards provide performance requirements for the design and construction of particular safeguards (for example, two-hand control devices, interlocking devices, pressure-sensitive protective devices, guards). They can be applied either directly by the designer/ manufacturer or by reference

    e.g., EN 418 (Emergency stop equipment)

- Machine safety standards (type C): They provide detailed safety requirements for particular machinery or group of machinery, where the term "group of machinery" means machinery having a similar intended use and similar hazards, hazardous situations, or hazardous events. Type C standards are machine-specific: their scope is determining the limits of the machinery and the significant hazards covered.

  e.g., EN 1218 (Safety requirements related to wood treatment machinery)

Risk Assessment

Machinery under the scope of the machinery directive must comply with the ESRs (Essential Safety Requirements) of Annex I of the Directive concerning design and construction. The following methods are proposed in ISO 12100 (EN 1050):

- Preliminary hazard analysis (PHA)
- What-if analysis
- Failure modes and effects analysis. Fault simulation for control systems. Method Organized for Systematic Analysis of Risk (MOSAR)
- Fault tree analysis
- Delphi technique
- A detailed list of relevant hazards is provided in ISO 12100

For simple machinery systems, it is often sufficient to use a version of preliminary hazard analysis (PHA) for the risk analysis. Additional data is captured to document risk reduction in (i) design, (ii) guards and protective measures, and (iii) information about risk and special requirements, like certificates.

Conformity Assessment

There are three kinds of conformity assessment:

1. *Self-assessment:* Used for machinery not included in Annex-IV[7] of the regulation. If machinery is designed in accordance with the relevant harmonised standards, the manufacturers can self-certify, thereby avoiding the requirement to deposit the technical file with a notified body.
2. *EC type examination:* Used where machinery is listed in Annex-IV of the regulation but is not manufactured wholly in accordance with harmonized standards. The machinery is to be assessed by a "notified body". If compliant, the notified body will issue an EC type examination certificate.
3. *Full quality assurance:* Used where machinery is listed in Annex-IV of the regulation and manufactured using full quality assurance. The 'responsible person'/manufacturer is required to have their system assessed by a notified body, which will issue necessary documentation and CE marking.

7. Categories of machinery to which one of the procedures referred to in Article 12(3) and (4) must be applied

Illustration from 2006/42/EC

CE marking:

- The CE Conformity marking shall consist of the initials 'CE' as shown left;
- The CE marking shall be affixed to the machinery visibly, legibly and indelibly;
- The CE marking must include the minimum particulars (on the machine e.g. labelled, printed, embossed, etc.);
- The CE marking must be affixed in the immediate vicinity of the name of the manufacturer or his authorised representative, using the same technique.

Marking of machinery:

- Business name and address of the manufacturer or his authorised representative;
- Designation of the machinery (may be indicated by a code);
- Designation of series or type (may be indicated by a code and may be combined with the designation of the machinery);
- Serial number, if any;
- Year of construction/assembly;
- Mass of the machine, in kg.

Figure 18: CE marking for machinery

Korea

Korea is the 9th largest importer of machinery in the world. It imported about USD 57.36 billion of machinery under chapter 84 in 2020 with major imports from China (USD 15.28 billion) followed by Japan (USD 9.7 billion) and the USA (USD 8 billion). Its major imports from China are under HS 8471, similar to the USA.

Regulatory regime

Regulator

Workers' health and safety on the work floor is overseen by the Korea Occupational Safety and Health Agency (KOSHA). It is also responsible for implementing the Occupational Safety and Health Act. This act requires products to be certified by KCs Mark which is different from the KC mark.

Certification

KC certification, or Korea Certification, is a product certification, which ensures the conformity of products to Korean safety standards—called K Standards. It focuses on prevention and reduction of risks regarding safety, health, or impact on the environment for products such as toys, consumer goods, etc.

However, for machine safety, the KCs mark is used where 's' depicts safety. This is a test mark of the "Korea Occupational Safety and Health Agency" (KOSHA) which shows that the machine has been tested and approved for safe operation.

Before 2009, there were 13 different certification systems by different government organizations with some partially overlapping each other. In 2009, the government of Korea decided to introduce the KC Mark Certification to replace the previous 140 different test marks.

The KC Mark and the corresponding KC Certificate are similar to the European CE mark and are valid for 730 different products such as automotive parts, machines, and many electronic products.

KCs certification can be separated into two types, based on certification processes: Certification of Compliance (CoC) and Declaration of Conformity (DoC).

Some products that require a safety certification (CoC) include	*Some products, that require a self-declaration (DoC) include*
• Cranes • Pressure Vessels • Lifts • Presses, Shearing/Press Brakes • Rollers • Injection Moulding Machines • Mobile Elevated Work Platforms • Gondola Lifts • Sawing Machines	• Grinders • Industrial Robots • Mixers • Crushers • Food Processing Machines • Conveyors • Automobile lifts

Figure 19: Examples of KCs certification

If the process of a machine is potentially harmful (e.g., with a pressure vessel) a Certification of Compliance (CoC) is necessary. As part of the CoC approval, an annual factory inspection is required. Products, which are related to safety (e.g., personal protective equipment) are also required to have a KC Certification and a CoC.

Products for which there is only a risk of injury when safety-related components fail (e.g., machine tools or industrial robots), require a Declaration of Conformity (DoC).

The KCs Mark certification is normally a manufacturer's certification, which is especially understandable when factory audits are required. However, foreign manufacturers of products or components that require a KCs and / or CoC certification can also choose to obtain a so-called import certification via their importer. This requires the collaboration of the importer and allows for a one-time import of 10 products as a maximum quantity. Under this certification, a factory audit is not required.

There are three main organisations that are accredited to certify and permitted to conduct product tests, factory audits, and issue certificates. These are as follows:

- Korea Testing and Research Institute (KTR)
- Korea Testing Laboratory (KTL)
- Korea Testing Certification (KTC)

Japan

Traditionally, Japan is famed to have quality and a reliable machinery-manufacturing sector. It is the 7th largest importer of machinery in the world with imports of USD 67 billion in 2020. Almost half of its imports are from China with the majority related to the semiconductor manufacturing industry. Japan exports almost double of the machinery it imports with major export destinations being China and the USA.

The Japan Machinery Federation (JMF) distinguishes between general machinery, electrical machinery, information and communication equipment, electronic parts and devices, transport equipment, and precision machinery. The highest production value among machinery is of transport equipment, especially automobiles. General machinery refers to machines mainly for industrial use, generally aiming at facilitating production.

Electrical machinery includes, *inter alia,* household appliances. Information and communications equipment is a subcategory of electrical machinery but separately listed due to its particular purpose. Electronic parts and devices are the basic components used to build electronic circuits, thereby distinguishing themselves from other machinery composed of numerous parts.

Regulatory regime

Regulator

The governing ministry is the Ministry of Health, Labour and Welfare (MHLW).

Regulation

Japan has regulated its machinery under the Industrial Safety and Health Act, 1972 (ISH) with amendments from time to time. The purpose of the Act is to ensure the safety and health of workers in workplaces, as well as to facilitate the establishment of a comfortable working environment by promoting comprehensive and systematic countermeasures concerning the prevention of industrial accidents, such as taking measures for the establishment of standards for hazard prevention, clarifying the safety and health management responsibility and the promotion of voluntary activities to prevent industrial accidents.

However, while importing, there are additional regulations to be followed for certain machine categories such as food processing machines, packaging machines, machines for book binding, etc.

For certain machines, even the Industrial Safety and Health Act, 1972, is not applicable, e.g. printing machinery, book binding machines, cutting machines, moulding machines, etc. For such machines, the Electrical Appliance and Material Safety Law is to be complied with. The ISH is a holistic act covering workers' safety, health hazards posed by harmful chemicals, etc. Chapter V in particular lays down regulations concerning machinery and harmful substances.

Risk Assessment

Machinery that pose a higher risk during operation are called "specified machines" and are subject to inspection. Based on risk profiles of the machines, they have been classified in various categories listed in the appended table of the Act. Subject to the risk associated, the machines may have to undergo either inspection or individual examination or type examination or self-inspection. Separate guidelines have been issued for assessing the risks.

Certification

To certify compliance to the set standards, the JIS mark is used. It is a Japanese quality certification mark and is needed for many different kinds of products. JIS is an acronym for "Japan International Standards" and the mark is managed by a committee with the same name, Japan International Standards Committee (JISC). It is similar to the CE mark by the EU. The mark is issued by the Japanese Standards Association Group that is responsible for developing draft JIS, management techniques, standardization, and conformity assessment.

Fees for Certification

The fees for certification include:

- *Application fee – ¥ 70,000: Administrative costs that are charged only for the first application*
- *The factory audit fee – On-site audit ¥ 140,000 (per person-day) or ¥ 20,000 (per person-hour): Administrative costs when your documents are reviewed and costs that arise when the auditors visit the factory*
- *Product testing fee – Estimated individually*
- *Certification costs – ¥ 150,000: Costs for arranging the audit, evaluate and issue the certificate*
- *Renewal of certification fee – ¥ 50,000 (per year): To be paid within the same month as the certificate is issued, every year*

Travel fees for the certification company: You are obliged to pay for accommodation, daily allowances and transportation fees

There may be additional marking requirements for electrical appliances and machines used in the food sector.

China

China was the largest exporter of machinery under chapter 84 of USD 440.25 billion in 2020. In terms of imports, it was the second largest importer of USD 191 billion during the same period. Its major imports are from Japan, Germany, and Korea. At the 4-digit level, it imports components of products under HS 8471. China has many of its own heavy-duty manufacturers in many sectors such as milling machines, heavy equipment machines, etc.

The low-end machinery market is dominated by SMEs, mainly due to their cost-cutting structures, price-based competition, and ability to crowd out larger enterprises to some extent. The high-end machinery market is largely composed of state-owned enterprises and international market players. These companies can differentiate their products beyond the reach and capabilities of local, smaller competitors and, therefore, possess significant intellectual property assets in terms of patents, licences, and trademarks while leveraging their globally recognized brands.

Regulatory regime

Similar to developed countries, China also has a regulation on machine safety, keeping in mind workplace safety.

Regulator

The State Council's two departments, namely, the State Administration on Work Safety (SAWS) and the National Health and Family Planning Commission (NHFPC) are responsible for governing occupational health work.

Regulation

The Law on Prevention and Control of Occupational Diseases and the Work Safety Law are the two most important laws in China that highlight the responsibilities of the employer, employee, governmental agencies, authorized occupational health service agency, and other stakeholders.

Based on its Occupational Safety and Health Act (OSHA), China has enacted regulations governing the registration of safety information for machinery, equipment, and tools. As per OSHA, machinery, equipment, or tools specified by the central competent authority and whose structures, functions, or safeguards do not fulfil safety standards shall not be manufactured and shipped from the factory, nor imported, rented out, supplied or installed by manufacturers, importers, suppliers, or employers.

The applicant shall designate a responsible person to take care of registration of safety information and subsequent updates. The technical files for the registered product may be kept for a period of not less than 10 years after the products are no longer manufactured. All the documents uploaded on the website must in be Chinese and may be supplemented by information in English or in other languages.

Such machinery shall be registered by manufacturers or importers on the information reporting website, specified by the central competent authority. When the applicant completes registration of safety information, he will be assigned a registration number and issue a registration-completed notice that will contain information about the applicant, basic data of the product, product specifications, information about the production premises, references to safety standards, registration number, registration date, period of validity, etc.

What is to be uploaded on the website?

1. Declaration of conformity: A document signed to declare compliance with safety standards.

2. Registration documents: Factory registration, company registration, business registration or other equivalent documents that demonstrate official approval for establishment of the factory, company, or business, except where registration is not required by law or the registration information has already been uploaded on the Information Website without changes.

3. Testing documents. Specified below that demonstrate compliance with safety standards and are valid for more than three months. Where registration is sought for a single article, the validity period of testing documents is not of concern and the certification of production consistency is not required.

(a) type verification certificate or self-inspection/self-test reports; and

(b) certificate of production consistency.

4. Basic information about the products:

(a) Description of the product type, including catalogue, product name, illustration of the appearance of the product, product classification code (HS code or CCC code), specification of the main processing unit and control unit, etc. Where it is not possible to identify the type of a product by its type number, a determination of the same type description may be used.

(b) Instructions of the installation, operation, maintenance, and repair of the product and recommended practices for responding to hazards, including illustration of the location of the product safety devices and their functions.

5. Information about the product safety devices and accessories:

(a) Brand name, specifications, descriptions of the safety structure, performance and protection, compliance; and

(b) Certification or test reports for critical components and relevant strength calculations. Where the products are single articles to be sold after further processing or repairmen and it is difficult to obtain relevant documents, other testing documents that can demonstrate compliance of the article can be provided.

6. Other conformity assessment procedure documents or technical files required by the central competent authority.

Once certified, the manufacturer has to put up a safety label in a prominent place on the product for identification. Based on the level of risk associated with the machinery, the manufacturer/importer shall either obtain a type certificate (highest risk), or product certificate from a certification body accredited by domestic/foreign accreditation bodies or self-declaration[8] (lowest risk).

For products requiring type certification, the certification has to be obtained from a certification body. In certain cases, safety assessment reports may also be required. If the following conditions are met, the requirement for type certification may be waived:

- Those that have undergone inspections, examination, certification, or approval as products in 'dangerous' category
- Those that are provided for military or national defence use, with documentation to this effect issued by the Ministry of National Defence or a subordinate body thereof.
- Those that are special models manufactured or imported in limited quantities for the sole purpose of technological R&D or testing, and have been authorized by the central competent authority.
- Those that are used for commercial sample or exhibition and not for actual use or operation purposes, and have been authorized by the central competent authority.

Vietnam

Vietnam imported about USD 21.5 billion worth of machinery in 2020, primarily from China, Korea, and Japan. Vietnam is not a major importer of first-hand machinery but a lot of second-hand machinery has been imported into the country over the past decades. As a result of this, Vietnam brought in revised regulations banning import of used or second hand machinery which has been discarded or banned by other countries because of its obsolescence, low quality, etc.

Regulatory regime

Regulator

The Ministry of Labourers, Invalids and Social Affairs enacted regulation on the list of machinery, equipment, materials, and substances subject to

8. Self-inspection shall be performed by testing laboratories accredited by accreditation organisations; self-check of production consistency shall be performed by units accredited by accreditation bodies; and the qualification of testing personnel of testing laboratories shall comply with criteria specified

strict requirements. Nearly 105 items have been divided into the following three groups:

GROUP 1	Machinery, equipment and materials subject to strict requirements for occupational safety (45 types)
GROUP 2	Machinery, equipment and materials subject to strict requirements for occupational safety in the military sector (45 types)
GROUP 3	Machinery, equipment, materials and substances subject to strict requirements for occupational safety in the public security sector (15 types)

Figure 20: Machinery classification by Vietnam

Regulation

There is no regulation on the import of new machinery in Vietnam. For decades, the import of used machinery has supported the economy, as it is cheaper. However, this has led to dumping of old, dangerous and environmentally harmful machines by China. In 2018, Vietnam spent over USD 32 billion on imports of machinery with nearly 40 per cent coming from China as per the General Department of Customs. On an average, Vietnam spends approximately USD 1 billion per month on machinery and equipment from China.

Thus, a new regulation was introduced in 2019 for regulating the import of used machinery or equipment. As per the new regulation, only used machinery can be imported and has to have a life of less than 10 manufacturing years.

Standards

The used machinery or equipment must satisfy safety, energy-saving, and environmental protection requirements as per the National Technical Regulation, Vietnam's Standard or standards of G7 countries. It should have at least 85 per cent of original capacity and energy consumption should not be more than 15 per cent of the original design. The approval is given on a case-by-case basis by the Ministry of Science and Technology.

The technology present in the machinery must be in use in at least three production facilities in a member-state of the Organization for Economic Cooperation and Development (OECD).

The following import documents are required for import of used machinery/equipment:

(i) Original certificate of manufacture about manufacturing year and standards of the used machinery/equipment being compliant with the above-mentioned import criteria for used machinery/equipment that has been manufactured in any G7 country or Korea

(ii) Inspection certificate issued by a designated inspection body for used machinery/equipment that has been manufactured in any G7 country or Korea without certificate of manufacture, or for used machinery/equipment that has been manufactured in a country other than G7 countries and Korea

Looking ahead

The biggest challenge in the Indian market is that it is currently unregulated. This leaves no benchmark or common standards to manufacture machines, thus, making the manufactured goods uncompetitive. Although the exporter does not have to comply with domestic regulations, the condition of the market determines the overall maturity of the sector. Since the quality of machinery made in India is not perceived as 'good', there is a low demand for Indian machinery. This makes capturing new markets challenging and retaining old ones difficult.

In other instances, the industry has complained of flooding of the Indian market with second-hand unsafe machines owning to lack of safety regulations even though the machines may be complying with environmental norms.

Given the wide variety of machines, an over-arching regulation that focuses on the safety of the machinery, irrespective of its usage, is required in India. The regulation also needs to have provisions in the TR to take care of import of second-hand machines and the use of machines beyond its useful life beyond which it may be rendered dangerous to use. Compliance and monitoring will determine the success of the regulation. This might require distribution of power to seize such machines that flout TRs.

Developed countries like Japan and the USA have had decades-old regulations realizing early on the necessity of having safe machinery for use. Their regulations have grown and matured over time, like old wine. The distribution of power at different levels of agencies responsible for compliance and monitoring of the regulations has been well established and appears to be working well.

Developing countries, on the other hand, may not have an established manufacturing sector and thus may have to import machinery suited to their requirements. Import of second-hand machinery may be more than first-hand machinery. In such situations, developing countries may act as dumping grounds for machines that are deemed to be no longer safe in the manufactured or country using them or may have lower compliance with environmental norms. A classic case is that of Vietnam, wherein the country realized the dumping of dangerous machines and amended its regulation to have specific TRs on import on second-hand machinery. Import of first-hand machinery may still be unregulated.

Not many developing countries have regulations governing the entire sector of machinery from the safety perspective. Many have piecemeal regulations for products, e.g., cranes, pulleys, etc. Developed countries have linked the welfare of labour to machine safety and have enforced it strictly.

In India, regulators of machinery are spread across ministries/ departments. It is necessary that a product that is critical for the development of the economy serves its purpose well by operating efficiently. It is thus essential that a common nodal ministry/department may be given charge to prepare an omnibus regulation on machinery safety.

REFERENCES

- https://www.thebalance.com/capital-goods-examples-effect-on-economy-3306224
- https://www.investindia.gov.in/sector/capital-goods
- https://www.trademap.org/Product_SelProductCountry.aspx?nvpm= 1%7c%7c%7c%7c%7c%7c84%7c%7c%7c4%7c1%7c1%7c1%7c1%7c1%7c1%7c1%7c1%7c1
- https://www.counterpointresearch.com/6-8-million-connected-heavy-construction-machines-shipped-till-2025/
- https://blog.assentcompliance.com/index.php/ce-marking-electrical-equipment/
- https://www.safetymanualosha.com/hand-tool-safety/
- http://www.sme.in/esfourengineering/Process-Plant.html

- https://www.rapiddirect.com/blog/cnc-machine-tools/
- https://www.sinotextilemachinery.com/weaving-machinery/
- https://www.marketsandmarkets.com/Market-Reports/construction-mining-equipment-market-179948937.html
- https://www.mordorintelligence.com/industry-reports/construction-machinery-equipment-market
- https://www.autocarpro.in/feature/india%E2%80%99s-construction-equipment-sector-headed-for-washout-in-q1-fy2022-79258
- https://www.mordorintelligence.com/industry-reports/construction-machinery-equipment-market
- https://www.industrialtechnology.co.uk/products—exporting-machinery-to-the-north-american-market.html
- https://www.holtca.com/company/news/construction-equipment-safety-tips
- https://www.gt-engineering.it/en/Insights/machinery-safety-usa
- https://www.machinesafetyspecialists.com/u-s-safety-standards/
- https://ec.europa.eu/info/strategy/priorities-2019-2024/europe-fit-digital-age/european-industrial-strategy_en
- https://www.cece.eu/industry-and-market/european-industrial-policy
- https://ec.europa.eu/growth/sectors/mechanical-engineering/machinery_en
- https://blog.assentcompliance.com/index.php/ce-marking-electrical-equipment/
- https://www.alliedmarketresearch.com/hand-tools-market
- https://www.osha.gov/nationally-recognized-testing-laboratory-program
- Presentation on Risk Assessment Section 17.10-The EU Machinery Directive by Stein Haugen & Marvin Rausand, RAMS Group, Department of Production and Quality Engineering NTNU, (Version 0.1)
- https://www.slideserve.com/izzy/the-supply-of-machinery-safety-regulations-2008
- https://www.ivg.org/fileadmin/downloads/Leitfaeden/leitfaden-englisch-handgefuehrte-rm-elektro-netz.pdf
- https://www.machinesafety.co.uk/free-downloads/directive-guide/
- https://www.korea-certification.com/en/kcs/kcs-mark/
- https://www.korea-certification.com/en/kc/what-is-kc-certification/
- https://www.jniosh.johas.go.jp/icpro/jicosh-old/english/guideline/Machinery/index.html
- https://www.ncbi.nlm.nih.gov/pmc/articles/PMC5886879/#:~:text= Occupational%20Diseases2).-,The%20Work%20Safety%20Law% 20of%20 the%20 People's %20Republic%20of%20China,both%20the%20employer%20and%20employee
- https://law.moj.gov.tw/ENG/LawClass/LawAll.aspx?pcode=N0060056
- https://law.moj.gov.tw/ENG/LawClass/LawAll.aspx?pcode=N0060001
- https://www.ditp.go.th/contents_attach/358257/358257.pdf
- https://www.global-regulation.com/translation/vietnam/2952995/circular-23-2015-tt-bkhcn%253a-regulating-the-import-of-machinery%252c-equipment%252c-technological-lines-have-through-the-use.html
- https://www.statista.com/topics/7931/machinery-industry-in-japan/#dossierKeyfigures
- https://www.export2asia.com/blog/jis-mark/
- https://www.vietnam-briefing.com/news/vietnam-bans-import-used-machinery-june-15.html/

CHEMICALS

The global chemicals industry is a complex and critical sector of the global economy and supply chain network. Products such as plastic resins, petrochemicals, and synthetic rubber are included in the basic chemicals segment, and products such as adhesives, sealants, and coatings are among the products included in the specialty chemicals segment.

The region-wise value of global chemical exports in 2021 is illustrated below:

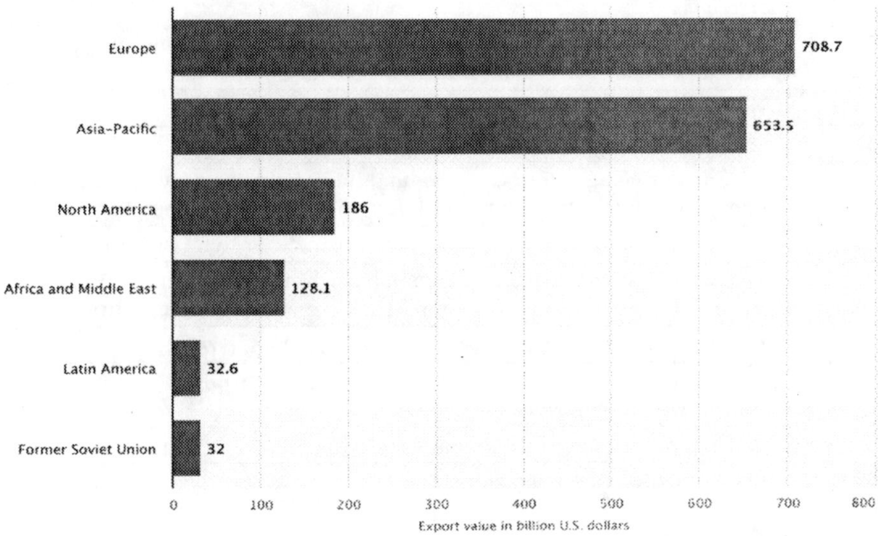

Figure 21: Region-wise export value of chemicals in 2021

The five leading chemical companies in the world based on revenue as of 2021 were BASF, Dow, Mitsubishi Chemical Holdings, LG Chem, and LyondellBasell Industries. German company BASF generated a revenue of more than € 59 million in 2020. Many of the leading chemical companies in the world have been established for a considerable length of time. BASF, for example, was founded in Mannheim, Germany in 1865. Similarly, Dow was founded in Midland, Michigan, in 1897.

Europe is the largest exporter of chemicals, thanks to companies in Germany followed by the Asia-Pacific region. The 3rd largest region exporting chemicals is the North America.

The chemicals are traded under HS codes of chapters 28 to 38 (excluding chapter 30: pharmaceuticals). The leading export destinations are the USA, China, Germany and Switzerland, whereas, leading import destinations are the USA, Germany, China and Ireland. The global trade during 2020 was USD 1.12 trillion of chemicals under HS codes of chapters 28 to 38 (excluding chapter 30: pharmaceuticals).

In the following section, chemicals refer to HS codes of chapters 28 to 38 (excluding chapter 30: pharmaceuticals).

Table 6: Chapters 28 to 38 for chemicals

Hs code	*Description*
28	Inorganic chemicals; organic or inorganic compounds of precious metals, of rare-earth metals, or radiation Elements Or of isotopes.
29	Organic chemicals
31	Fertilizers
32	Tanning or dyeing extracts; tannins and their derivatives Dyes, pigments and other colouring matter; paints and ver; putty and other mastics; inks.
33	Essential oils and resinoids; perfumery, cosmetic or toilet preparations.
34	Soap, organic surface-active agents, washing preparations, lubricating preparations, artificial waxes, prepared waxes, polishing or scouring prep.
35	Albuminoidal substances; modified starches; glues; enzymes.
36	Explosives; pyrotechnic products; matches; pyrophoric alloys; certain combustible preparations.
37	Photographic or cinematographic goods.
38	Miscellaneous chemical products.

India

Chemicals industry is highly diversified, covering more than 80,000 commercial products. It is broadly classified as mentioned in Figure 23.

India's proximity to the Middle East, the world's source of petrochemicals feedstock, makes for economies of scale. It ranks 11th in the world exports of chemicals and ranks 6th in the world imports of chemicals. The industry employs more than 2 million people.

The total export of chemicals by India during 2020 was USD 29.8 billion, whereas imports were USD 41.1 billion. The major export destinations for India were the USA and China. The major exports were for organic chemicals under chapter 29 of HS codes.

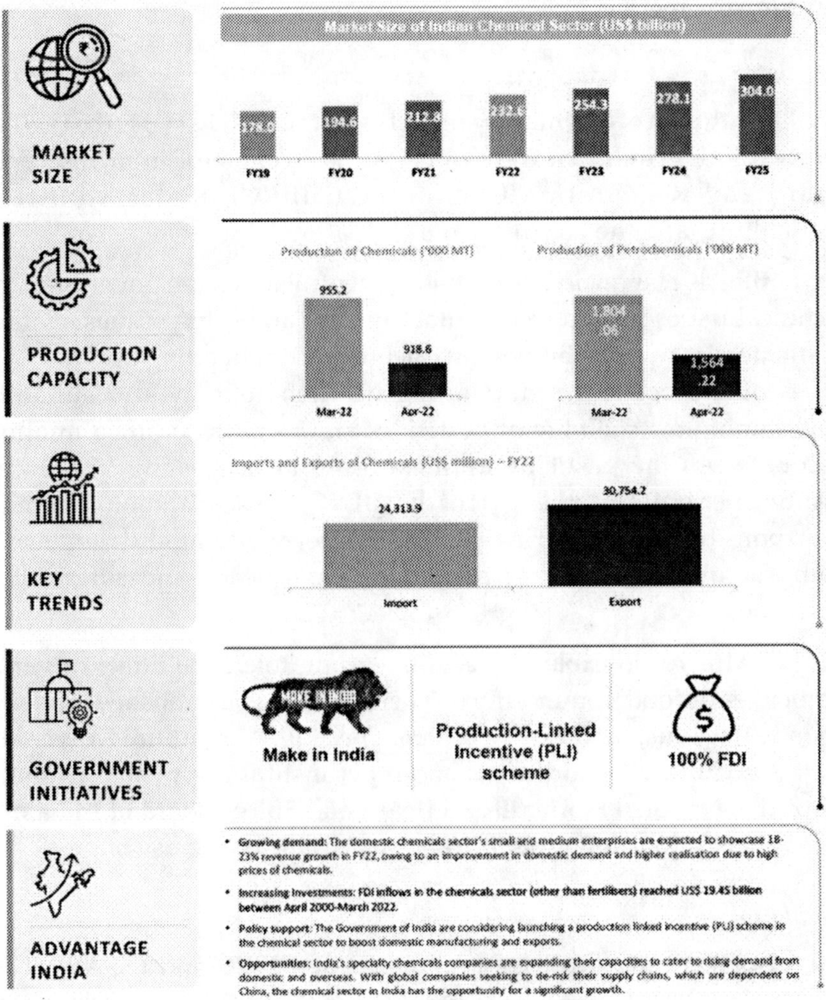

Figure 22: IBEF snapshot: chemicals

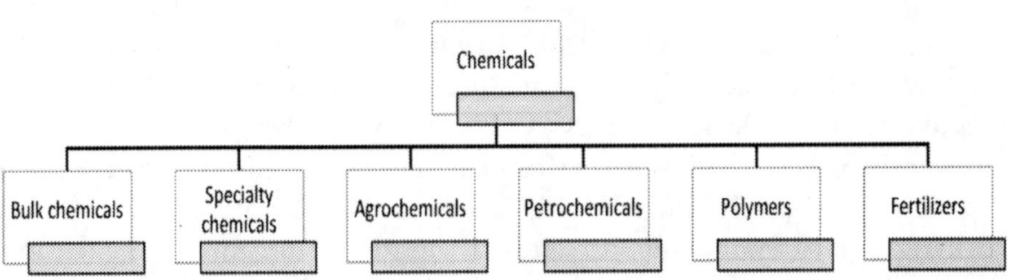

Figure 23: Classification of chemicals in India

Regulatory regime

Regulator

The Department of Chemicals and Petrochemicals (DCPC) is the regulator for chemicals in India. However for agrochemicals, the Central Insecticides Board and Registration Committee (CIBRC), under Ministry of Agriculture, and the FSSAI are the regulators.

CIBRC is responsible for advising central and state governments on technical issues related to manufacture, use and safety issues related to pesticides. Its responsibilities also include recommending uses of various types of the pesticides depending on their toxicity and suitability, determining the shelf life of pesticides and recommending a minimum gap between the pesticide applications and harvesting of the crops (waiting period). The other part of the CIBRC, the Registration Committee, is responsible for registering pesticides after verifying the claims of the manufacturer or importer related to the efficacy and safety of the pesticides.

FSSAI is responsible for recommending tolerance limits of various pesticides in food commodities. The FSSAI was established under the Food Safety and Standards Act, 2006. The State Agriculture Universities, State Agriculture Departments and other institutions related to specific crops like National Horticultural Board and Spices Board of India make recommendations for agricultural practices including use of pesticides.

Regulation

The agrochemicals are strictly regulated by CIBRC and FSSAI. Most of the regulations by FSSAI regarding tolerance limits of pesticides in food are harmonized with the global standards. The scope of agrochemicals are more aligned for regulation through SPS measures.

The regulation of chemicals, other than agrochemicals is a new concept and started only recently since 2018. As part of the initiative to regulate non-industrial products, DCPC has notified 60 product categories under BIS Act, 2016 with different national standards. These are specification based standards and do not necessarily pertain to the safety during use of chemicals, as against the global norm of registration, evaluation and assessment of chemicals. Globally, the regulation is focused on the hazard and nature of the chemicals. This approach of piecemeal regulation of chemicals has been a source of discomfort for many countries and have been raised at TBT Committee as Specific Trade Concerns demanding India to work on a holistic solution similar to REACH regulation.

> ***TBT Committee and STCs***
>
> *TBT Committee is an institutional mechanism in-built in the WTO system to address two major issues:*
>
> *(i) Review of specific laws, regulations or procedures that affect their trade, usually in response to notifications. These are called as Specific Trade Concerns (STCs). Essentially, members raise STCs to find out more about the scope and implementation of each other's regulations in light of the core TBT obligations. The discussion is mostly about measures in the pipeline, but can also be about the implementation of existing measures. To date, more than 700 STCs have been raised globally of which 27 are against India*
>
> *(ii) Strengthening implementation of the TBT Agreement: Members exchange experiences on the implementation of the Agreement with a view to making implementation more effective and efficient. This discussion revolves around generic, cross-cutting themes, including transparency, standards, conformity assessment and good regulatory practice.*
>
> *The Committee usually holds three formal meetings per year. These are sometimes preceded by workshops or thematic sessions. Meetings are open to all the WTO members and observer governments. International inter-governmental organizations—several of them standardizing bodies—also participate as observers in the Committee.*

Apart from the piecemeal regulations by DCPC, after extensive consultation with stakeholders, an omnibus draft regulation on the hazardous nature of chemicals is under discussion by the DCPC. The draft was placed in the public domain for comments. It is yet to be notified to the WTO for comments from other countries.

United States of America

The USA is one of the largest consumers of chemicals in the world. It imported USD 258.9 billion worth of chemicals with organic chemicals occupying the largest amount of value i.e. USD 56.4 billion with the major import destination being Ireland, followed by China. It exported USD 111.9 billion of chemicals with majority being organic chemicals and miscellaneous chemicals. The leading countries of destination for U.S. chemical exports were Mexico, Canada, and China.

Dow is the largest U.S. chemical company, and the world's second largest behind German chemical company BASF. Other leading U.S. chemical companies are LyondellBasell, and DuPont.

Regulatory regime

The regulations on chemicals are largely concerned with the health and safety of the individuals who use them, guard employee safety, and hold employers accountable for keeping their workers safe.

Regulator

One of the most important pieces of legislation regarding chemical safety in the U.S., Toxic Substances Control Act (TSCA) ensures that chemicals are used, stored, and disposed of in ways that are safe for human health and the environment. Passed in 1976, this Act regulates the use, importation, and disposal of a wide range of new and existing commercial chemicals in the U.S. It does not regulate food, food packaging, pharmaceuticals, pesticides, and chemicals used in cosmetics and personal care products. The TSCA gives the Environmental Protection Agency (EPA) the authority to request reports and impose restrictions concerning chemical substances and mixtures.

Regulation

The TSCA provides EPA with authority to require reporting, record-keeping and testing requirements, and restrictions relating to chemical substances and/or mixtures. TSCA addresses the production, importation, use, and disposal of specific chemicals including polychlorinated biphenyls (PCBs), asbestos, radon and lead-based paint.

The TSCA's requirements for importers or manufacturers include:

- Reporting the products to the EPA
- Keeping records (e.g. records related to purchasing, or sales)
- Testing products according to required standards or test methods
- Obtaining specific certifications for the products
- Correctly label the products and their packaging

Additionally, importers and manufacturers of new chemical substances must submit a new chemicals notice to the EPA. The TSCA lists 86,607 chemicals under the "TSCA Inventory". The public can get access to the non-confidential part of the TSCA Inventory on the EPA's official website.

Due to the large number of chemicals recorded in the Inventory, the TSCA uses special flags to identify and group the chemicals for easier management. For flagged chemicals, different requirements might apply according to the flag, including testing, reporting, labeling, or certification. Examples of flagged chemicals include:

- Polychlorinated biphenyls (PCBs)
- Asbestos
- Radon
- Lead

If a chemical is listed in the inventory but is not flagged, importers or manufacturers must issue a negative certification statement and submit it to the CBP, declaring that the chemicals in the shipment are not subject to the TSCA.

Chemicals that are not listed in the inventory are deemed as "new". Importers or manufacturers of "new" chemicals must submit a pre-manufacture notice ("PMN") to EPA at least 90-days before manufacturing or importing them.

Certification

Importers must certify that imported chemicals either comply with TSCA (positive certification) or, if not otherwise clearly identified as a chemical excluded from TSCA, are not subject to TSCA (negative certification).

A certificate must be signed and filed electronically or in writing with CBP by the importer or an authorized agent of the importer. It must also include the certifier's name, email address, and telephone number. It is required for substances that are imported and are received by mail or commercial carrier, including those intended for research and development.

Substances Restrictions in Articles (Products)

Some TSCA's substance restrictions apply to articles in general, such as the restrictions of PBT. Some restrictions only apply to certain categories of products, such as the restriction of formaldehyde level in composite wood products.

Persistent, Bioaccumulative, and Toxic (PBT)

The TSCA prohibits the use of five persistent, bioaccumulative, and toxic chemicals under Part 751 of the CFR. These prohibited PBTs might be used in various consumer and industrial products as plasticizers, flame retardants, anti-wear additives, or an anti-compressibility additive.

These five restricted PBT and their maximum allowable limit on articles are:

- *2,4,6-TTBP d" 0.3% by weight*
- *DecaBDE: Prohibited*
- *PIP 3:1: Prohibited)*
- *PCT d" 1% by weight*
- *HCBD: Prohibited*

Product examples:

- *Power sockets*
- *Plastic electronic components*
- *Plastic enclosures for electronic equipment*
- *Wire and cables*
- *Textiles and apparels*
- *Upholstered furniture*

Certificate filed electronically must be filed in the Automated Commercial Environment (ACE). For paper certification, the statement must be typed, pre-printed on the invoice, or otherwise included in the entry documentation and must be filed with the director of the port of entry before release of the shipment. An importer's statement must certify either that the chemical shipment is either accompanied by positive certification or negative certification.

> ***Positive Certification Statement for Chemicals***
>
> *The TSCA positive certification statement is meant to declare that the chemical complies with all applicable TSCA requirements, and should include the following wording:*
>
> *"I certify that all chemical substances in this shipment comply with all applicable rules or orders under TSCA and that I am not offering a chemical substance for entry in violation of TSCA or any applicable rule or order thereunder."*
>
> ***Negative Certification Statement for Chemicals***
>
> *On the other hand, if the chemicals are not flagged in the TSCA inventory, importers and manufacturers need to issue a negative certification, which should include the following wording:*
>
> *"I certify that all chemicals in this shipment are not subject to TSCA."*

Some chemicals have specific import and export requirements under section 6 of TSCA such as PCBs, mercury, and, asbestos.

Under the TSCA Title VI regulation, importers must also:

- Keep Records: For three years, bills of lading, invoices, or comparable documents that include a written statement from the supplier that the composite wood products (or component parts/ finished goods) are TSCA Title VI compliant.
- Provide Records on Request: When EPA requests, make available within 30 days records identifying 1) the panel producer and the date the composite wood products were produced; and 2) records identifying the supplier, if different, and the date the composite wood products (or component parts/finished goods) were purchased.

Labelling

The TSCA specifies labeling requirements for certain chemicals and products:

(i) Articles Labeling: The regulation sets labeling requirements for some products, such as composite wood products. For this type of product, the label should contain the following information:
   (a) Panel producer's name
   (b) Lot number

(c) Third-party certification number accredited by the EPA

(d) A statement to clarify that the products are TSCA Title VI compliant

(ii) Chemicals labelling: Labeling might be necessary for some chemicals as well. For example, the TSCA requires that whoever distributes metalworking fluid containing mixed mono and diamides of organic acid must affix a label to each container containing the fluid. The label should contain carcinogenic warnings and icons.

Reporting requirements

The TSCA requires importers and manufacturers of the following products to report to the EPA:

- Mercury-added products
- Composite wood products
- Products containing PCB
- PFAS
- Formaldehyde
- Some classes of phthalates (for example BBP, DBP, Dicyclohexyl phthalate, DEHP, DIBP)
- Some classes of flame retardants (for example TBBPA, TPP, TCEP)

Under the TSCA, lab testing might be explicitly required for some products (e.g. composite wood products). Even if testing is not explicitly required, it may be needed to make sure it doesn't contain restricted substances above the limits.

European Union

The EU exported USD 432 billion of chemicals to the world, the major segment being of organic chemicals and, imported USD 389 billion. Germany and France are the two largest chemicals producers in Europe, followed by Italy and the Netherlands. These four countries accounted for more than 60 per cent of EU chemical sales.

The EU chemicals industry:

- represents around 7.5 per cent of EU manufacturing by turnover
- has sales amounting to €565 billion (2018), which is about 17 per cent of global chemicals sales

- creates an estimated 3.6 million indirect jobs and supports around 19 million jobs across all value supply chains
- has a labour productivity 77 per cent higher than the manufacturing average

Regulatory regime

The EU was one of the first countries to come with a comprehensive regulation for the chemicals sector. REACH is a European regulation and is an acronym for the Registration, Evaluation, Authorization and Restriction of Chemicals. The overall aims of REACH are to:

- Provide a high level of protection of human health and the environment from the use of chemicals
- Allow free movement of substances on the EU market
- Enhance innovation and the competitiveness of the EU chemicals industry
- Reduce animal testing by promoting the use of alternative methods of assessing chemicals

It entered into force on 1 June 2007 and replaced a large number of European Directives and Regulations in a single system.

Regulator

The European Chemicals Agency (ECHA) is the body responsible for the administration of REACH in the EU. It manages the submission of data in the form of dossiers from industry and provides guidance and assistance to industry.

Regulation

REACH has a very wide scope as it applies to all chemical substances that are manufactured, imported, placed on the market or used within the European Community, either on their own or as mixtures or in other products.

Some substances are exempted from the overall scope of REACH, while others are exempted from certain parts of the regulation. They are as follows:

- Radioactive substances
- Those under customs supervision

- Non-isolated intermediates
- Transport of substances
- Waste

Other substances can be exempted from certain provisions of REACH provided they are regulated under other existing EU legislation, such as medicinal products for human or veterinary use, food or feeding stuffs, plant protection products and biocides etc.

Substances listed in Annexes IV and V of REACH are exempted from registration.

An exporter has to appoint an Only Representative (OR) within the EU who completes the registration dossier on behalf of all of the EU importers. Appointment of the OR must be made in writing by the exporter; the EU importers must have confirmation of this appointment and that their tonnage is covered by the arrangement.

A flowchart to explain the process is given below:

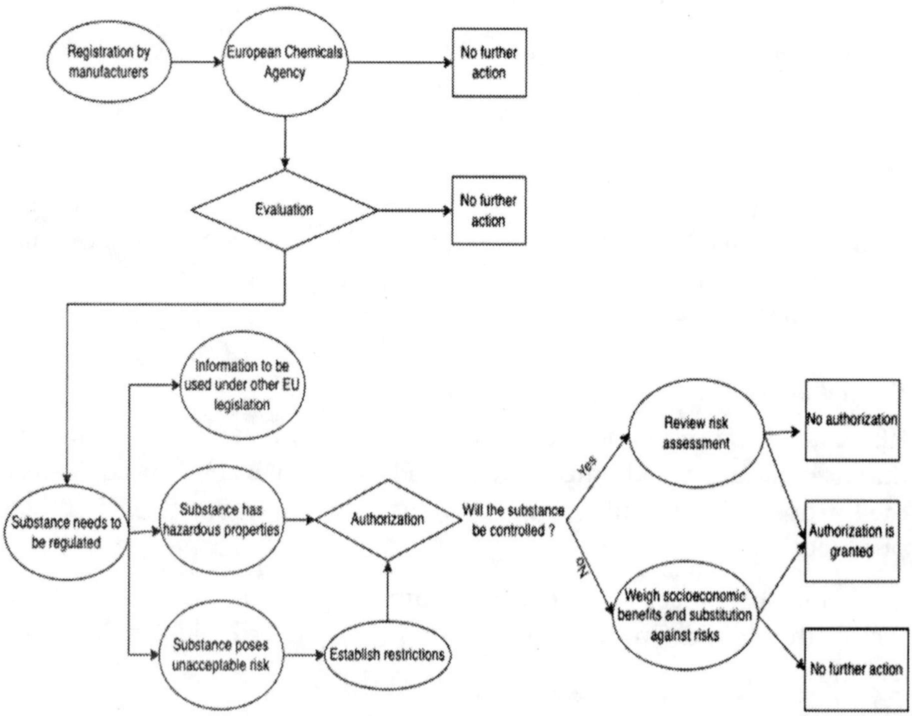

Figure 24: REACH flowchart

Evaluation

Evaluation is a process under REACH which involves ECHA, Member State Competent Authorities and registrants. There are two types of evaluation which can be carried out: dossier evaluation and substance evaluation.

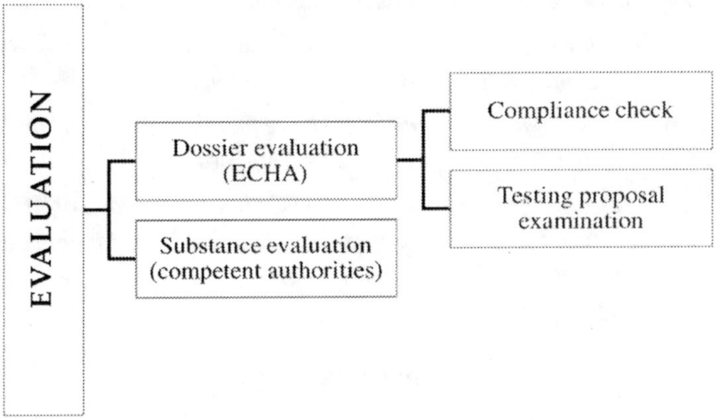

Figure 25: Evaluation under REACH

There are two processes under dossier evaluation:

(i) Compliance check: ECHA examines the registration dossier to check if the information provided is compliant with the standard information requirements of REACH.

(ii) Testing proposal examination: This applies only to registration dossiers at 100 tonnes or more. Where a registrant identifies the need to perform new testing to meet the standard information requirements of REACH, they are required to submit a testing proposal to ECHA prior to commencing the study.

Substance evaluation applies to any registered substance. It is undertaken by Member State Competent Authorities. Its aim is to clarify whether the use of a particular substance/group of substances poses a risk to human health or the environment and to decide if further information should be requested from the registrants of the substance(s) to verify the suspected concerns. Substance evaluation takes into account all registrations of the substance(s), regardless of the tonnage band.

Substance of Very High Concern (SVHC)

Certain substances which may have serious or irreversible effects on human health or the environment can be identified as Substances of Very High Concern (SVHC). In particular, Article 57 of REACH outlines specific criteria for the identification of SVHCs:

- *Substances classified as carcinogenic, mutagenic or toxic to reproduction (CMRs)*
- *Substances that are persistent, bio-accumulative and toxic (PBT) or very persistent and very bio-accumulative (vPvB) to the environment*
- *Substances for which there is scientific evidence that they give rise to an equivalent level of concern to CMRs, PBTs or vPvB substances*

A Member State or ECHA (on request of the EU Commission) may prepare a proposal to identify a substance as a SVHC when it considers that it meets the above criteria. Such proposals are subject to a public consultation on ECHA's website. All agreed SVHCs are included in the Candidate List.

Candidate List

It is a list of all agreed SVHCs. It is periodically updated and the latest version can be found on the ECHA website. The inclusion of a substance on the Candidate List results in a number of immediate legal obligations on the use of the substance on its own, in mixtures or in articles:

- *Notification: producers and importers of articles containing candidate list substance(s) in a concentration above 0.1% (w/w) and where the quantities of SVHC in the articles is greater than 1 tonne per year must submit a notification to ECHA*
- *Information on substances in articles: suppliers of articles which contain candidate list substance(s) in a concentration above 0.1% (w/w) have to provide sufficient information to allow safe use of the article to their customers or, upon request, to a consumer*
- *Information on mixtures: suppliers of a mixture not classified as dangerous, but containing at least one substance on the candidate list at a concentration of at least 0.1%, must provide a safety data sheet to recipients on requests*
- *Information on substances: Suppliers of a substance that appears on the candidate list must provide a safety data sheet to their customer*

Authorization

Authorization is a licensing system, whereby chemical substances which are included on the Authorization List (Annex XIV of the REACH Regulation) may not be used or placed on the market for use in the EU, unless an authorization has been granted for that specific use. The aim of authorization is to promote substitution of such hazardous substances with less hazardous substances or technologies.

The first step in this process is the identification of a chemical as a Substance of Very High Concern (SVHC) and its inclusion on the Candidate List.

Periodically, ECHA reviews the substances on the Candidate List and recommends some for inclusion in the Authorization List. The final decision on whether a substance is added to the Authorization List is taken by the European Commission.

Registration

REACH requires each manufacturer and importer of a substance from outside the EU, and each producer and importer of articles containing a substance intended to be released, to submit a registration dossier to the European Chemicals Agency (ECHA) once the manufacture or import reaches one tonne or more per year. Companies must collect information on the properties and uses of the substance they manufacture or import, and assess the hazards and potential risks posed. This information is submitted to ECHA in a registration dossier via a specific IT system, known as REACH-IT. A standard set of data is required for each substance – the amount of information depending on the tonnage of the substance.

Labelling

The two main instruments used to communicate the hazards of chemicals are labels and safety data sheets. Provisions for labels are regulated by Classification, Packaging and Labelling (CLP) regulations. While the label is the primary tool for communication of hazard information to the consumer, the safety data sheet provides more detailed information on hazards and control measures for the worker. Safety Data Sheets should accompany chemicals throughout the supply chain, providing information to users in order to ensure that the chemicals are safely managed.

China

China is the world's largest chemicals market. Globally, the chemical industry generates a total revenue of approximately USD 4 trillion every year. Almost 45 per cent of that amount came from China alone as of 2020. Not only does China generate the highest revenue from the chemical industry in the world, but it is also a leader in chemical exports, with an annual export value of over USD 72 billion. At the same time, China's domestic chemical consumption amounted to USD 1.77 trillion in 2020.

With USD 330 billion of total revenue and over 725,000 people employed, organic chemical material manufacturing is an important part of China's chemical industry. Organic chemicals are also China's largest chemical export category, accounting for over 75 per cent of Chinese chemical exports based on value. The top destinations for Chinese chemical exports as of 2019 were the United States and India, while other major destinations were predominantly emerging countries. On the other hand, the largest importers of chemicals from China were Japan and Korea, each importing over USD 20 billion worth of chemicals in 2019, followed by the USA and Germany.

Regulatory regime

Chemical regulations are implemented under two primary enabling Decrees/Orders:

(i) The "Decree of the State Council—People's Republic of China—Number 591—Regulations on Safe Management of Hazardous Chemicals" (Decree No. 591)

(ii) The "Order of the Ministry of Ecology and Environment (MEE) Number 12—Measures on the Environmental Management Registration of New Chemical Substances" (MEE Order No. 12).

Decree No. 591 is currently under revision with the second draft revision, "Law on Safety of Hazardous Chemicals," issued on October 2, 2020. The third draft revision is expected in 2022. In addition, China currently implements the 4th revised edition of the United Nations Globally Harmonized System of Classification and Labelling of Chemicals (GHS) through a series of national standards (GB30000 series, GB15258, GB/T16483, and GB/T17519), and adoption of the 7th revised edition of GHS and the 20th revised edition of the United Nations Recommendations on the Transport of Dangerous Goods is under consultation.

Regulator

The Ministry of Ecology and Environment is primarily in charge of the complete management of new chemical substances, and the Ministry of Ecology and Environment's Solid Waste and Chemicals Management Technology Center is in charge of routine administrative activities such as receiving and processing documents submitted by the applicants.

Regulation

The "Order of the Ministry of Ecology and Environment (MEE) Number 12—Measures on the Environmental Management Registration of New Chemical Substances" (MEE Order No. 12) came into effect from 1 January 2021.

MEE is sometimes also called the 'China REACH' for short. 'China REACH' references the EU Regulation No. 1907/2006 concerning the Registration, Evaluation, Authorization and Restriction of Chemicals.

Under MEE Order 12, any entity involved in research, production, importation and processing of new chemicals in China (except for areas under special customs regulation, such as a bonded area) shall obtain filing or registration of such new chemicals prior to production or importation. New chemicals refer to chemicals not yet included in the Inventory of Existing Chemical Substances in China (IECSC). "New chemicals" do not include medicine, pesticide, veterinary medicine, cosmetics, food, food additives, fodder, fodder additives and fertilizers, except when they are used for other industrial usage.

When applying for filing or registration, the applicant may also apply for trade secret protection on information related to the new chemicals. MEE Order 12 provides the longest protection term – five years from the date of filing or registration.

According to the Order, a new chemical will automatically be added by MEE to IECSC after five years of regular registration. As such, a new hazardous chemical will also be added to IECSC after five years of regular registration but may be further subject to its restricted usage, as mentioned below:

- New chemicals subject to filing or simplified registration will not be listed in IECSC. Being listed in IECSC means the use of such chemical in China is in principle not subject to the regulation of

MEE Order 12 (i.e., no registration or filing under MEE Order 12 is required), and only ordinary environmental regulation applies to it.

- However, as to highly hazardous chemicals, PBT, their restricted usage will be recorded in IECSC, and new usage chemicals be regulated. Under the Order, if the holder of the registration of a highly hazardous chemical proposes to change the usage of such chemical, or any other entity proposes to use it for any usage, a new usage registration must be obtained; if any entity proposes to use a registered PBT chemical for a new usage, a new usage registration must also be obtained.

Japan

In recent years, the Japanese chemical industry was the 4th largest worldwide, following China, the United States, and Germany. Since other industries such as the transportation machinery industry and the automotive industry are dependent on materials provided by the chemical industry, it is one of the most important and largest manufacturing industries in Japan. Furthermore, the chemical industry was one of the largest employers of the manufacturing industries in Japan, providing employment to over 9 lac people.

In 2020, Japan imported 36 billion worth of chemicals and exported chemicals worth USD 53.8 billion. Its major trading partners are China, the USA, Germany and Korea.

Regulatory regime

The Japan Chemical Substances Control Law (CSCL) was enacted on 16 October 1973 to prevent environmental pollution and control chemical risks to human health. The Law is intended to manage risks of industrial chemicals manufactured and imported in Japan.

Regulator

The regulatory authorities are the Ministry of Health, Labor and Welfare (MHLW), Ministry of Environment (MOE) and Ministry of Economy, Trade and Industry (METI).

Regulation

New Substance Notification under Japan CSCL

An exporter who intends to export a new chemical substance to Japan shall notify it to MHLW, MOE and METI (all three) at least three months prior to the manufacture or importation. These ministries have appointed National Institute of Technology and Evaluation (NITE) as the main body to evaluate new substance notifications under CSCL.

A new substance is defined as a chemical substance other than the following substances:

- A substance that is on the list of existing and new chemical substances (ENCS)
- Monitoring chemical substances
- Priority assessment chemical substances
- Class I or II specified chemical substance

Japan ENCS consists of two parts:

- Existing chemical substances placed on Japanese market before 16 Oct 1973 (approximately 20,600 substances)
- New chemical substances that have been notified under the CSCL, determined to be "safe" and published in the government Gazette (more than 8,000 substances)

The outline of the regulation is given on next page.

Korea

Korea is one of the world's leading chemical exporters. Most of its export partners are other Asian countries, with China importing more Korean chemicals than the other top nine partners combined. Additionally, the country is also an active importer of chemicals. As Korea lacks natural sources of oil and gas, the import of petrochemicals for domestic use and further processing is vital.

Korea imported chemicals worth USD 35 billion and exported worth USD 40.7 billion. Its major export destinations are China, Chinese Taipei and Japan whereas import destinations are China, Japan and the USA.

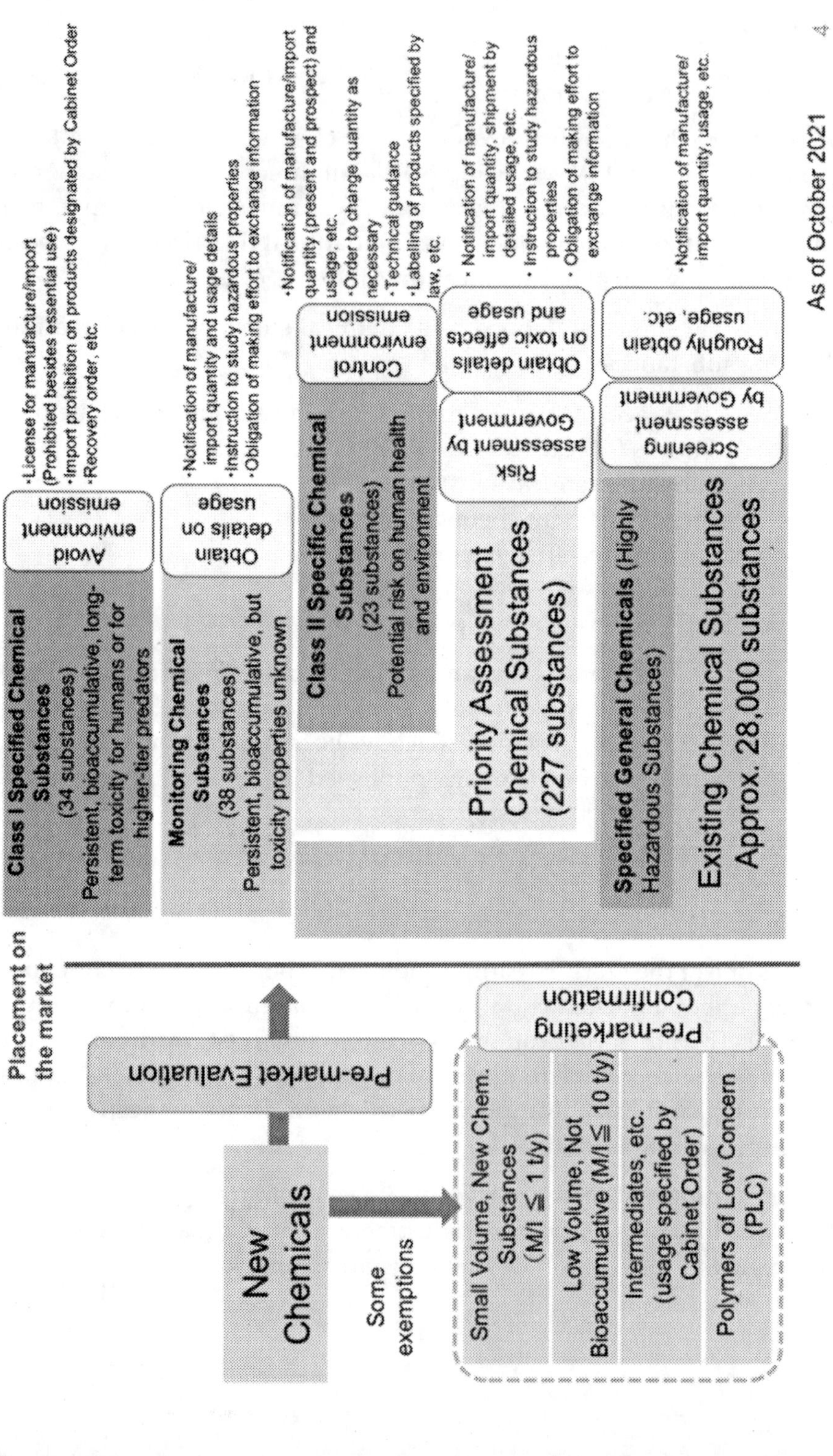

Figure 26: Outline of CSCL, Japan

Regulatory regime

Similar to EU, Korea also has a REACH regulation, called as K-REACH. On 1 January 2015, Korea revised its laws with respect to "new" chemical notifications. In this revision, the former Toxic Chemical Control Act (TCCA) was divided and recast into the following:

- The Act on the Registration and Evaluation of Chemicals (K-REACH, also known as ARECS) and
- The Chemicals Control Act (CCA)

K-REACH, which was promulgated on 22 May 2013, regulates the designation of hazardous chemical substances through registration and evaluation. The CCA regulates the control and follow-up management of hazardous chemicals designated by K-REACH.

Based on the results of a hazard and risk assessment, chemicals can be placed into one of four categories: toxic substance, authorization substance, restricted substance, or prohibited substance under CCA. The chemicals will then be subject to further regulations as applicable.

Regulator

The Ministry of Environment (MoE) is the regulator for K-REACH. It is supported by:

- The National Institute of Environmental Research (NIER): Responsible for registrations, reduced registrations, amendments to registrations, and registration enquiries.
- The Korea Environment Corporation (KECO): Responsible for applications for pre-registration and confirmation of exemptions from registration.
- The Ministry of Environment and Labor (MoEL): Responsible for the associated Korea Occupational Safety and Health Act (OSHA) and the regulation of chemicals in the workplace (e.g., United Nations Globally Harmonized System of Classification and Labelling of Chemicals [UN GHS] implementation).

Some key dates are mentioned in Table 7.

Table 7: K-REACH deadlines

31 December 2030	Deadline for registration of substances exceeding 1t/y.
31 December 2027	Deadline for registration of substances exceeding 10t/y.
31 December 2024	Deadline for registration of substances exceeding 100t/y.
31 December 2021	Deadline for registration of CMR substances exceeding 1t/y and substances exceeding 1000t/y
30 June 2019	Deadline for K-REACH pre-registration
1 January 2019	Commencement of the amended K-REACH
21 November 2015	K-REACH: new substances notification leniency programme ends
1 January 2015	"K-REACH" comes into force

Regulation

The K-REACH regulation is similar to EU-REACH.

Registration

The exporters have to complete K-REACH registration for the following products:

- At least 0.1 ton/y of a new chemical substance;
- Existing substances manufactured, imported or sold more than 1 ton per year

New substances manufactured or imported at least 0.1 ton/y shall be registered prior to manufacturing or importation. A grace period (given to pre-registered substances) will be granted to existing substances to be manufactured/ imported at least 1 ton/y.

Foreign manufacturers exporting chemical substances or products containing hazardous chemical substance may appoint an Only Representative to fulfill relevant obligations under K-REACH.

New Substance

A new substance is defined as a substance that is not on the following lists:

- *Chemical substances which were placed on Korean market before 2 February 1991, and notified by the Ministry of Environment on 23 December 1996; and*
- *Chemical substances which have undergone the examination of toxicity under the former provisions or the provisions of this Act after 2 February 1991 and were announced by the Minister of Environment.*

Looking ahead

Chemicals are an integral part of our life is an undeniable fact and cannot be wiped off from use in daily activities, despite their hazardous nature. Their usage and exposure, however, have to be controlled.

During COVID-19, the sale of chemicals was affected as manufacturing in various sectors had nearly halted and supply chain disrupted but post COVID-19, the manufacturing of chemicals is bouncing back. The recovery road is not the same as earlier. Changes are being seen in terms of digitalization, human resources deployment, environmental concerns and supply chain localization.

The developed countries through REACH-like regulations and inventorization have ensured that all chemicals placed in their market are accounted for. It is similar to establishing traceability of chemicals as is present in agricultural products.

The developing countries are also realizing the importance of the REACH regulation but the process of complete implementation will take almost a decade. EU took 10 years to implement the regulation in a phased manner. The K-REACH will be implemented by 2030. Other countries that have REACH-like regulations are Turkey and the UK. Several countries around the world, including the United States, Australia, Japan, Philippines, Canada, Taiwan, New Zealand, Switzerland and China have chemical registration protocols under which chemical registrations and notifications only have to be submitted for new substances and SVHCs.

India has a large manufacturing base and is a prominent exporter of chemicals. Therefore, any regulation that has to be prepared has to be prepared keeping industry's readiness to adopt to the regulation without much disruption. The exporters who are already exporting to countries such as EU, China and the USA are well aware of the operation of REACH-like regulations in these countries. The domestic manufacturers, downstream users and other consumers have to be taken on-board for bringing similar regulation in India. Enough buffer also has to be built into the timeline for registration such that very little damage to the manufacturers is incurred during the transition from no regulation to complete monitoring system.

REFERENCES

- https://www.statista.com/statistics/302018/global-chemical-exports-by-region/
- https://www.investindia.gov.in/sector/chemicals
- https://www.ibef.org/industry/chemical-industry-india/infographic
- https://www.cseindia.org/state-of-pesticide-regulations-in-india-7611#:~:text=The%20pesticides'%20regulations%20in%20India,operation%20of%20Ministry%20of%20Agriculture.
- https://www.bis.gov.in/index.php/product-certification/products-under-compulsory-certification/scheme-i-mark-scheme/
- https://www.statista.com/topics/1526/chemical-industry-in-the-us/
- https://www.chemwatch.net/blog/chemical-acts-regulatory-bodies-codes-and-standards-usa/
- https://www.epa.gov/laws-regulations/summary-toxic-substances-control-act
- https://www.epa.gov/compliance/compliance-monitoring-strategy-toxic-substances-control-act-tsca
- https://www.epa.gov/tsca-import-export-requirements/tsca-requirements-importing-chemicals#who
- https://www.hsa.ie/eng/your_industry/chemicals/legislation_enforcement/reach/#:~:text=The%20European%20Chemicals%20Agency%20(ECHA,its%20website%2C%20guidance%20and%20helpdesk.
- https://www.hsa.ie/eng/your_industry/chemicals/legislation_enforcement/reach/evaluation/
- https://www.hsa.ie/eng/your_industry/chemicals/legislation_enforcement/reach/svhcs_and_authorisation/
- https://www.hsa.ie/eng/your_industry/chemicals/legislation_enforcement/reach/registration/
- https://www.hsa.ie/eng/your_industry/chemicals/legislation_enforcement/reach/information_in_the_supply_chain/
- https://www.statista.com/topics/8167/chemical-industry-in-china/
- https://www.actagroup.com/practices/chemical-regulation-in-china#:~:text=Chemical%20regulations%20in%20China%20currently,Hazardous%20Chemicals%E2%80%9 D%20(Decree%20No.
- https://www.natlawreview.com/article/china-s-new-regulation-new-chemicals-aims-to-make-life-easier
- https://enviliance.com/regions/east-asia/cn/cn-chemical
- https://www.statista.com/topics/7733/chemical-industry-in-japan/#dossierKeyfigures
- https://www.cirs-group.com/en/chemicals/japan-cscl-and-ishl
- https://www.statista.com/topics/8673/chemical-industry-in-south-korea/#dossierContents__outerWrapper
- https://www.cirs-group.com/en/chemicals/revised-k-reach-the-act-on-the-registration-and-evaluation-of-chemicals
- https://www.intertek.com/assuris/chemicals/regulatory/k-reach/#:~:text=K%2DREACH%2C%20which%20was%20promulgated,chemicals%20designated%20by%20K%2DREACH.
- https://www.compliancegate.com/toxic-substances-control-act/

COSMETICS

Cosmetics is the 24th largest sector traded across the globe with an export of USD 144.7 billion in 2020, the major exporters being France, the USA, and Germany. The major import destinations are China and the USA.

The production of cosmetics and beauty products is controlled by a handful of multi-national corporations—L'Oréal, Unilever, Procter & Gamble, Estee Lauder, Shiseido, and Lancôme, to name just a few. As of 2021, the French cosmetics company, L'Oréal, was the leading beauty manufacturer in the world, generating about USD 34 billion in revenue that year.

The International Cooperation on Cosmetics Regulation (ICCR) is a voluntary international group of cosmetics regulatory authorities from Brazil, Canada, Chinese Taipei, the European Union, Japan, the Republic of Korea, and the USA that meet on an annual basis to discuss cosmetics safety and regulation, as well as enter into a constructive dialogue with relevant cosmetics industry trade associations.

The products are traded under chapter 33 of the HS code. A broad scope of coverage is given below:

Item	*Definition*	*HS code*
Perfume and eau de cologne	Perfume and eau de cologne	3303
Make up cosmetics	Foundation creams, lipsticks, eye makeup, etc.	3304
Skin care cosmetics	Skin lotions, essence, skin milk, cleansing creams, etc.	3304
Hair care cosmetics	Hair dyes, shampoos, hair treatments, etc.	3305
Special purpose cosmetics	Sunscreens, shaving creams, etc.	3307
Cosmetic soaps	Soaps for cosmetics	3401

Figure 27: HS classification for cosmetics

With work from home becoming the new norm in the COVID-19 era, the consumption of cosmetics has gone down, especially when consumers prefer to work in a comfortable environment. The largest affected segment is that of lipsticks, whose market has been nearly washed out by the use of COVID-19 masks. However, there are efforts by the industry to revive usage, but until the waves of infection keep on returning, the industry will have a challenging time ahead.

India

The Indian cosmetics industry is a small one with very few recognized brands of its own. Most of the brands are domestically established. The current market size is only USD 26.8 billion. Exports were USD 1.84 billion for 2020 and imports were USD 661 million, with imports primarily from China, the USA, and France. The bulk of exports go to the USA, UAE, and China.

Regulatory regime

Regulator

The Central Drugs Standard Control Organization (CDSCO) is the regulator for cosmetics and pharmaceuticals that issues licences for cosmetics. Registration and import of cosmetic products is governed by the Drugs and Cosmetics Act, 1945, and the new Cosmetics Rules, 2020.

> **Cosmetics: definition**
>
> *It means any article, which is intended to be poured, scrubbed sprayed, or introduced into the human body which is used for cleansing, beautifying, or altering the appearance, which also includes any article used as a component of cosmetics products.*
>
> *The new Cosmetic Rules, 2020, introduces the concept of "New Cosmetics", which refers to a cosmetic, which contains a novel ingredient that has not been used anywhere else in the world or is not recognized for use in cosmetics in any national or international literature.*

Regulation

The applicant is first required to register on the online 'Sugam' portal. All imports must also be registered through the SUGAM portal in Form COS-1 with the following documents:

- A valid manufacturing licence for the complete formulation of the cosmetic with details in a form from the State Licensing Authority
- Details of registered brand owners of the finished product in India

A fee of USD 1,000 is charged per category, USD 50 per variant, and USD 500 per manufacturing site.

Step 1: Determination of classification of cosmetics
When a manufacturer decides to get their products registered in India, he/she must review the CDSCO's gazette notifications prior to making a final determination of a product's regulatory status

↓

Step 2: Appointment of Indian agent
The agent must have a wholesale licence (Forms 20B and 21B/C) who will then be granted the power of attorney to manage registration and importation in India

↓

Step 3: Compilation of documents and process to obtain certificate for import
A number of documents are required*

Figure 28: Procedure for import of cosmetics in India

*Form COS 1/2, Challan, Power of Attorney, Schedule III, original copy of label, FSC, product specifications and testing protocol, list of countries where marketing permit/ authorization has been granted, receipt of application form, fee, etc.

Following the evaluation of the application, the CDSCO will either make a request for additional papers or issue the import Registration Certificate within six months from the date of application. The Registration Certificate granted to an importer shall remain valid for a period of five years from the date of its issuance, unless suspended or cancelled by the authority.

Animal testing

No cosmetics that have been tested on animals after 12 November 2012 can be imported into India

What are prohibited cosmetics?

1. *Manufacture or sale of the cosmetic that is prohibited in the country of origin*
2. *'Use Before or Use by Date' is less than six months from the date of import*
3. *Cosmetics that contain 'hexachlorophene' (considered harmful on humans) and*
4. *Cosmetics that have been tested on animals*

Labelling

Labelling has been revised and made stricter in the amended rules of 2020. The rules mandate importers to ensure that the following requirements are complied with on both the inner and outer coverings of cosmetics:

- The name of the cosmetic, name of legal manufacturer, complete address of the manufacturing site and date of expiry must be stated on both the inner and outer labels
- A declaration on the outer label specifying the net content in terms of weight, fluid measures, and numerical count used in manufacturing the product
- A distinctive Batch number, Lot number, Manufacturing licence number and Registration Certificate number in a proper manner as required under the 2020 Rules
- Names of ingredients present in concentration of more than 1 per cent must be listed in descending order of weight or volume at the time they are added, followed by those in concentration of less than or equal to 1 per cent, in any order, and preceded by the word "INGREDIENTS"
- In case of cosmetic products containing hazardous ingredients, the label for 'Direction for safe use' or any such caution or warning must be specified on the inner label of the product
- Details of the importer must be stated, along with any other information necessary to be disclosed under the 2020 Rules and rules stipulated by the BIS for a few specific categories of cosmetic products

United States of America

The USA is the largest trader in cosmetics. It exported USD 12.3 billion of cosmetics to countries like Canada, China, and Mexico and imported USD 13.5 billion from Ireland, France, Canada, etc., during 2020.

Regulatory regime

Regulator

As far as the regulation aspect goes, the Food and Drug Administration (FDA) regulates all imports of cosmetics before they are cleared by Customs and Border Protection (CBP).

Cosmetics: definition

The Food, Drugs & Cosmetics Act of the USA defines cosmetics by their intended use, as "articles intended to be rubbed, poured, sprinkled, or sprayed on, introduced into, or otherwise applied to the human body...for cleansing, beautifying, promoting attractiveness, or altering appearance".

However, if the product is intended for therapeutic use, such as treating or preventing disease, or to affect the structure or function of the body, it is a drug, or in some cases, a medical device, even if it affects the appearance.

Regulation

Cosmetic products and ingredients are not subject to pre-market approval by the FDA. Colour additives are an exception. However, these additives must be safe and must be properly labelled. The colour additives must be approved for the intended use while some must be from batches certified by the FDA.

Under the law, manufacturers are not required to register their cosmetic establishments or file their product formulations with the FDA. No registration number is required to import cosmetics into the USA.

However, cosmetic firms can register with FDA's Voluntary Cosmetic Registration Program (VCRP) using an online registration system. Cosmetic manufacturers, distributors, and packers can file information on their products that are currently being marketed to consumers in the USA and register their manufacturing and/or packaging facility locations in the VCRP database.

In order to focus inspection efforts more efficiently, the FDA issues import alerts to advise inspectors of trends in violations. Among the products addressed in import alerts are those marketed with therapeutic claims that are considered unapproved new drugs under the law, cosmetics that are adulterated because of microbial contamination, failure to meet USA requirements for colour additives, and bulk shipments of high-risk bovine tissue from BSE (bovine spongiform encephalopathy) countries. With the exception of colour additives and those ingredients that are prohibited or restricted by FDA regulations, a cosmetic firm may use any ingredient, as long as it does not cause the product to be adulterated in any way.

Labelling

Since cosmetics are not regulated per se, some requirements are still necessary to be followed such as labelling. The following are some of them:

- All required label information must be in English. However, if some labelling information appears in another language, all required label information must also appear in that language
- Under the Fair Packaging and Labelling Act (FPLA), ingredients must be identified by their "common or usual names". Terms such as "aqua," "mel," or "parfum" are permitted only in parentheses following their common or usual names in English, such as "water," "honey," and "fragrance"
- The regulations require use of common or usual names. Latin terms may be included parenthetically following the common or usual name of an ingredient. Example: Aloe (Aloe barbadensis) Extract
- C.I. (Cosmetic Ingredients) numbers are not acceptable on product labelling unless they are preceded by the colour additive names accepted in the country followed by the C.I. number in parentheses as they do not indicate FDA approval or FDA colour certification
- Bulk cosmetics do not have to comply with the cosmetic labelling regulations if the person introducing the shipment is the operator of the establishment where the shipment is going to be repackaged and labelled, or, in a case where someone else is going to introduce the shipment into the country, if a written agreement signed by the establishment operator is available for customs officials at the time the shipment is offered for import. The labelling exemption will be void, however, if the product is shifted from the establishment without the required labelling.
- There are no regulations to print expiration dates
- As part of the prohibition against false or misleading information, no cosmetic can be labelled or advertised with statements suggesting that the FDA has approved the product
- The following information must appear on the principal display panel[9]
    - o An identity statement, indicating the nature and use of the product by means of either the common or usual name, a

9. This is the part of the label most likely displayed or examined under customary conditions of display for sale

descriptive name, a fanciful name understood by the public, or an illustration

- o An accurate statement of the net quantity of contents in terms of weight, measure, numerical count or a combination of numerical count and weight or measure
- o The declaration must be distinct, placed in the bottom area of the panel in line generally parallel to the base on which the package rests, and in a type size commensurate with the size of the container as prescribed by regulation. The net quantity of contents may be stated in terms of the metric system of weights or measures

- The following information must appear on an information panel:[10]
    - o Name and place of business for manufacturer, packer, or distributor
    - o Distributor statement: If the name and address are not those of the manufacturer, the label must say "Manufactured for..." or "Distributed by...," or similar wording
    - o Material facts: Failure to reveal material facts is one form of misleading labelling and therefore makes a product misbranded. An example is directions for safe use if a product could be unsafe if used incorrectly
    - o Warning and caution statements: They must be prominent and conspicuous
    - o Ingredients: If the product is sold on a retail basis to consumers, even if it is labelled "For professional use only" or words to that effect, the ingredients must appear on an information panel, in descending order of predominance.

Companies and individuals who manufacture or market cosmetics have a legal responsibility to ensure the safety of their products. Neither the law nor FDA regulations require specific tests to demonstrate the safety of individual products or ingredients. The law also does not require cosmetic companies to share their safety information with the FDA.

10. Refers to a panel other than the PDP that can accommodate label information where the consumer is likely to see it

Use of colour additives

If a product contains a colour additive, the following points have to be kept in mind:

- *Approval:* All colour additives used in cosmetics (or any other FDA-regulated product) must be approved by the FDA. There are regulations specifically addressing a substance's use as a colour additive, specifications, and restrictions.
- *Certification:* In addition to approval, a number of colour additives must be batch certified by the FDA if they are to be used.
- *Identity and Specifications:* All colour additives must meet technical requirements mentioned in the CFR.
- *Use and Restrictions:* Colour additives may be used only for the intended uses stated in the regulations that pertain to them.

How are colour additives recognized?

The FD&C Act, Section 721[21 U.S. C. 3(c)] and colour additive regulations [21 CFR, Parts 70 and 80] distinguish colour additives into two main categories: those subject to certification and those exempt from certification. In addition, the regulations refer to other classifications, such as straight colours and lakes.

- **Colours subject to certification:** *These colour additives are derived primarily from petroleum and are sometimes known as "coal-tar dye" or "synthetic-organic" colours.*
  - o *Except in the case of coal-tar hair dyes, these colours must not be used unless FDA has certified that the batch in question has passed analysis of its composition and purity in FDA's own labs.*
  - o *These certified colours generally have three-part names. The names include a prefix FD&C, D&C, or External D&C; a colour; and a number. An example is "FD&C Yellow no. 5". Certified colours also may be identified in cosmetic ingredient declarations by colour and number alone, without a prefix (such as "Yellow 5").*
- **Colours exempt from certification:** *These colour additives are obtained primarily from mineral, plant, or animal sources. They are not subject to batch certification requirements. However, they are still considered artificial colours, and when used in cosmetics or other FDA-regulated products, they must comply with the identity, specifications, uses, restrictions, and labelling requirements stated in the regulations.*

European Union

At an aggregate level, EU imported USD 47.9 billion of cosmetics with the major importers being Germany and France and exports of USD 71.5 billion, the majority of it from the same two countries in 2020. Almost 30 per cent of global imports are made by the EU and, hence, it is important to understand the regulatory environment in the EU.

In the current regulation, the following are the most significant changes that have been brought about:

Strengthened safety requirements for cosmetic products

- Manufacturers need to follow specific requirements in the preparation of a product safety report prior to placing a product on the market.

Introduction of the notion of 'responsible person'

- Only cosmetic products for which a legal or natural person is designated within the EU as a 'responsible person' can be placed on the market. The new cosmetics regulation allows precise identification of the responsible person and clearly outlines their obligations.

Centralised notification of all cosmetic products placed on the EU market

- Manufacturers need to notify their products only once – via the EU- CPNP

Introduction of reporting of Serious Undesirable Effects (SUE)

- A responsible person has an obligation to notify serious undesirable effects to national authorities. The authorities also collect information coming from users, health professionals, and others that can be shared with other EU countries.

New rules for the use of nanomaterials in cosmetic products

- Colourants, preservatives and UV-filters, including those that are nanomaterials, must be explicitly authorised. Products containing other nanomaterials not otherwise restricted by the cosmetics regulation will be the object of a full safety assessment at the EU level if the Commission has concerns. Nanomaterials must be labelled in the list of ingredients with the word 'nano' in brackets following the name of the substance, e.g., 'titanium dioxide (nano)'.

Figure 29: EU regulation (cosmetics)

Regulatory regime

Regulation

The overall regulation governing the EU market is Regulation No. 1223/ 2009 but national regulations also apply. That means in addition to a common regulation across EU, country specific regulations will also have to be complied with. Every cosmetic placed on the EU market must have a Product Information File (PIF) which includes a Safety Assessment (SA) and must comply with Good Manufacturing Practices (GMP). Not just the cosmetic, but the ingredients contained in the cosmetic formula must also be authorized in the EU. Apart from EU regulations on cosmetics, requirements of the REACH regulation also have to be followed.

> ***Cosmetics: definition***
>
> *"Any substance or mixture intended to be placed in contact with the external parts of the human body (epidermis, hair system, nails, lips, and external genital organs) or with the teeth and the mucous membranes of the oral cavity with a view exclusively or mainly to cleaning them, perfuming them, changing their appearance, protecting them, keeping them in good condition or correcting body odours" (Article 2 Regulation 1223/2009).*

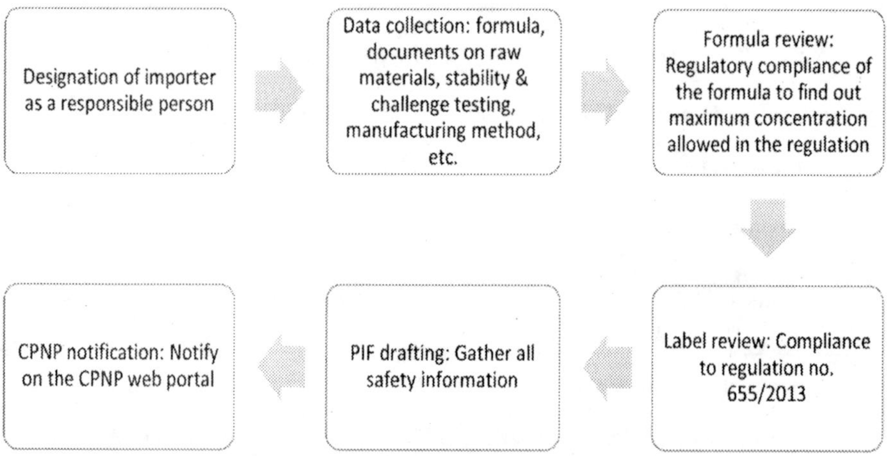

Figure 30: Compliance in EU with cosmetics regulation

The responsible person is not only indicated on the cosmetic packaging; he or she also has obligations (such as safety of the product, GMP, safety assessment, notification, etc.). Every paid and free supply of a cosmetic product for distribution, consumption, or use in the context of a commercial activity, even promotional gifts at trade fairs, is considered to be placing the product on the market.

A PIF is to be created by the manufacturer. It has two parts: part A includes product safety information and part B includes product safety assessment. The PIF also contains a declaration that GMP (CEN ISO 22716: Cosmetics—Good Manufacturing Practices (GMP)—Guidelines on Good Manufacturing Practices) have been complied with and that no animal testing has been done. Some of the information required are as follows:

- Raw material breakdown formula (Quantitative and Qualitative formula)
- International Nomenclature Cosmetic ingredient name
- Function
- CAS number
- Exact percentage
- Certificate of analysis
- Impurity Profile
- Safety Data Sheets (MSDS)
- Technical data sheets
- PAO and challenge test
- Stability test and DOMD (data of minimum durability) conclusion
- Standard Operating Procedures

Animal testing

According to the EU Cosmetics Regulation, animal testing is prohibited, both with the finished product and with the raw materials used.

This must also be proven.

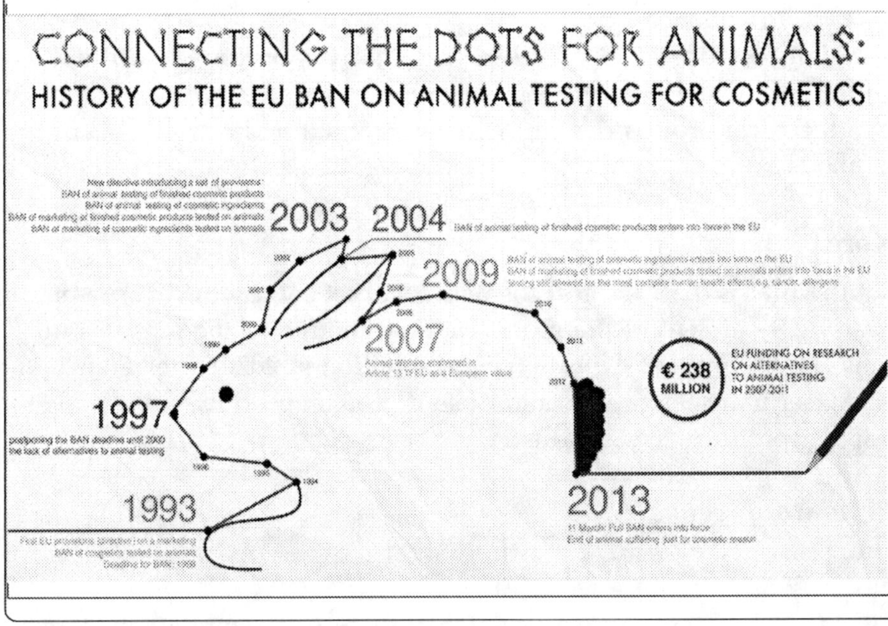

Labelling

There are mandatory requirements such as name and purpose, nominal content, list of ingredients, shelf life, batch, and the address of the responsible person in the EU. Unlike in the USA, the expiry date is required to be mentioned on the product. It is also important that statements about the product be made in the national language of the respective country. Certain products, such as aerosols, hair colours and sunscreens, require additional notices and warnings. The language of the labelling and packaging is determined by the laws in the member-state where the product is intended to be marketed and sold.

Market surveillance

EU countries are responsible for the surveillance of their own markets for cosmetics. In order to ensure a coherent approach to consumer product issues, the market surveillance authorities of all EU countries established the Platform of European Market Surveillance Authorities for Cosmetics (PEMSAC). The aim of this network is to facilitate cooperation by:

- coordinating activities
- exchanging information
- developing and implementing joint projects
- exchanging expertise and best practices in cosmetics market surveillance

Members of PEMSAC are representatives of market surveillance authorities in all EU countries. They meet twice a year in plenary and in two technical groups dealing with market surveillance and analytical methods.

Korea

South Korea is the 9th largest cosmetics market in the world, representing nearly 2.8 per cent of the global market, though in the global trade, it ranks 6th in terms of exports (USD 7.4 billion in 2020) after France, the USA, Germany, Singapore, and Ireland. Korean products are among the popular products in the industry.

Regulatory regime

Regulator

The Ministry of Food and Drug Safety (MFDS) is the competent authority that enacts and executes cosmetic regulations. The South Korean Pharmaceutical Traders Association (KPTA) is responsible for issuing importing cosmetic approvals and supervising cosmetics trading.

Regulation

The Cosmetics Act represents the main legal regulatory framework and provides standards for the manufacture, import, and sale of cosmetics and cosmetic ingredients, including detailed requirements for the labelling and advertising of products.

Cosmetics: definition

According to the Cosmetics Act, cosmetic products are defined as "products/articles intended to be applied to the human body by friction, spraying or other means, in order to cleanse it, beautify it, make it more attractive, improve its appearance, maintain, or improve the state of health of the skin or hair, and which has surface effects".

In Korea, cosmetics are divided into 'general' and 'functional' cosmetics:

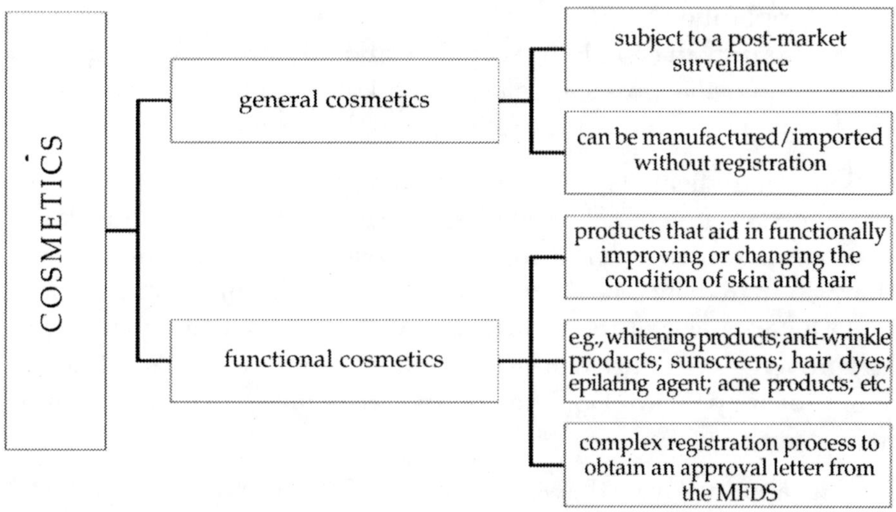

Figure 31: Classification of cosmetics in Korea

A company has to register its type of cosmetics business and the product before it can be placed in the market. A manufacturer has to register as a "manufacturer" whereas an importer has to register as "marketing authorization holder (MAH)". A cosmetics supervisor needs to be designated by the MAH and registered with MFDS. An MAH can be an importer or a third-party like a registration company or shipping and warehousing company.

Functional cosmetics

Functional cosmetics, which previously comprised of 4 categories, viz., whitening, anti-wrinkle, sunscreen, and tanning products, were extended to 10 categories in 2017. The new categories include hair colorants, hair nutrients, and cosmetics that help protect damaged skin. The MFDS only reviews functional cosmetics for pre-market approval. For all other regular cosmetics, the KPTA has been authorized by the MFDS to review and certify import permission requests submitted by the importer.

As per the latest amendment to the regulations, functional products can no longer make any claims on atopic skin, as the term 'atopic' now can only be used in the pharmaceutical product category. The company shall apply to the MFDS for the registration of "Responsible Cosmetic Distribution Business" with the following documents:

- Application letter
- Proof about complying with the standards for quality control and responsible post-sale safety control of cosmetics
- Qualification certificate of responsible distribution manager

Some ingredients have already been approved by the MFDS to be used in certain functional cosmetics. This means that if a manufacturer or importer wants to sell a functional cosmetic which contains only approved ingredients, he does not need to provide clinical and efficacy data. The approval of these products will take about seven days. For unapproved ingredients, clinical and efficacy data have to be submitted for approval by the MFDS. The approval may take 4 to 6 months to be concluded.

After approval from the MFDS (and the KPTA for imported products) and according to the type of cosmetic product, the product needs to be tested in a lab located in Korea.

Prohibited ingredients

The MFDS has issued a list of about 1,032 prohibited ingredients that cannot be added in cosmetics. Furthermore, the manufacturer shall only use restricted preservatives, restricted UV-filter ingredients, restricted hair dye ingredients, and other restricted ingredients under the specific conditions given in the relevant requirements due to safety concerns. If the manufacturer intends to use a non-specified restricted ingredient, it has to apply to the MFDS for approval. The application documents should include:

- Application letter
- A summary of all submitting documents
- The origin, development process, usage standard, and usage situation of the ingredient
- Properties of the ingredient
- Safety and efficacy documents (if necessary)
- Data of the ingredient standard and test method

Labelling

Similar to the practice in the USA, labelling is an important aspect of regulation in Korea. Not just the product, but safe containers that are used to prevent children poisoning themselves by misuse have also been stipulated in the labelling.

The information that is required on the label depends on the category of the cosmetic and its volume, among other parameters. The product's name, name of the MAH, the expiry date and lot number are mandatory on the labels of all products. For functional cosmetics, the MFDS has strict rules on what the product claims and what it can be labelled as, e.g., an "anti-wrinkle" product may claim "anti-wrinkle" or "dine lines" but it cannot claim "anti-aging".

For products with volume content over 10 g, the following labelling requirements prevail:

- Name of product
- Name & address of MAH and Manufacturer
- Names of all ingredients (descending order) for products exceeding 50 ml(g)
- Name of designated ingredients for products exceeding 10 ml(g) and 50 ml(g) and less
- The volume or weight of contents (it should be in ml or g.)
- Price
- In case of functional cosmetics, the word "기능성화장품" (functional cosmetic)

- Cautions in use that is designated by enforcement regulation of cosmetic law
- In the case of functional cosmetics, efficacy, how to use, cautions approved by MFDS
- Bar code
- Call centre information and home page address and phrase ("Exchange or refund if the product has problems")

Animal testing

Animal testing on cosmetics and ingredients was banned in 2017

For general cosmetics (skin care and hair care), the KPTA is the relevant organization for registration and it usually takes seven days to complete the process.

"Organic cosmetics"

In July 2019, the MFDS implemented the Regulations on the Standards of Natural and Organic Cosmetic Products. This Regulation specified "organic" and "natural" definitions, permitted ingredients, manufacturing processes, and requirements for the business entity. For example, the concentration of natural raw materials should exceed 95 per cent in a natural cosmetic. Organic cosmetics, besides the 95 per cent concentration in natural raw materials, have to contain over 10 per cent organic ingredients.

In January 2021, Korea introduced a new certification mechanism, which inspects raw materials instead of the final products.

Recycling Act

The Recycling Act, 2019 is applicable and impacts all products, including cosmetics. Under the said Act, the usage of plastic materials that are difficult to recycle such as PVC and coloured PET bottles has been banned.

In March 2020, the Korean government introduced the world's first customized cosmetics system, which mixes cosmetics at stores according to the individual skin condition and preference. For example, a local cosmetics flagship store now offers a tailored 3D mask. A skincare product utilizes a smart phone app that measures a customer's facial dimensions, generates a skin diagnosis, and sends the information to a special 3D printer, which then prints a hydrogel facial mask that is tailored to the user's face shape and skin conditions.

Japan

Japan is the 7th largest exporter of cosmetics with exports of USD 6.5 billion in 2020 to China. It has a trade surplus in this sector with imports of only USD 3.3 billion during the same period. It primarily imports from France, Korea, and China.

Benefitting from the strict regulations, J-beauty products are valued for their high quality and product safety hidden in a minimalistic design in the global market. Home to large cosmetics manufacturers like Shiseido, Kao Corporation, and Kosé Corporation, J-beauty is particularly represented in the prestige segment overseas. Within the domestic market, the enterprises are covering the mass and high prestige markets through their extended brand portfolios, meeting the broad demand of Japanese consumers.

Regulatory regime

Regulators

The Ministry of Health, Labour, and Welfare (MHLW) under the Pharmaceutical and Medical Devices Law regulates cosmetics. The Pharmaceutical Affairs and Food Sanitation Council is the MHLW's backup expert panel. Prefectural governments are responsible for licensing, inspection, and guidance.

Segmentation

Cosmetics are classified in two broad types: cosmetics and quasi-drugs.

Cosmetics

Cosmetics are products that have a mild action on the human body and are applied by rubbing, sprinkling, or other methods, which aim to clean, beautify and increase attractiveness, alter the appearance, or keep the skin or hair in good condition. In the Japanese market, "cosmetics" are further classified into six different categories:

- Perfume and eau de cologne: Perfume and eau de cologne
- Makeup cosmetics: Foundation creams, lipsticks, eye makeup, and others

- Skincare cosmetics: Skin lotions, essence, skin milk, cleansing creams, and others
- Hair care products: Hair dyes, shampoos, hair treatments, and others
- Special-purpose cosmetics: Sunscreens, shaving creams, and others
- Cosmetic soaps: Soaps for cosmetics

Quasi-drugs

Quasi-drugs have mild effects on the human body, and the MHLW designates them based on their characteristics. Generally, quasi-drugs include deodorants, depilatories, hair growth treatments, hair dyes, bath products, dentifrices, perms, and straightening products as well as medicated cosmetics. Cosmetic products that come under quasi-drugs include:

- Whitening products
- Anti-aging products
- Oily skin or acne treatment products
- Anti-dandruff or anti-itching products
- Freckle-removing products
- Shaving products
- Anti-sunburn or "snow burn" products
- Anti-bactericide products

Cosmetics: definition

The Pharmaceutical Affairs Act defines cosmetics as "Articles with mild action on the human body, which are intended to be applied to the human body through rubbing, sprinkling or other methods, aiming to clean, beautify and increase attractiveness, alter the appearance or to keep the skin or hair in good condition."

The Pharmaceutical Affairs Act defines "Quasi-drug" as an item for the purpose of:

- *Preventing nausea and other discomfort*
- *Preventing heat rash, soreness, etc.*
- *Encouraging hair growth or removing hair*
- *Exterminating and preventing mice, flies, mosquitoes, fleas, etc.*

Importing cosmetics

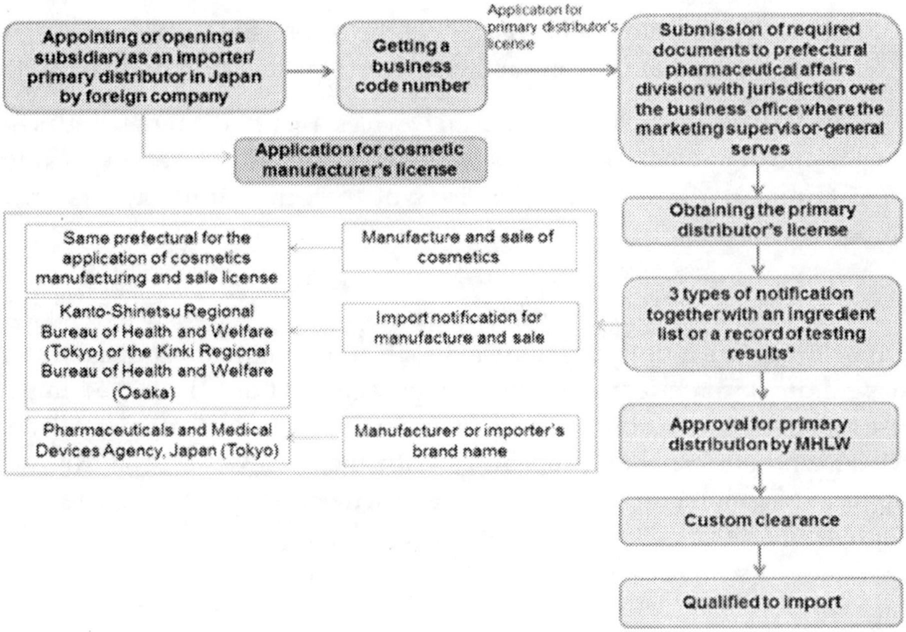

Figure 32: Importing cosmetics in Japan

The following documents are required with the application for a primary distributor's licence and cosmetics manufacturer's licence:

(i) Primary distributor's licence
  (a) A copy of the corporate registration (in the case of a corporation)
  (b) A list of duty specifications
  (c) A medical certificate specifying the applicant
  (d) Documents certifying the qualifications of the marketing supervisor-general
  (e) An employment contract of the marketing supervisor-general
  (f) Documents disclosing the quality management system
  (g) Documents disclosing the post-marketing safety management system
  (h) A floor plan of the business office and storage facility

(ii) Cosmetics manufacturer's licence
  (a) An outline of the physical facility
  (b) A floor plan of the manufacturing facility

(c) Documents certifying the qualifications of the responsible engineer
(d) The employment contract of the responsible engineer
(e) A copy of the contract with a testing laboratory (when used)

The Pharmaceuticals and Medical Devices Agency (PMDA) conducts on-site and document-based inspections, evaluates adverse effects, if any, reports and reviews the applications of foreign manufacturers and importers.

How to export quasi-drugs to Japan?

Quasi-drugs are a unique product classification in Japan. A quasi-drug has minimal to moderate pharmacologic activity but is restricted in its use for specific indications. A foreign manufacturer must appoint a drug MAH who performs all procedures with the MHLW on behalf of the applicant for marketing approval. Moreover, the MAH must have a quality representative, medical safety officer and General Manager who are qualified to take responsibility for release of the medicinal product in Japan.

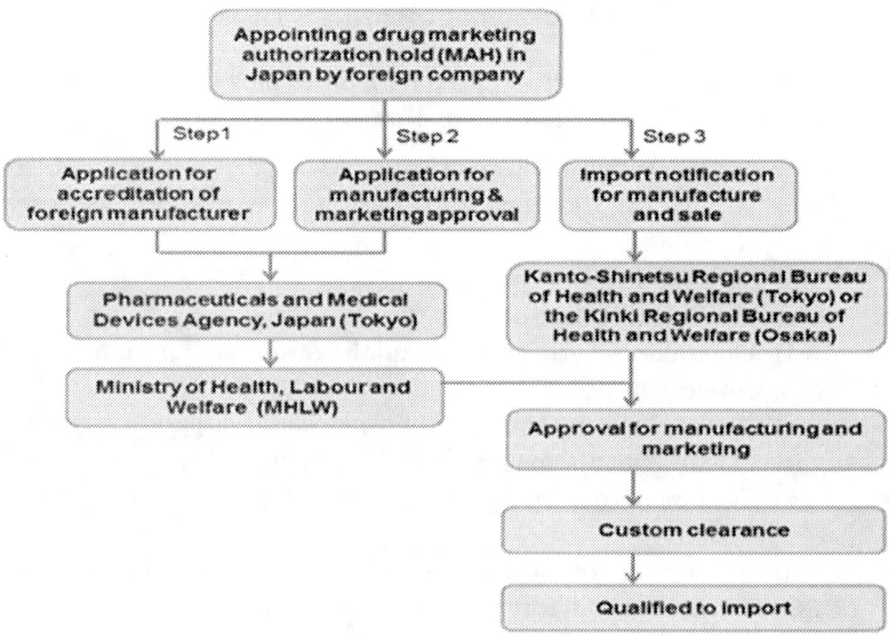

Figure 33: Importing quasi-drugs in Japan

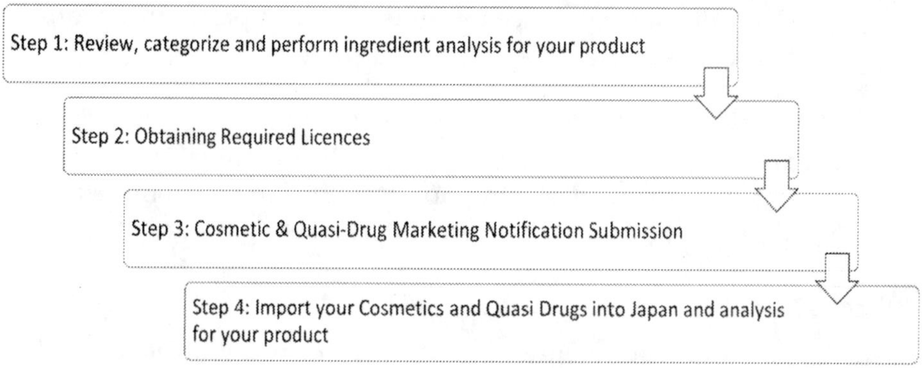

Figure 34: How to market cosmetics in Japan?

Step 1: Review, categorize and perform ingredient analysis

The application process for marketing licences and manufacturing licences for quasi-drugs is the same as for cosmetics. However, the requirements and regulators vary as the quasi-drugs are examined more from the safety and efficacy points of view.

Therefore, before initiating any process of registration, the product needs to be reviewed and the category selected. Thereafter, ingredient analysis of samples by testing is done by the MHLW at designated facilities, owned or contracted by manufacturers/importers. It includes analyzing the list of ingredients, and whether it complies with Japanese standards for cosmetics. This is not a mandatory process but the authorities may ask for these reports during inspection.

Step 2: Obtaining the Required Licences

The next step is obtaining the required licences such as Cosmetics Manufacturing Licence and Cosmetics Marketing Licence from the respective regulatory authorities.

In the case of foreign manufacturers, they need to be accredited by the MHLW as an "Accredited Foreign Manufacturer". A Japanese marketing licence holder who markets quasi-drugs manufactured by a foreign manufacturer can make an accreditation application on the manufacturer's behalf. Marketing Licence holders have to implement a set of standards called:

- Good Quality Practice for maintaining the quality of products, and

- Good Vigilance Practice for undertaking appropriate actions for safety management.

Step 3: Cosmetic & Quasi-Drug Marketing Notification Submission

After manufacturers obtain the licence and before initiating the import and selling, a cosmetic marketing notification is to be submitted to the same authority who issued the cosmetics marketing licence.

Step 4: Import of Cosmetics and Quasi-Drugs

All the requirements mentioned above have to be implemented by importers with slight differences. For import of cosmetics and quasi-drugs into Japan, the following are required:

- Primary distribution approval
- Cosmetics Manufacturing Licence (packaging, labelling, and storage)

Labelling Cosmetics

Cosmetic labels are required to be in Japanese with full ingredient labelling (also in Japanese) and is mandatory on the outer package of cosmetics. Labelling with misleading expressions and unapproved claims of functionality or efficacy are prohibited.

The Japan Cosmetic Industry Association (JCIA) has compiled a Japanese version of the "List of Cosmetic Ingredient Label Names" to use in compliance with the PMDL's requirements to list all ingredient names on the labelling.

Labelling of Quasi-drugs

For quasi-drugs, the label should contain the names of specific ingredients prescribed by the MHLW. It does not offer a reference list of permitted or prohibited claims for quasi-drugs.

Brazil

Brazil has a small segment in exports but is coming up in a big way. It exported USD 782 million cosmetics in 2020 to the USA and Argentina, and imported USD 582 million during the same period from the USA, France, and Spain. The Brazilian cosmetic industry represents more than 2 per cent of the country's GDP. Its market is projected to exceed Japan's and become the second highest in the world.

Regulatory regime

Regulator

The Ministry of Health is the regulator while the Brazilian Health Surveillance Agency (ANVISA) is responsible for sanitary surveillance and for cosmetic products. Another organization, the Hygiene, Perfume, Cosmetics and Sanitizing Products Management is tasked with coordinating, supervising, and controlling the activities related to registration, information, inspection, norms and standards establishments, compliance with regulations concerning the sanitary surveillance of personal care products, cosmetics, perfumes, and sanitizers.

Regulation

Cosmetics: definition

Personal Care Products, Cosmetics and perfumes, are defined as "Preparations consisting of natural or synthetic substances for external use on various parts of the human body, skin, capillary system, nails, lips, external genital organs, teeth, and mucous membranes of the oral cavity, with the sole or main purpose of cleaning them, perfuming them, altering their appearance, correcting body odours, and or protecting or maintaining them in good condition."

Cosmetics are classified under Class I and Class II:

Table 8: Classification of cosmetics in Brazil

Classification	*Description*	*Examples*
Class I	• Products with basic or elementary properties • They do not require detailed information on their labelling regarding their mode of use and their restrictions of use	• Skin moisturizers (without sunscreen; except those for stretch marks) • Face cleansing creams • Lotions • Gels and oils (except those for acne skin) • Perfumes, lipsticks (without sunscreen) • Fingernail polishes • Eye and facial makeup • Preparations (without sunscreen) • Eyelash mascara • Cleansing shampoos and • Hair conditioners.

Classification	Description	Examples
Class II	• Products have specific indications that require proof of safety and/ or efficacy, as well as more information on their labelling on their mode of use and restrictions of use.	• Children's products; sunscreen lotions and creams • Products for straightening, curling and/or dyeing hair products and for wrinkles • Antiseptic soap • Insect repellent products

Overview of registration process

The registration of cosmetics in Brazil depends on their classification. In general, cosmetics from Class I are exempted from registration and require notification to ANVISA only whereas those under Class II require registration.

Notification Process of Class I Cosmetics

The notification process is known as 'Prior Communication'. It is an administrative procedure that consists of informing ANVISA about the intention of commercializing these products. This 'Prior Communication' is performed through ANVISA's electronic platform known as the Cosmetic Automation System (SGAS). Once the notification process is completed, the company can commercialize its products after the notification is published on ANVISA's website. The notification fees depend on the size of the company and the fee ranges between R$ 175.72 and R$ 3,414.32 Brazilian Reais. ANVISA takes about two months to publish the notification on its website.

Registration Process of Class II Cosmetics

The registration process requires an application through ANVISA's electronic platform. After receiving the application, the registration dossier is reviewed and an inspection of the manufacturing site is carried out to ensure compliance with GMP. After finishing the review and inspection, ANVISA publishes its decision in the Official Journal (Diario Oficial da UniaÞo - DOU). The registration process may take up to 90 days. Similar to the fees in notification of Class I products, the fees for registration of Class II products depend on the size the company submitting the application. The range of the fees is between R$ 244.05 and R$ 4.881,00 Brazilian Reais. The registration licence is valid for five years from the date of publication in the Official Journal.

According to Law No. 6.360/76, only companies authorized by the Ministry of Health and licensed by ANVISA can extract, produce, manufacture, process, synthesize, purify fraction, pack, repack, import, export, store or ship cosmetics in Brazil.

Vietnam

Similar to Brazil, Vietnam is a small player in the cosmetics industry with an export of USD 324 million and imports of USD 900 million. It exports primarily to the USA and France and imports from Singapore, etc.

According to the Society of Cosmetics in Ho Chi Minh City, over 400 cosmetic businesses have been registered in Vietnam and 90 per cent of the market share is dominated by foreign brands, including Korean, European, and Japanese ones.

Regulatory regime

Regulator

Cosmetics registration is managed by the Drug Administration of Vietnam (DAV), under the Vietnam Ministry of Health (MOH), that issues safety regulations and certificates. Besides, every importer and exporter is required to obtain the relevant local certificates.

Regulation

Cosmetics: definition

Cosmetics are defined as substances or a preparation used for touch the outer parts of a human body (skin, hair system, fingernails, toenails, lips, and external reproductive organs) or teeth and mouth mucous membrane, whose purpose is to cleanse, aromatize, change the external characteristics or form, adjust body smell, safeguard the body, or maintain the human body in a good condition.

According to Circular No. 06/2011/TT-BYT, there are 21 product types of cosmetic product as below:

1. Creams, emulsions, lotions, gels and oils for skin (hands, face, feet, etc.)
2. Face masks (with the exception of chemical peeling products)
3. Tinted bases (liquids, pastes, powders)
4. Make-up powders, after-bath powders, hygienic powders, etc.

5. Toilet soaps, deodorant soaps, etc
6. Perfumes, toilet waters, and eau de Cologne
7. Bath or shower preparations (salts, foams, oils. gels, etc.)
8. Depilatories
9. Deodorants and anti-perspirants
10. Hair care products
11. Shaving product (creams, foams, lotions, etc.)
12. Products for making-up and removing make-up from the face and eyes
13. Products intended for application to lips
14. Products for the care of the teeth and the mouth
15. Products for nail care and make-up
16. Products for external intimate hygiene
17. Sunbathing products
18. Products for tanning without sun
19. Skin whitening products
20. Anti-wrinkle products
21. Others

To ensure quality assurance and product identification, it is mandatory for all products to be registered with the MOH in Vietnam. However, there are no specific regulations to regulate foreign companies that export cosmetics to Vietnam.

Every stock-keeping unit (SKU) needs a separate registration. In other words, if there are any differences in a cosmetic product's shape, colour, or ingredients, all variations need to be registered as separate items. For example, different shades of lipsticks require separate registration.

The cosmetics registration procedure in Vietnam is called the Cosmetic Product Proclamation. All imported cosmetic products must have valid Cosmetic Product Proclamation receipt number.

Cosmetics producers and owners are responsible to assess and evaluate product safety in accordance with the ASEAN safety guidelines and attributes specified in Annex 06-MP. In this annex, restrictions are set out for heavy metals and microbial parameters in cosmetic products. All other requirements concerning cosmetic ingredients can be found in the latest version of the ASEAN Cosmetic Treaty.

All entrepreneurs who import products into Vietnam and sell them in Vietnamese markets shall apply for DAV registration documents.

Applicants will receive a registration number from the authority within three business days following full submission of required registration documents and registration fee payment. The registration number is valid for five years from the issuance date.

According to Vietnam's Law, notification numbers are not required on cosmetic packages. The information (clearly displayed and printed) that is required on the label, in accordance to ASEAN regulations, is as follows:

- Name and functions of product
- Complete ingredients formula
- Instruction of usage
- Country of origin (where cosmetics are made)
- Name and address of company or individual responsible for product sales (must be written in Vietnamese)
- Weight or volume
- Manufacturing date or expiry date and best-use-before date (DD/MM/YYYY)—for product stability less than 30 months, expiry date is mandatory.
- Warning about usage safety
- Manufacturing lot number

Looking ahead

Cosmetics is a dynamic sector. There are countries like Korea with an established reputation for good quality products, and countries like Brazil that are newcomers in this sector having evolving markets.

The biggest challenge for exporters is of labelling and its changing requirements. Exports to different countries require compliance to different labelling. For exporting to countries like the EU, the REACH regulation has also to be complied with. Therefore, it is not just a regulation related to cosmetics that has to be complied with but chemical-related regulations also.

The COVID-19 pandemic forced cosmetics sector players to relook at the way the sector functions. During the lockdown, consumers opted for a minimalist lifestyle. At one point in time, it appeared that lipsticks will go completely out of fashion. Speaking of fashion, fashion events could not be held and, hence, innovations in this field could not be showcased to appropriate audiences. The brick-and-mortar sales came down and so did e-commerce sales with the focus shifting from non-essential products to essential goods.

From the regulation point of view, the rules have become stricter. In 2020, Korea came up with custom cosmetics, the first of its kind. Even for innovation, compliance to TRs has to be mandatorily affected.

Consumers across countries are alike. All wish to look beautiful. However, the quality of the products available in the market also depends on the consumer spending capacity. The more they can spend, the more high-end products are sold. In the use of cosmetics, culture and social aspects also play a major role.

There is no such differences between developed or developing countries in this sector as there are keen consumers everywhere. Many manufacturers in developing countries such as Brazil are making their mark as producers to cater to their domestic market as well as international consumers. Korean products have made a mark in this segment and are very popular in India. Anything that is tagged as 'Made in Korea' is bought with closed eyes by consumers who are aware of the quality of Korean cosmetics. The same goes for other brands with a 'Made in USA' tag. Acceptance of products made in China is yet to grow in India but it is seeing growth in other countries

In the Indian market, there are no specific TRs for this sector. What is more challenging is that both the states and the centre are empowered to legislate. We, therefore, see cheap versions of high-end brands being sold on the streets of major cities. They sell because there is a demand for cheaper knockouts. There is a segment of customers that are not conscious or do not care about the effects of harmful substances used in these products that can damage the skin.

There are numerous small players who thrive on copying branded products and selling cheaper and fake versions. There are no effective enforcement mechanisms. Regulation of cosmetics may also not be on the priority list of states.

It is, thus, important that regulation be made at the central level with compliance by state governments. This includes amendment to the existing rules in line with the global trend. This will ensure uniformity in the quality of products across the country and a greater variety of products for consumers. Labelling requirements need to reflect the true picture of what the product contains and what it can do, and not false claims.

Regulation will not only discipline the domestic industry but will, in a way, also help them to step up their quality to international standards.

REFERENCES

- https://www.fda.gov/cosmetics/cosmetics-international-activities/cosmetics-importers
- https://www.shippabo.com/logistics-knowledge/cosmetics-for-resale
- https://www.fda.gov/cosmetics/cosmetics-laws-regulations/fda-authority-over-cosmetics-how-cosmetics-are-not-fda-approved-are-fda-regulated
- https://www.fda.gov/cosmetics/cosmetics-laws-regulations/it-cosmetic-drug-or-both-or-it-soap
- https://www.fda.gov/cosmetics/cosmetics-labeling/cosmetics-labeling-regulations
- https://www.fda.gov/cosmetics/cosmetics-labeling-regulations/summary-cosmetics-labeling-requirements
- https://www.fda.gov/industry/color-additives-specific-products/color-additives-and-cosmetics-fact-sheet
- https://www.fda.gov/regulatory-information/search-fda-guidance-documents/draft-guidance-industry-cosmetic-good-manufacturing-practices
- https://www.ecomundo.eu/en/blog/steps-import-cosmetic-product-europe
- https://www.cossma.com/business/article/importing-cosmetics-from-outside-the-eu-36160.html
- https://www.compliancegate.com/cosmetics-regulations-european-union/
- https://ec.europa.eu/growth/sectors/cosmetics/legislation_en
- https://ec.europa.eu/growth/sectors/cosmetics/ban-animal-testing_en
- https://ec.europa.eu/growth/sectors/cosmetics/market-surveillance_en
- https://criticalcatalyst.com/regulatory-framework-cosmetic-products-south-korea/#:~:text=General%20cosmetics%20are%20subject%20to,importing%20processes% 20can%20be%20made.
- https://www.export.gov/apex/article2?id=Korea-Cosmetics
- https://www.trade.gov/country-commercial-guides/south-korea-cosmetics
- https://www.cosmeticsbridge.com/overview-on-south-korea-cosmetics-regulations-the-cosmetics-act/
- https://cosmetic.chemlinked.com/cosmepedia/cosmepedia-south-korea-cosmetic-regulation
- https://credevo.com/articles/2020/12/15/japan-cosmetics-registration-and-market-approval-process/
- https://globalregulatorypartners.com/wp-content/uploads/Registration-of-Cosmetics-in-Brazil-v2-002.pdf
- http://antigo.anvisa.gov.br/en/cosmetics
- https://www.ditp.go.th/contents_attach/223344/223344.pdf
- https://www.export.gov.il/files/cosmetics/VietnamCosmeticPresenttion Jan2017.pdf
- https://www.cirs-group.com/en/cosmetics/a-comprehensive-guide-to-cosmetics-registration-in-vietnam#:~:text=Cosmetics%20Import,the%20registration%20certificate%20to%20DAV.
- https://emerhub.com/vietnam/cosmetic-product-registration-vietnam/

- https://www.iccr-cosmetics.org/
- https://morulaa.com/blog-morulaa/blog/registration-and-importation-of-cosmetic-products/
- https://www.meilin-law.jp/en/importation-of-cosmetic-products-in-india-2/
- https://www.statista.com/topics/3137/cosmetics-industry/#dossierKeyfigures
- https://cliniexperts.com/india-regulatory-services/cosmetic/for-importer/

ORGANIC PRODUCTS

Increasing health concerns due to the growing number of chemical poisoning cases globally is acting as a driver in the organic food market. Consumers are becoming more health-conscious. The toxicity of chemical pesticides in food products can cause cancer, hormone disruption, and birth defects. According to a UN report, around 200,000 people die every year due to the toxic effects of pesticides in food products.

The organic food market consists of sales of organic food and beverages and related services. The production of organic food involves practices that promote ecological balance and aim to conserve biodiversity. These food products do not use any food additive or industrial solvent. Major players in the organic food market are General Mills Inc., Cargill, Inc., Danone, United Natural Foods Inc., and Amy's Kitchen.

India

It is widely known that despite being a leader in the production of several agricultural commodities, India's agriculture sector is primarily characterized by high wastage post-harvest (up to 16 per cent in perishable products such as fruits and vegetables), lack of mechanization, low yield, and lower levels of value addition compared to its global counterparts. This has prevented farmers from realizing the true potential of their crops resulting in significantly lower incomes. As per available statistics, India ranks 8th in terms of the World's Organic Agricultural Land and 1st in terms of the total number of producers, as per 2020 data (Source: FIBL & IFOAM Year Book, 2020).

The total volume of exports of organic products in 2020-21 was 888,179.68 MT. The organic food export realization was around INR 7,07,849.52 lakh (USD 1,040.95 million). Organic products are exported to the USA, the European Union, Canada, Great Britain, Republic of Korea, Israel, Switzerland, Ecuador, Vietnam, Australia, etc.

In terms of export value realization, processed foods including soya meal (57 per cent) lead followed by oilseeds (9 per cent), cereals and millets (7 per cent), plantation crop products such as tea and coffee (6 per cent), spices and condiments (5 per cent), medicinal plants (5 per cent), dry fruits (3 per cent), sugar (3 per cent), and others.

Regulatory regime

Regulator

The APEDA, Ministry of Commerce & Industries, Government of India, implements the National Programme for Organic Production (NPOP).

Regulation

The programme involves accreditation of certification organisations, standards for organic production, promotion of organic farming and marketing, etc. The NPOP standards for a production and accreditation system have been recognized by the European Commission and Switzerland for unprocessed plant products as equivalent to their country standards. With these recognitions, Indian organic products, duly certified by the accredited certification bodies of India, are accepted by the importing countries. APEDA is also in the process of negotiations with Korea, Taiwan, Canada, Japan, etc.

A product will be allowed to be exported as an "organic product" only when accompanied by a Transaction Certificate[11] issued by a certification body accredited by the National Accreditation Body for organic products under the NPOP.

United States of America

Organic farming and food are regulated by the United States Department of Agriculture's National Organic Program (USDA NOP) under the Organic Foods Production Act of 1990. An easier way to export an organic product to the USA, is to get the product certified by a government agency of the exporting country that has entered into a recognition agreement for specific product exports.

Regulatory regime

The accreditation of certification bodies is done by the USDA and are called Accredited Certification Agents (ACAs). These include state and local government agencies, for-profit enterprises, and non-profit non-governmental organizations. For exporters in countries or in regions with

11. A transaction certificate is issued to certify that the products sold (can be to another operator in the country of export) in each consignment are certified organic products

recognition arrangements with the USDA NOP, compliance with the equivalent standards and certification by a USDA ACA or an equivalent accredited certification body is sufficient when accompanied by an NOP import certificate and attestation statement.

The other method, where a recognition agreement does not exist or the product is not listed in the agreed list of organic products under the recognition agreement, is to apply directly to USDA accredited certifiers. This requires complete compliance with the USDA NOP and certification by an ACA according to the USDA NOP.

A similar agreement existed between India's APEDA and the USA's USDA. Under this agreement, the USDA recognized certificates issued by agencies accredited by the APEDA under its TraceNET. However, the USDA's organic program (NOP) has ended its recognition agreement with the APEDA that allowed accredited certifiers to provide USDA organic certification in India. Now, exporters desirous of exporting organic products to the USA will have to apply directly to the USDA accredited certifiers for their standards. This will lead to heightened market surveillance for the export of organic products from India to the USA while this transition arrangement is in place.

Uptil now

- By July 12, 2021, to continue to export to theUSA, the current organic operations in India will need to have applied for certification with a USDA-accredited organic certifier.
- By mid-March 2021, USDA certifiers will be able to list these organic operation applicants in India in the Organic Integrity Database, to help U.S. buyers verify that a farm or business in India has applied for NOP certification.

after July 12, 2022

- USDA organic certification by a USDA-accredited certifier will be required to import organic products from India to the USA
- APEDA-accredited certifiers may apply to the NOP for direct accreditation by the USDA organic program at any time.
- Organic certifiers and operations in India are responsible for ensuring compliance to any additional Government of India export requirements, including TraceNet reporting and documentation

Figure 35: USDA transition arrangement for organic exports from India

How to Become a Certified Organic producer for exports to the USA (no recognition agreement)

Certifiers are responsible for making sure that USDA organic products meet all organic standards. There are five basic steps to organic certification:

- *The farm or business adopts organic practices, selects a USDA-accredited certifying agent, and submits an application and fees (USD 325, one time) to the certifying agent (nearly USD 750 in the first year and approximately USD 375-575 in later years).*
- *The certifying agent reviews the application to verify that practices comply with USDA organic regulations.*
- *An inspector conducts an on-site inspection of the applicant's operation.*
- *The certifying agent reviews the application and the inspector's report to determine if the applicant complies with USDA organic regulations.*
- *The certifying agent issues an organic certificate.*

There is an annual review and inspection procedure for continuing organic certification for a farm.

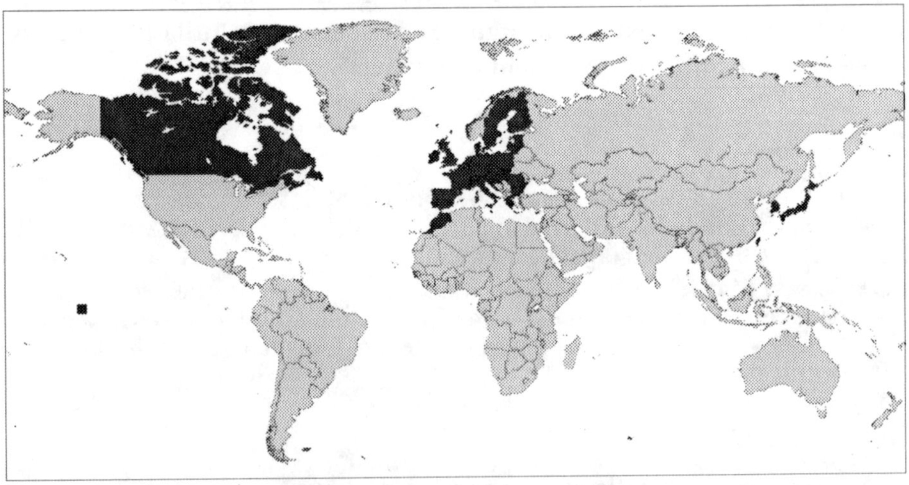

Figure 36: Countries with which the USA has a recognition agreement for organic exports

European Union

The EU is the second-largest consumer of organic food in the world, with € 37.4 billion in retail sales. The Commission has set out a comprehensive organic action plan for the European Union. Through it, the Commission aims to achieve the European Green Deal target of 25 per cent of agricultural land under organic farming by 2030.

The organic logo can only be used on products that have been certified as organic by an authorised control agency or body. This means that they have fulfilled strict conditions on how they are produced, transported and stored

Figure 37: EU organic logo

The European Green Deal will improve the well-being and health of citizens and future generations by providing:

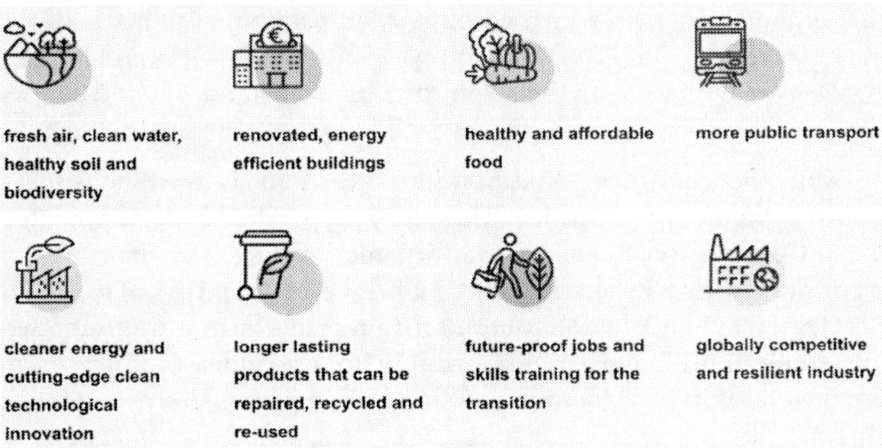

Figure 38: EU Green Deal

The new organic legislation came into force on 1 January 2022, following the postponement of its implementation for a year. The rules reflect the changing nature of this rapidly growing sector. Producers in third countries will have to comply with the same set of rules as producers in the EU.

Regulatory regime

All food producers, processors, or traders who wish to market their food as organic need to be registered with a control agency or body. The control agency or body is responsible for verifying that the exporter acts in compliance with organic rules. Each EU country can decide whether this is a public or a private body but they check that the European Union's rules on organic production are followed.

EU regulations on organic production exclude products from fishing and hunting of wild animals but include harvests of wild plants when certain natural habitat conditions are respected.

Regulation

The import must conform to equivalent standards for goods produced in the European Union. To ensure this, there are procedures that all importers have to follow when they wish to market a product as organic. These procedures depend on where the goods have originated. The EU has concluded agreements on trade in organic products with Chile, Switzerland, and the United Kingdom. Inspection and certification of most organic products is carried out by the national authorities of the country of origin. This is because arrangements for the imports of organic products are in place with these countries as their standards and control measures have been assessed as equivalent to those in place in the EU.

In all other countries, inspection and certification is the responsibility of 'control bodies or authorities'. These are independent bodies appointed by the Commission to ensure that organic producers in their area of responsibility follow standards and control measures equivalent to the EU ones. There may be additional controls or requirements on products imported from some non-EU countries. Currently, this includes products from Ukraine, Kazakhstan, Moldova, the Russian Federation, China, and India.

General requirements

• following documents to be verified at border:
  • certificate of inspection
  • documents of customs declaration
  • transport documents
  • operators & product traceability: verification of names, addresses & valid certification of each operator, from farmer to exporter
• atleast 1 representative sample to be taken from each consignment & tested in accredited labs in EU

Country specific scope of import
• Ukraine, Kazakhstan, Moldova, Turkey, and Russia: Ch 10, 11 (ex 1105 to 09), 12 (ex 1211 to 1214) & 23 (ex 2307) • China: Ch 10, 11 (ex 1105 to 09), 12 (ex 1211 to 1214) & 23 (ex 2307), 08109075 (Goji berries) • India- HS code 12074090 – sesame seeds

Figure 39: Requirements for import of organic products by EU

> ***Certification***
>
> *All organic products imported into the EU must have appropriate electronic Certificate of Inspection (e-COI). These are administered through the Trade Control and Expert System (TRACES).*

China

Following government reorganization, the SAMR is responsible for managing organic food certification and accreditation, including the issuance of national standards and certification regulations for organic food. The SAMR is responsible for maintaining the list of certified organic products. This list (in Chinese) is published on the website of the CNCA.

Regulatory regime

In China, organic food production is regulated under Organic Products (GB/T19630-2011), which is a national standard. The standard was published in 2005 by the Standardization Administration of the People's Republic of China (SAC), a revised version of which was published in 2011. Additionally, Administrative Measures for Organic Product Certification (AQSIQ Decree No. 155), implemented on 1 April 2014, define rules for the certification, production, processing, import, and sales of organic products in China. The newly-established General Administration of Market Supervision (GAMR) has absorbed the duties of the AQSIQ and the SAC.

Regulator

The responsibility for organic agriculture in China is shared between the Ministry of Agriculture, the Ministry of Ecology and Environment and the General Administration of Quality Supervision, Inspection and Quarantine (AQSIQ). The competent authority responsible for the implementation of the organic production standard is the CNCA, now under the supervision of the GAMR.

Regulation

There is a mandatory national organic logo for organic products certified according to the National Standards (GB/T19630.1-2011 and GB/T19630.2-2011). Part 3 of the standards sets out the general specifications and requirements for the use of the logo (GB/T 19630.3-2011).

The control and certification process is performed by private and state-owned control units, which are authorized by the CNCA and accredited by the China National Accreditation Service for Conformity Assessment (CNAS).

For countries or regions exporting organic products to China, whose certification system is accepted to be equivalent to China's product certification system, the CNCA may sign a cooperation agreement or memorandum with the competent authority of the country. Organic products exported to China from these countries or regions have to be managed in accordance with the requirements set up in the cooperation agreement or memorandum. So far, only New Zealand has signed an equivalency agreement with China, which is not yet in force.

Brazil

The market for organic products in Brazil recorded a value of USD 81 million in 2021, representing 0.1 per cent of the global market value with a per capita consumption of USD 0.38.

Regulatory regime

Regulator

The competent authority in Brazil is the Ministry of Agriculture, Livestock, and Food Supply (MAPA).

Regulation

Organic production in Brazil is regulated by Organic Law 10.831 2003, updated in 2017, which outlines the basic requirements for organic production. Decree 6 323 2007 provides details on how the law is applied whilst a series of eight Normative Instructions from 2009 and 2011 establishes control mechanisms, technical standards, and procedures, including for accreditation, certification, marketing, labelling, inputs, and organic production standards for plants, animals, and aquaculture.

The mandatory national organic logo, must be used for all domestic and imported organic products. The official label is mandatory, with two versions (one for audit certification and one for the Participatory Guarantee Systems (PGS) system).

There are three permitted approaches for organic quality assurance:

(i) certification by approved third-party certification bodies accredited by the National Institute of Metrology, Quality, and Technology (INMETRO)

(ii) by Participatory Guarantee Systems (PGS) through a participatory conformity assessment body (OPAC), which is certified and supervised by the MAPA with no need for accreditation by the INMETRO

(iii) restricted to small farmers selling directly to consumers under the control of a social control body wherein no certification is required

Brazil does not have an equivalence agreement with any country. All importers must be certified by a third party certification body approved to operate in Brazil. Organic products imported to Brazil must be certified by an organization registered at the INMETRO (Accreditation Body approved by the Brazilian government) and the MAPA. Therefore, each country interested in exporting organic products to the Brazilian market should make sure that its certification body is registered.

They must comply with Brazilian production standards and be certified by a MAPA-accredited compliance organisation. Foreign producers must be listed in the National Register of Organic Producers. In practical terms, this means that exporters must contract a local accrediting body to certify each organic product they intend to sell in Brazil.

Labelling

Labelling of organic products must follow the requirements below:

- Single-ingredient products may be labelled as "organic product" once certified
- Products made of more than one ingredient, including additives, in which not all the ingredients are of certified-organic origin, must be labelled in the following manner:
  - Mixed products with a minimum of 95 per cent of ingredients from certified-organic origin may be labelled "organic"
  - Products made with 70-95 per cent of ingredients from certified-organic origin may be labelled as "products with

organic ingredients," and must include the proportions of the organic and non-organic ingredients on their labels, excluding water and salt from the calculation

Any imported product subjected to quarantine treatment not compatible with Brazilian organic production regulation will lose its organic status. Since 2011, all organic products sold in Brazil must have the organic seal. The only exception is for products sold at street fairs or farmers' markets, where the producer has been previously authorized by the MAPA and the products produced or imported before 2011.

Korea

The demand for organic foods in Korea is on the rise following growing concerns about food safety and food quality. Since organic foods are/ recognized as being a healthier option, families in particular, are looking at buying organic. A strong example is organic baby food products. Despite the/low birth rate, the/organic baby food market grew notably between 2013 and 2017 and was expected to grow further until 2022.

Regulatory regime

In Korea, organic agriculture is regulated by the Act on Promotion of Environment-friendly Agriculture and Fisheries and Management and Support for Organic Food, etc. The legislation requires that organic products are free from residues of pesticides, with zero tolerance.

Regulator

The competent authority is the Korean Ministry of Agriculture, Food and Rural Affairs (MAFRA), which is responsible for the implementation of organic legislation as well as for the accreditation of the private certification organisations. Within MAFRA, the Korean National Agricultural Products Quality Management Service (NAQS) is responsible for the audit of MAFRA-accredited certification bodies. The NAQS also administers the organic import control procedures. There is a voluntary national logo owned by the government. Additionally, imported products can be labelled with logos from other countries according to the conditions laid out in the relevant legislation of the USA, Japan, Australia, and the EU.

Regulation

Equivalence agreements exist between Korea and the USA and between Korea and the EU. The equivalence agreements cover only products that are classified as 'processed' according to the Korean Food Code. These products are permitted to be imported to Korea without being certified by a MAFRA-accredited certification body. Organic products from the USA and EU that are not classified as 'processed', but are classified as either 'agricultural products' or 'simple agricultural processed products' must be certified by a Korean-based organic certification body accredited and approved by the MAFRA.

According to the Korean Food Code 'processed' essentially means that the food should not be recognisable as in its original form and has been transformed. Typically, multi-ingredient products will be considered to be processed. Some parts of the definition of 'processed' are open to interpretation. In such cases, the Ministry of Food and Drug Safety (MFDS) clarifies whether or not the product is considered as 'processed'. To explain how the criteria are applied, the MFDS published a note ("Criteria and standards for processed food—guidelines and definitions"), which is only available in Korean.

Japan

The organic food market is an emerging segment within the Japanese food market. Even though the first regulation for agricultural produce from plant origins were implemented in 2000, the share of organic vegetables in the agriculture sector remains low.

Japan ranks 14th in market size globally with a value of USD 602.6 million in 2021. In the fiscal year 2020, around 105,000 tons of organic agricultural products were imported to Japan, of which fruits made up the largest share, with around 75,000 tons.

Regulatory regime

Regulator

In Japan, organic food production is regulated by the Ministry of Agriculture, Forestry and Fisheries (MAFF) through the Japanese Agricultural Standard (JAS) system, which covers general and specific standards for food, non-alcoholic beverages, and forestry products.

Regulation

Specific JAS organic standards cover plants, processed foods, organic feeds and organic livestock products. The standards were introduced in 2005 and updated in 2012 (organic feeds and organic livestock) and 2017 (organic plants and organic processed foods). The MAFF is the competent authority, the Food and Agriculture Materials Inspection Centre (FAMIC) is responsible for accreditation and auditing of certification bodies in Japan. Organic agricultural products and processed products from countries that have their organic system recognized as being equivalent to the JAS system, are able to export their products with the organic JAS logo. For this, a certificate that has been issued by a government agency or an organization in the country with organic equivalency is required.

Those who wish to export organic products to Japan must be compliant with the JAS standard and be certified by a Japanese registered certification body. Import of livestock products is not permitted.

Japan has equivalency agreements with the USA, Argentina, Australia, Canada, Switzerland, New Zealand, and member-states of the European Union. Eligible organic products from these countries are permitted to be imported to Japan and must be labelled with the JAS organic Logo. Organic standards in these countries are considered equivalent to JAS Organic Standards. Export certificates issued by relevant national government authorities must accompany consignments of the imported products.

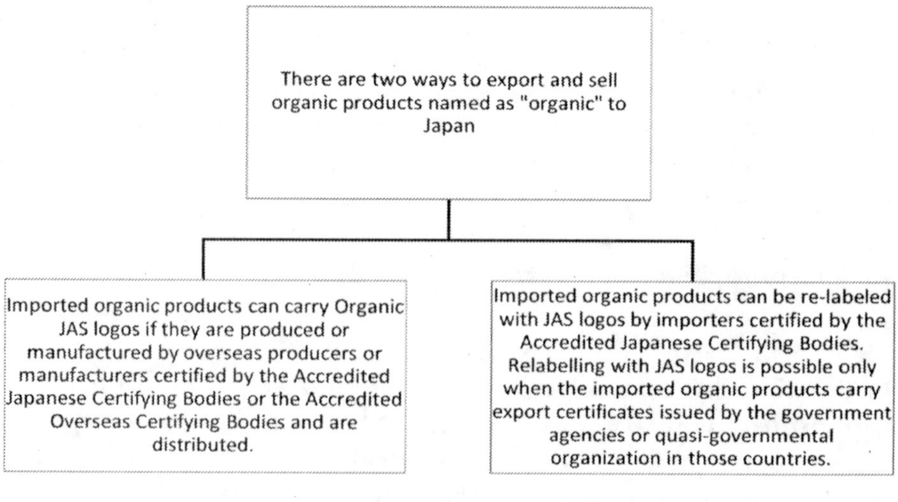

Figure 40: Organic products export to Japan

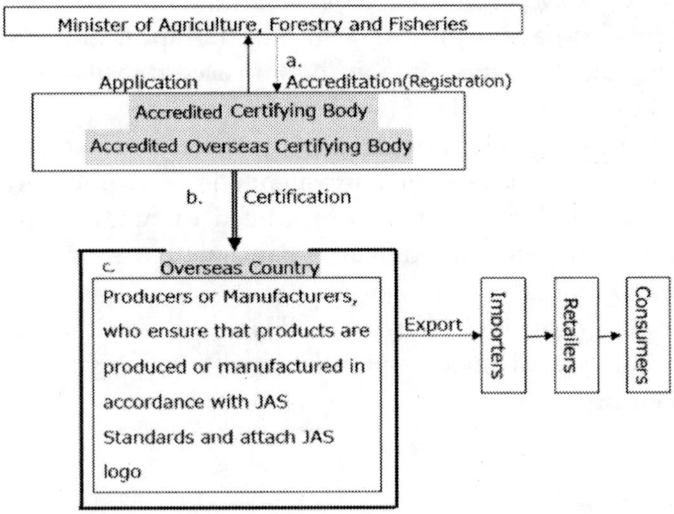

Figure 41: Grading by Accredited Japanese Certifying Bodies or Accredited Overseas Certifying Bodies

The MAFF registers Japanese certifying bodies or overseas certifying bodies. Those Accredited Certifying Bodies certify producers, manufacturers, and other business entities of agricultural and forestry products. Certified producers, manufacturers or other business entities that produce or manufacture products, and attach JAS logos to the products.

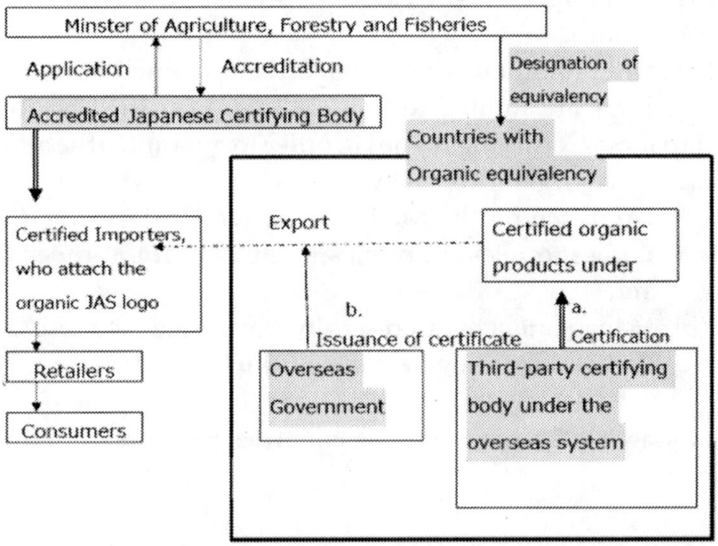

Figure 42: Labelling of Organic JAS Logos by Importers Certified by Accredited Japanese Certifying Bodies

— Third-party certificates under legislation of overseas countries, whose organic rules and standards Japan has approved as equivalent certified organic foods in accordance with the organic rules and standards of those countries.

— Government agencies or quasi-governmental organizations of countries with organic equivalency issue export certificates to certify the organic foods produced or manufactured in the countries were graded in accordance with the organic system of the countries.

— Importers certified by Accredited Japanese Certifying Bodies who import organic foods and re-label with the Organic JAS logo on their products in Japan.

Applied to the agricultural products and processed foods which conform to the Organic JAS. Without Organic JAS logo, no product can be labelled as "organic".

Figure 43: Japanese organic logo

— Countries whose organic rules and standards Japan has approved as equivalent as provided in Article 37 of the Ministerial Ordinance.

— Importers authorized to attach the Organic JAS logo to their products are limited to those who are certified by Accredited Japanese Certifying Bodies in order to guarantee the adequacy of imported organic foods by:

(a) Guidance by the MAFF or Accredited Japanese Certifying Bodies to relevant parties in the case of improper labelling; and

(b) Management of importers by Accredited Japanese Certifying Bodies, including keeping grading records.

As of March 2021, the following countries have organic equivalency with Japan:

USA, Canada, Australia, Switzerland

- organic products of plant origin
- organic livestock products
- organic processed foods

EU, Argentina, UK, New Zealand, Taiwan

- organic products of plant origin
- organic processed foods of plant origin

Figure 44: Organic equivalency by Japan

The Japanese government has been making an effort to raise awareness about the organic food sector by enforcing strict labelling regulations to prevent misleading advertisements. To further stimulate domestic demand, the MAFF launched the "Japanese Organic Supporters" platform for businesses actively handling organic food. However, despite the promotion activities and rising awareness levels, only a minority of consumers understand the added value of the Organic JAS logo. While the health food sector has been benefitting from the growing demand for a healthy lifestyle and healthy eating habits, the organic food segment is challenged by distinguishing itself from conventional food segments.

On the other hand, organic non-food products are attracting consumer interest. Consumer goods, apart from foodstuff, are not subjected to Organic JAS regulations, resulting in the rise of new market segments like organic cosmetics and organic cotton. While organic cotton is not eligible for organic certification, it can still be marketed as "organic" and has gained popularity as a sustainable material in the fashion industry.

Looking ahead

The export of organic products is a niche segment. The de-recognition of Indian organic products by the U.S. authorities has been a setback to exporters as it affects their global image. Since organic certification requires end-to-end transparency, strict monitoring is required. Not all products are organic certified for export. It is a tedious process to get accredited for certification by organizations designated for certification in exporting countries.

The demand for organic products is going to continue increasing in coming times as people become more and more concerned about their health and how the use of pesticides and insecticides is harmful in the long run.

Lack of awareness also causes loss of premium to farmers and exporters, even though the market is export oriented. The same product may have a higher value in the export market than in the Indian market.

Developing countries have the potential for export of organic products but the biggest hurdle is the use of chemicals in farming to increase produce and protect it from pests, insects, and fungus. Once the chemical is sprayed, the "organic" nature of the plantation made is lost.

There is a high demand in developed countries for organic products and they have adequate disposable income to buy them, It is believed that organic farming is appreciated more in developed nations and works better there, but recent studies have shown that this belief is not true.

According to a research, organic agriculture yields 92 per cent of the production of conventional farming in developed countries, whereas in developing nations, this figure is 80 per cent. The disparity in yields is caused by access to materials needed for organic farming. For example, in developing countries, chemical pesticides, insecticides, and fertilizers are expensive. This may be challenging for conventional farmers but for organic farming, it becomes much easier.

Organic farming may not be able to replace conventional farming in the near future, but the trend is fast catching up in the world. On Indian shelves, the consumer understands that organic products will have a mark-up over other products, but the awareness of what is genuine and what is not, is not known to many. This is something that the government could raise awareness about.

For faster access to Indian organic products in the international market, the farm-to-fork chain needs to be strengthened, reviewed, and revised periodically. The mutual agreements, that guarantee a faster market access, have to be taken up on a fast-track basis so that exporters can focus more on the product than on the processes for approval. This may mean making them a part of FTA proposal also, apart from standalone initiatives.

REFERENCES

- https://www.globenewswire.com/news-release/2021/11/23/2339637/28124/en/Global-Organic-Food-Market-Report-2021-to-2030-Featuring-General-Mills-Cargill-and-Danone-Among-Others.html
- https://home.kpmg/in/en/blogs/home/posts/2021/07/food-processing-key-doubling-farmers-income.html
- https://www.foodsafetynews.com/2021/01/usda-increasing-certification-requirements-for-organic-imports-from-india/
- https://www.organicexport.info/usa.html
- https://www.ams.usda.gov/services/organic-certification/international-trade
- https://www.ams.usda.gov/services/organic-certification/becoming-certified
- https://www.ccof.org/page/organic-certification-fees#:~:text=Many%20 small%20farms%20 can%20be,size%20operations%20receive%20 competitive%20 fees.
- https://www.unep.org/explore-topics/green-economy/what-we-do/advisory-services/eap-green-organic-agriculture/exporter-0#:~:text=The%20import %20of%20 organic%20products,country%20recognised%20by%20the%20EU.
- https://ec.europa.eu/info/food-farming-fisheries/farming/organic-farming/organics-glance_en
- https://www.maff.go.jp/e/policies/standard/specific/Export_of_ Organic_products.html
- https://www.maff.go.jp/e/policies/standard/jas/specific/attach/pdf/Organic _equivalency-1.pdf
- https://ec.europa.eu/info/food-farming-fisheries/farming/organic-farming/organic-logo_en
- https://ec.europa.eu/info/sites/default/files/food-farming-fisheries/farming/documents/factsheet-organic-farming-in-numbers_en.pdf
- https://ec.europa.eu/info/sites/default/files/food-farming-fisheries/farming/documents/guidelines-imports-organic-products_en.pdf
- https://ec.europa.eu/info/food-farming-fisheries/farming/organic-farming/organic-action-plan_en
- https://ec.europa.eu/info/food-farming-fisheries/farming/organic-farming/future-organics_en
- https://ec.europa.eu/info/food-farming-fisheries/farming/organic-farming/becoming-organic-farmer_en
- https://ec.europa.eu/info/food-farming-fisheries/farming/organic-farming/organic-production-and-products_en
- https://ec.europa.eu/info/food-farming-fisheries/farming/organic-farming/trade_en
- https://www.organicexport.info/japan.html
- https://www.organicexport.info/korea.html#:~:text= Import%20 Requirements, Agreement%20with%20the%20European%20Union
- https://www.ccpb.it/en/blog/certificazione/organic-in-south-korea/
- https://www.organicexport.info/china.html
- https://www.organicexport.info/brazil.html#:~:text=All%20importers%20must %20be%20certified,Ministry%20of%20Agriculture%20(MAPA).
- https://apeda.gov.in/apedawebsite/organic/PresentStatus.htm

- https://globalorganictrade.com/country/japan
- https://www.statista.com/statistics/1280512/japan-import-volume-organic-agricultural-products-by-type/
- https://www.statista.com/topics/5756/organic-food-market-in-south-korea/#dossierKeyfigures
- https://bsranchandfarm.com/organic-farming-is-easier-in-developing-countries/

PHARMACEUTICALS

Pharmaceuticals sector is the fifth-largest sector traded globally after machinery (electrical & mechanical), mineral fuels, and automobiles with a total trade value of USD 724 billion. The largest importers are the USA, Germany, Belgium, Switzerland, and China, the USA being the largest with imports of USD 139 billion in 2020. The largest exporters for the same period were Germany, Switzerland, Ireland, Belgium, and the USA.

The pharmaceutical industry is responsible for R&D, manufacturing, and distribution of medications. Based on the prescription drugs market, Pfizer is the largest pharmaceutical company in the world. Even though the USA is the largest market and the fact that some of the largest pharma companies hail from the USA, the EU is another big source of medicines in this sector. Some of the major European companies are GSK, Roche, and Novartis.

The industry is highly dependent on R&D with big companies investing around 20 per cent of their sales revenue on it. R&D helps in formulation of new products that in turn earn more revenue for the pharmaceutical companies. However, the revenue model is not just based on plain sales; it has a component of patents also. After the expiration of the patent period, which is usually 20 years, revenues from that product drop drastically as generic forms hit the market.

In this sector, there are three major forms of companies in the market: pharmaceutical companies, biotech companies[12] and generic companies.[13]

India

India has the 3rd largest pharmaceuticals industry in the world by volume and the 14th largest by value. It is the largest producer of generic medicines having a share of 20 per cent in supply. India has the highest number of USFDA compliant pharma plants outside the USA and has more than 3,000 pharma companies located in the country.

12. Deals with biological treatments and biological therapies
13. Manufactures of off-patent medicines to provide consumers at a cheaper cost, called generics

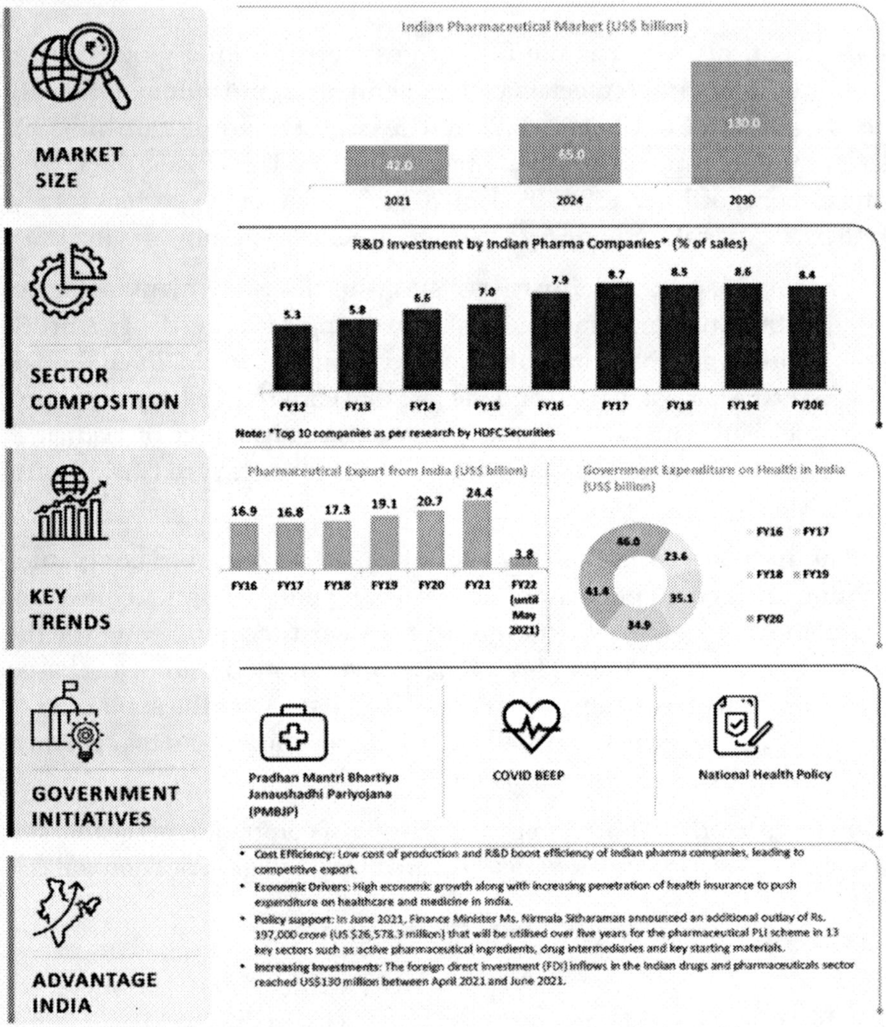

Figure 45: IBEF Snapshot: Pharmaceuticals

The Indian pharma industry (API) manufactures 60,000 generic brands across various categories occupying 70 to 80 per cent of the retail market. The API industry is the third world's largest, and has 57 per cent of APIs in the WHO.

It is expected to reach USD 65 billion by 2024 and about USD 120-130 billion by 2030 with a growth of 10 to 12 per cent. India is a preferred choice for manufacturers as compared to Western markets as the cost of manufacturing is almost one-third lower. The major pharmaceutical clusters in India are given below:

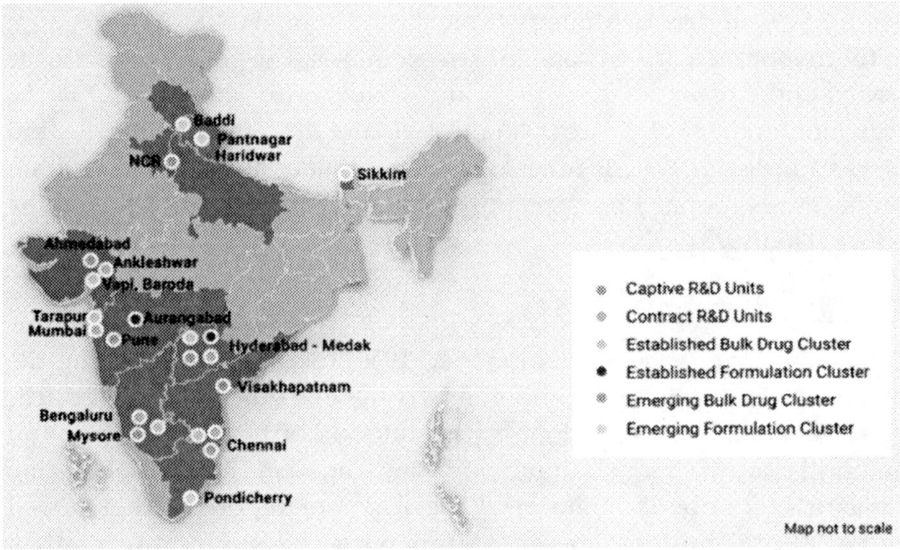

Figure 46: Pharmaceutical clusters in India

strength	weakness	opportunity	threat
•lower cost of manufacturing than other nations •diversified ecosystem •workforce	•lack of R&D •absence of collaboration between industry & academicians •insignificant health care costs as compared to other household expenses	•greater export possibilities	•product patent possibilities •small businesses face danger from MRP-based excise duty structure

Figure 47: SWOT analysis of Indian pharmaceutical sector

India's drugs and pharmaceuticals exports stood at USD 24.44 billion in FY21. The country's pharmaceutical sector contributes 6.6 per cent to the total merchandise exports. Indian drugs are exported to more than 200 countries in the world, with the USA being the key market.

Regulatory regime

Regulator

The CDSCO under the Ministry of Health & Family Welfare is the central authority for regulating drugs/pharmaceuticals. The governing act is the Drugs and Cosmetics Act, 1940, and Rules 1945. The CDSCO is the regulator for medical devices also and regulates them through the Medical Devices Rules, 2017. For other domestic regulations on pricing within India, the National Pharmaceutical Pricing Authority (NPPA) is the relevant authority.

Regulation

Under the Drugs and Cosmetics Act, 1940, the task of regulating the manufacturing, sale, and distribution of drugs and other related products, and issuance of licences is done by the state authorities, while the central authorities are in charge of approving new drugs and clinical trials, listing standards for drugs, administering the quality of imported drugs as well as collaborating and co-ordinating with the state drug control organisations.

Central level	State level
• New Drug Approvals/Medical Devices • Import of Drugs/Medical Devices • Clinical Trials • Standards for Drugs • Amendments to Act and Rules • Pharmaco vigilance	• Licence for Manufacture, Sale, and Distribution • Monitoring quality of Drugs and Cosmetics • Investigations and Prosecutions

Figure 48: Distribution of powers at state and central level in pharmaceutical sector in India

Registration

The government has launched an online licensing portal called "SUGAM" in line with e-governance initiatives. The same portal is used by CDSCO for regulating cosmetics. The portal allows manufacturers to upload permissions and licences received from state FDAs (Food & Drug Administration) and details about manufacturing sites and formulation data.

After applying online, hard copies of documents have to be submitted in the CDSCO's office for verification of registration.

Once verification is completed, login credentials are shared on the registered mail id. The fee applicable for registration is USD 1,000. Registration is valid for three years.

Licence

After obtaining the registration certificate, the importer must provide the following information to the licensing authority to obtain the import drug licence:

- name, full address, telephone number, fax number and email of the applicant;
- name of the drug to be imported; and
- a copy of the registration certificate obtained from the licensing authority.

The fee to obtain a licence to import a new drug and for permission for clinical trials is Rs. 50,000. The validity period of the licence to import drugs, including new ones, is three years.

To obtain a licence to sell, stock, exhibit, or distribute drugs, the following information must be provided to the licensing authority:

- the name of the applicant; and
- the names of the qualified persons under whose personal supervision the drugs will be sold.

The fee to obtain a licence to sell or distribute drugs is Rs. 1,500. The licence is valid for five years.

To obtain a licence to manufacture drugs, the following information must be provided to the licensing authority:

- name of the applicant;
- address of the premises where manufacturing will be done;
- name of the drug; and
- names, qualifications, and experience of technical staff employed for manufacturing and testing.

The fee to obtain a licence to manufacture drugs is Rs. 50,000. The validity period of the licence is five years.

The Drugs and Cosmetics Rules, 1945, do not prescribe a specific timeline for granting marketing approval of a drug. However, Table 9 below outlines the key applications to be filed for the import of drugs and marketing, applicable fees, the validity periods, and approximate timelines. The actual time taken depends on various factors, such as the amount and effectiveness of follow-up with the authorities concerned.

Table 9: Approximate timelines for drug marketing approval

Application	*Form No.*	*Fees*	*Validity (years)*	*Approximate timeline**
Import, manufacture of new drug and permission to undertake a clinical trial	44	Rs. 50,000	–	180 days
Registration for the import of drugs into India	40	$ 1,000	3	270 days
Import licence	8	Rs. 1,000	3	45 days
Licence to sell, stock, or exhibit	19	Rs. 1,500	5	30 days

Requirements for exporting drugs from India

The Drugs and Cosmetics Rules prescribe that a manufacturer with a valid licence to manufacture drugs may obtain a no-objection certificate (NOC) from the Drug Controller General of India (DCGI) to export drugs. 'Guidelines for the Export of Drug' issued by the MoHFW prescribe detailed guidelines for applicants for the export of drugs. The two primary conditions to obtain an NOC from the DCGI are that the applicant must:

- have a copy of the valid export order; and
- identify the premises where the drug will be manufactured

GMP & inspection

Schedule M of the Drugs and Cosmetics Rules, 1945, prescribes GMP and the obligatory requisites with respect to premises, plant, and equipment that should be maintained by the manufacturers of drugs or as a pre-condition to set up a new manufacturing unit. Officials undertaking the GMP inspection of manufacturing units include inspectors from the CDSCO, and the State Drug Control Office along with product experts from the Central Drug Laboratory. These inspections are usually carried out for a period of 2-5 days, depending on the quantity of products being manufactured in the unit, the complexity of products, as well as the size of the unit. Inspections can be conducted on several occasions, and for various reasons such as pre-approval inspection of the site, regular annual inspection, inspection for evaluation of post-approval changes and risk-based inspection. Inspections are also conducted for issuance of a Certificate of Pharmaceutical Product (COPP), when exports of pharmaceutical products are to be done.

United States of America

The US pharmaceutical market is the largest in the world and accounts for more than 40 per cent global pharmaceuticals sales. The USA pharmaceutical industry earned USD 425 billion in annual revenue in 2020. A household spends an average of USD 442 on Over-The-Counter (OTC) medications each year.

Regulatory regime

Regulator

The US FDA (Food and Drug Administration) is the agency responsible for regulating the pharma sector. It regulates a number of products such as food, human drugs (APIs and OTCs), cosmetics, vaccines (biological products such as blood, screening tests, tissue, embryo, etc.), medical devices, radiation-emitting electronic products, dietary supplements, and tobacco products through the Federal Food Drug and Cosmetic Act.

Regulation

Every drug, be it novel or generic, has to pass through four approval stages of pre-clinical, clinical, new drug application review, and post marketing. One of the primary steps is to get the establishment registered with the US FDA for a said drug. The process is known as 'registration'. For registration, a US agent has to be identified and include all known importers in drug registration. The establishment listing needs to include what drug is being manufactured, at what location for commercial distribution and submit updates to the FDA twice a year (in June and December). For registration, the Electronic Drug Registration and Listing System (eDRLS) is used.

Once an establishment has been registered, marketing approval of the drug is sought. A drug can be marketed either as a novel drug or as a generic drug or OTC or investigational drug. The following are the various types of applications that need to be submitted to the US FDA for drug development and approval. They include:

(i) New Drug application (NDA): by which a drug sponsor applies to the US FDA for approval of marketing and sales of the drug in the USA. It includes all information and data related to animal and human trials

(ii) Investigational NDA: This means the process after which a pharma company gets permission to transport an experimental drug across various states prior to the approval of marketing application of the drug

(iii) Abbreviated NDA: This is for marketing of generic drugs. They are called abbreviated because there is no compulsion of incorporating pre-clinical (animal) and clinical (human) data to demonstrate safety attributes. What pharma companies need to be concerned about is the performance of their product as compared to the innovator drug. Drug companies have to confirm scientifically that the performance of their product is comparable with that of the innovator drug. For the US FDA to grant approval, the generic version of the drug must deliver the same quantity of active ingredients in a patient's bloodstream, and it should take the same amount of time as taken by the innovator drug.

(iv) Over-the-counter drugs (OTC): These are available to consumers without a prescription and constitute an important segment of the market. The FDA evaluates the APIs and the labelling rather than the individual drug products for this category.

(v) Biologic licence application (BLA): These products are approved under the Public Health Service Act, which requires detailed information about the processes, chemistry, pharmacology, and medical impacts of the product.

Once the marketing approval for imports is received by the importer or its representative, called 'licensed customs broker', the following documents are required:

- Commodity and sub-type
- Product code
- Product description
- Country code identifying where the product was produced, sourced, grown, or harvested
- Names and addresses of manufacturer, shipper, importer, delivered to party
- Contact information
- Estimated arrival date and time
- FDA Affirmation of Compliance (mandatory in some instances)
- Quantity and value (voluntary submission)

The following requirements are verified at the time of importation:

- Registration
- Listing: at the time of import, registration information is checked against the FDA database of listings. Details of such information can be accessed at the Drugs Establishments Current Registration (DECRS) page
- Drug application: A marketing application is required before the import (NDA, ANDA, IND, etc.)
- Drug labelling: This depends on the type of drugs being imported. For example, over–the-counter drugs, prescription drugs, investigational drugs, and drugs imported for drug efficacy studies are subject to specific labelling requirements in addition to the general drug label provisions. The labelling requirements are given in the Code of Federal Regulations under Title 21 (Food & Drugs), chapter I.
- Drug current good manufacturing practices (cGMPs)

European Union

The EU had a share of 23.9 per cent of global pharma revenues in 2020. It imported pharmaceutical products worth USD 371.4 billion in 2021 and exported USD 522.9 billion during the same period with the bigger players being Belgium and Germany.

Switzerland is a long established player in this sector. Its pharmaceutical production value is larger than Germany's and Ireland's together. Major companies operating out of Germany are Roche and Novartis. EU member-countries spend a sizeable chunk of their sales revenue on R&D. Nearly 30 per cent of the clinical trials held across world are performed in the EU.

Around 8.30 lac people are working in the European pharmaceutical industry, a significant increase compared to around 5.57 lac employees back in 2000.

Regulatory regime

Regulator

The European Medicines Agency (EMA) was established to harmonize the approval process among EU countries. The advantage is that once approved, the drug can be marketed across all EU member-states. Those that do not follow the centralized procedure are approved individually by the member-states using their national processes.

Regulation

Given the vast landscape of the EU, drug manufacturers are organized within the EFPIA (European Federation of Pharmaceutical Industries and Association). Currently, it includes 36 national pharma associations and 39 companies.

The EU pharma industry is set for a change in the coming years as it intends to overhaul the current EU's legislation on medicines. In 2020, the pharma strategy for the EU was adopted. It aims at creating a future-proof regulatory framework and supporting industry in promoting research and technologies that reach patients in order to fulfil their therapeutic needs while addressing market failures. It will be based on four pillars, which include legislative and non-legislative action:

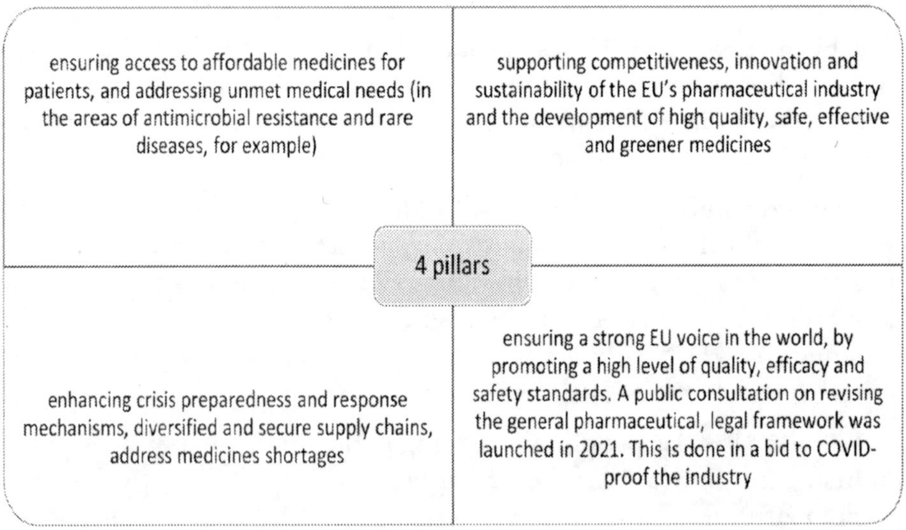

Figure 49: Four pillars of pharmaceutical strategy of EU

The regulatory system is managed by around 50 regulatory authorities from each member-state, the European Commission, and EMA, which includes experts. Similar to the USA, for placing an imported drug in the EU market, licence to manufacture is needed first, followed by an authorization.

Getting a licence

All manufacturers, importers, and distributors need to be licensed by the corresponding member-state. The details are entered in the EudraGMDP system that can be accessed online and is a publicly available database.

> ***EudraGMDP***
>
> *The EudraGMDP database is a community database on manufacturing, import and wholesale distribution authorisations, and good manufacturing practice (GMP) and good distribution practice (GDP) certificates. A public version of the database has been available since 2011, which allows public access to the information in the database that is not of a commercially or personally confidential nature.*
>
> *The database aims to:*
>
> - *improve the sharing of information between regulators and the public, including the pharmaceutical industry;*
> - *aid the coordination of inspections of manufacturers in Third World countries among national competent authorities;*
> - *eliminate the need for industry to submit paper documents to support marketing authorizations and variation applications;*
> - *help protect the medicine distribution chain and active substance supply chain by facilitating the verification of legitimate actors;*
> - *facilitate the sharing of information on the outcomes of inspections conducted by the European Economic Area (EEA) authorities with regulatory authorities elsewhere in the world.*

The units listed for licence are inspected by competent EU authorities. For foreign establishments, unless there is an MRA between the EU and the other country, carrying out inspection is mandatory. Inspection outcomes are also available on EudraGMP. All member-states have similar processes that are ensured by common legislation, common good manufacturing practice (cGMP), common procedures for inspectorates, technical support, meetings, trainings, and internal and external audits.

For an API, it is to be accompanied by a written confirmation issued by the competent authority of the country where it is produced, confirming that the GMP applied is at least equivalent to the recognised EU GMP standards. A waiver applies for some countries, which have applied to have their regulatory systems for the supervision of manufacturers of API by the EU and have been found to be equivalent to the EU.

How EMA evaluates medicines?

About six to seven months before submitting an application, manufacturers can meet the EMA to ensure that their application complies with legal and regulatory requirements. This means that the application includes all the different aspects required by EU legislation and is needed to demonstrate that a medicine works as intended. The companies pay an administrative fee upfront before EMA assessment starts. The administrative fee applicable for each procedure is defined by EU legislation.

The data submitted by medicine developers in their application for marketing authorization must comply with EU legislation and include information on:

- *the group of patients the medicine is proposed to treat, and whether there is an unmet medical need addressed by the medicine;*
- *the quality of the medicine including its chemical and physical properties, such as its stability, its purity and biological activity;*
- *compliance with international requirements for laboratory testing, medicine manufacture and conduct of clinical trials ('good laboratory practice', 'good clinical practice', and 'good manufacturing practice');*
- *the medicine's mechanism of action, as investigated in laboratory studies;*
- *how the medicine is distributed in, and eliminated by, the body;*
- *the benefits observed in the patient group at whom the medicine is aimed;*
- *the medicine's side effects observed in patients, including in special populations such as children or the elderly;*
- *the way risks will be managed and monitored once the medicine is authorised;*
- *what information is intended to be gathered from follow-up studies after authorization.*

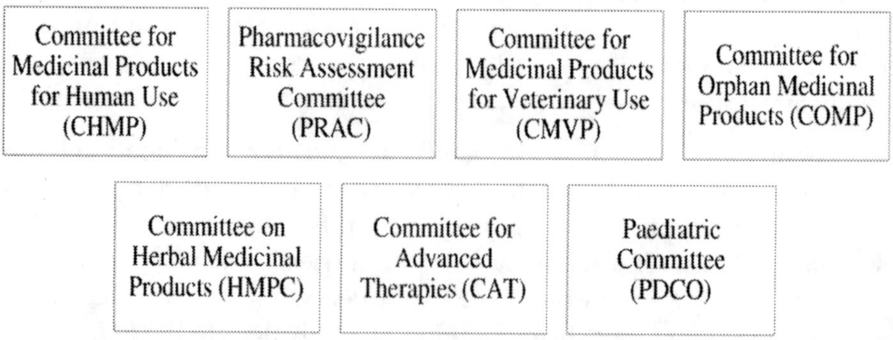

Figure 50: Seven scientific committees that carry out scientific assessments in EU pharmaceutical sector

Getting market authorization

The market authorization is granted to ensure availability of high quality, safe, and effective medicines. There are two ways to obtain a market authorization: centralized and de-centralized method:

(i) Under the centralized procedure, market authorization is granted based on a single EU-wide assessment and is applicable across the EU. A single application is submitted to the EMA based on which the Committee for Medicinal Products for Human Use (CHMP) carries out scientific assessment of the application and gives a recommendation to the EC to either grant or refuse market authorization. All innovator drugs have to compulsorily follow this route of authorization.

(ii) Decentralized procedure is used by companies when they apply for simultaneous authorizations of a medicine. While the majority of new, innovative medicines are evaluated by the EMA and authorized by the European Commission, most generic medicines and medicines available without a prescription are assessed and authorized at the national level in the EU.

(iii) Mutual recognition procedure in which companies that have a medicine authorized in one EU member-state can apply for this authorization to be recognized in other EU countries. This process allows member-states to rely on each other's scientific assessments.

Fees for marketing authorization by EMA

The EMA charges fees for applications for marketing authorization, and for variations and other changes to marketing authorizations, as well as annual fees for authorized medicines.

Examples of basic fees

Fee type	*Human medicines (€)*	*Veterinary medicines(€)*
Marketing-authorisation application (single strength, one pharmaceutical form, one presentation)	*From 296,500*	*From 148,400*
Scientific advice	*From 44,400 to 89,000*	*From 14,600 to 44,400*
Annual fee	*106,300*	*35,600*

The pricing and reimbursement is, however, decided at the state level depending on the importance of the medicine in the health system of that member-state. An EPAR (European Public Assessment Report) is published for every grant or refusal of marketing authorization.

Every batch of medicines must be certified by a Qualified Person (QP) as having been manufactured and tested in accordance with GMP and in conformance with the marketing authorisation before it is placed on the market. For imported drugs, it needs to undergo full analytical testing in the EU, unless an MRA is in place between the EU and the exporting country. India does not have an MRA with the EU in this field, hence, full testing is done. The EU has MRAs with Japan, Canada, Switzerland, Australia, and New Zealand.

China

China's pharmaceutical drug market is constantly growing and is the second-largest pharmaceutical industry in the world, after the USA. It is estimated to reach USD 161.8 billion by 2023, with an average growth rate of 5 per cent in the coming years, taking a 30 per cent share of the global market.

Currently, the pharma market is highly fragmented, comprising of approximately 5,000 manufacturers, a majority of which are small and medium-size companies. This fragmentation keeps the research and development spending to as low as 5 per cent of sales on average. The companies are mostly engaged in production of generics, therapeutic medicines, active pharmaceutical ingredients and traditional Chinese medicine. More than 90 per cent of drugs registered in China are generic ones.

Regulatory regime

Regulator

The regulatory agency in China is the National Medical Product Agency (NMPA) which was formed after disbanding and is now called the China Food and Drug Administration. It is responsible for drug registration management, formulating drug registration specifications, and organizing drug registration review and approval.

NMPA's Drug Evaluation Centre (CDE) is responsible for the review of drug clinical trial applications, drug marketing authorization applications, supplementary applications, and drug re-registration applications for overseas manufactured drugs.

Regulation

The requirements to develop and register a medicinal product in China depend on further classification:

- Chemical medicines
- Biological products
- Traditional Chinese medicines

Each type is then classified into three registration categories, which determine the documents that the applicant must provide as part of the registration process, e.g., clinical trial application, marketing authorization application, etc.

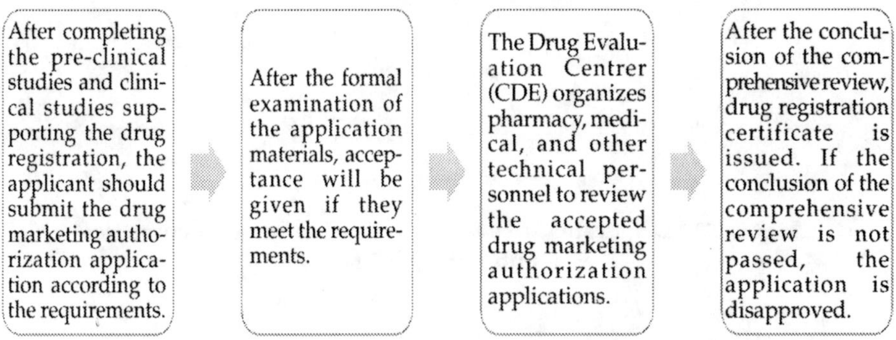

Figure 51: Review process for drug marketing authorization in EU

Recently, the Chinese regulatory regime has undergone a change with respect to generic drugs, on strengthening its clinical data, and encouraging the drug approval process. Its new drug review process is similar to the USFDA's process, which is divided into the following categories:

- Breakthrough
- Priority review
- Fast-track approval
- Special approval process

The usual timelines of three years has been reduced to 16 months in the case of fast track approvals. The following generic drug categories that have been previously approved in the USA, the EU or Japan and have not been approved in China for the last 10 years, are eligible for approval by any of the methods mentioned above:

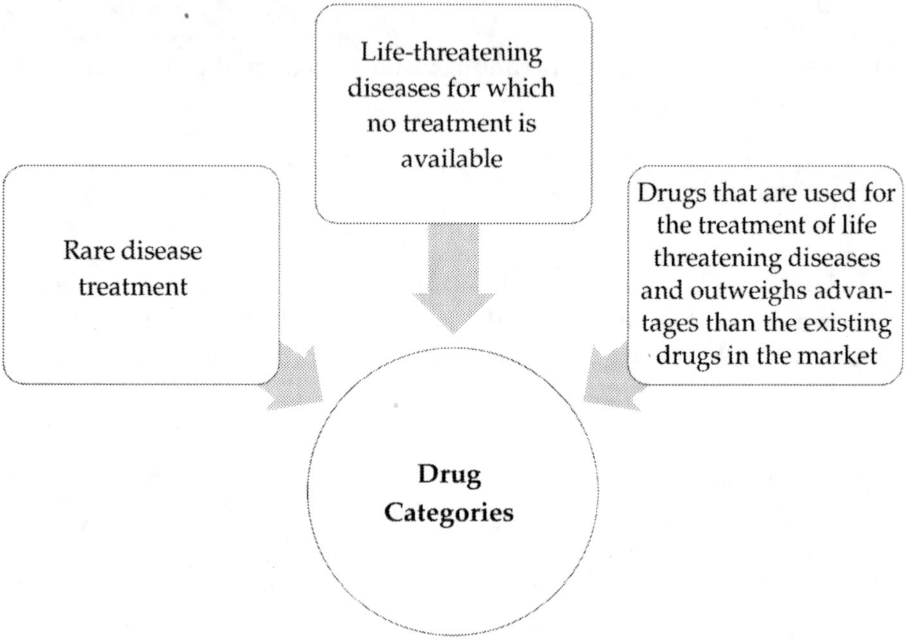

Figure 52: Drug categories approved earlier in other countries and not in China

Import of drugs

In the import of drugs that do not have import registration certificates but are of special requirement or short in domestic supply, importing units should apply to the Ministry of Public Health of the People's Republic of China for a "single permit for import of drug". The "permit" is applicable only to the drug, the country, the manufacturer, the quantity, and the terms indicated in the permit.

Registration certificates for imported drugs should be applied for by a foreign manufacturer or its agent with an application form filled in duplicate and submitted to the Bureau of Drug Administration of the Ministry of Public Health with all data and documents.

The following data and documents should be submitted when applying for a registration certificate:

1. Original certificate issued by the authority of the manufacturing country ratifying the production, sales, and export of the drug concerned as well as GMP inspection report with its Chinese version
2. Letters patent
3. Data sheets and their Chinese versions
4. Technical information:
   (a) Formula, names (including non-proprietary names, trade names, chemical names) of active ingredients and preservatives and dosages;
   (b) Brief description of the production process;
   (c) Specifications and quality control methods of the drug and their Chinese translations;
   (d) Abstracts of its pharmacological and toxicological experiments, and their information on literature;
   (e) Clinical data, including indications, dosages, route of administration, adverse and side-effects, contra-indications, and precautions;
   (f) Data on its stability studies.
5. Samples of the drug(s);
6. Packaging materials and their samples.

The Registration Certificate for imported drug is valid for three years from its date of issuance.

Looking ahead

Regulatory compliance has emerged as a critical challenge for the pharmaceutical industry, especially in the regulated markets. Non-compliance can lead to loss of reputation, patient safety issues, criminal sanctions, etc.

One of the cooperation areas at the international level is the presence of the Pharmaceutical Inspection Cooperation Scheme (PIC/S) which is an informal collaboration among member-economies spearheaded by the EU, seeking to improve the standards of manufacturing requirements amongst its members. India is not currently a member of the PIC/S. Membership requires countries to bring their GMP systems up to international standards.

There have been times when India has taken steps towards PIC/S membership. Although it will increase the visibility of India and build confidence in newer markets for Indian medicines and diagnostics, it will hamper the growth prospects of smaller industries that will have to abide by stricter compliance requirements. As of now, approximately two-thirds of pharmaceutical products exported from India are being supplied to PIC/S member-countries. Becoming a member of PIC/S will enhance exports.

Since products in this sector affect the health of humans, there is no difference in the importance assigned to regulations in this sector by countries. Developed and developing countries want alike.

Since developed countries put in more money in R&D (technically it is the companies based in those countries), they are less inclined to promote generic and off-patent drugs, but the latter are less expensive options, even for developed countries. For exporters, this may translate into a longer approval process with heavier documentation and fees.

One of the ways to facilitate exports is to have an MRA with EU. This will reduce the double cost that an exporter has to beat for double testing.

REFERENCES

- https://www.statista.com/topics/1764/global-pharmaceutical-industry/#dossierKeyfigures
- https://www.youtube.com/watch?v=JoX3xoCMW7g
- https://www.investindia.gov.in/sector/pharmaceuticals
- https://www.ibef.org/industry/pharmaceutical-india.aspx
- https://groww.in/blog/overview-of-pharma-industry-in-india/
- https://www.eximbankindia.in/Assets/Dynamic/PDF/Publication-Resources/ResearchPapers/92file.pdf
- https://www.fda.gov/industry/import-basics/regulated-products
- https://www.fda.gov/industry/import-program-food-and-drug-administration-fda/entry-process
- https://www.fda.gov/industry/entry-process/entry-submission-process
- https://www.fda.gov/industry/regulated-products/human-drugs
- https://www.fda.gov/drugs/guidance-compliance-regulatory-information/electronic-drug-registration-and-listing-system-edrls
- https://www.fda.gov/drugs/guidance-compliance-regulatory-information/human-drug-imports
- https://www.fda.gov/regulatory-information/laws-enforced-fda/federal-food-drug-and-cosmetic-act-fdc-act
- http://uscode.house.gov/browse/prelim@title21/chapter9/subchapter5&edition=prelim

- https://www.fda.gov/drugs/guidance-compliance-regulatory-information/human-drug-imports
- https://www.fda.gov/media/71146/download
- https://www.fda.gov/media/71129/download
- https://www.fda.gov/regulatory-information/federal-food-drug-and-cosmetic-act-fdc-act/fdc-act-chapter-v-drugs-and-devices
- https://www.fda.gov/industry/fda-resources-data-standards/structured-product-labeling-resources
- https://www.ecfr.gov/current/title-21
- https://www.fda.gov/media/91681/download
- https://www.statista.com/topics/8631/pharmaceutical-industry-in-europe/#dossierContents__outerWrapper
- https://www.euractiv.com/section/health-consumers/news/new-eus-pharma-rules-a-game-changer-for-strategic-autonomy-on-plasma/
- https://ec.europa.eu/health/sites/default/files/human-use/docs/pharma-strategy_report_en.pdf
- https://ec.europa.eu/health/human-use/strategy_en
- https://www.ema.europa.eu/en/documents/leaflet/european-regulatory-system-medicines-european-medicines-agency-consistent-approach-medicines_en.pdf
- https://www.ema.europa.eu/en/about-us/what-we-do/authorisation-medicines/how-ema-evaluates-medicines
- https://www.ema.europa.eu/en/about-us/what-we-do/legal-framework
- https://www.ema.europa.eu/en/human-regulatory/overview/fees-payable-european-medicines-agency
- https://www.ema.europa.eu/en/about-us/what-we-do/authorisation-medicines#centralised-authorisation-procedure-section
- https://www.slideshare.net/shettyuc/presentation-on-eu-regulatory-quality-system
- https://www.ema.europa.eu/en/documents/other/laboratory-patient-journey-centrally-authorised-medicine_en.pdf
- https://www.efpia.eu/media/602699/production-import-dependencies-and-export-vulnerabilities-of-pharmaceuticals-for-the-eu27-final.pdf
- https://www.fdli.org/2017/10/india-pharmaceutical-legal-regulatory-environment/
- https://www.drishtiias.com/daily-updates/daily-news-editorials/regulatory-issues-in-indian-pharmaceutical-sector
- https://cdscoonline.gov.in/CDSCO/FAQ
- https://www.pmda.go.jp/files/000234057.pdf
- https://www.lexology.com/library/detail.aspx?g=4279bcc1-b80e-47c6-ba13-4a83a6bff52a
- https://cdsco.gov.in/opencms/export/sites/CDSCO_WEB/Pdf-documents/import-registration/Import_guidance_doc.pdf
- https://globalregulatorypartners.com/chinas-nmpa-introduces-new-revised-regulation-for-drug-approval-by-foreign-companies/
- http://www.lehmanlaw.com/resource-centre/faqs/health-sciences/what-is-the-standard-registration-procedure-for-importing-drugs-into-china.html
- http://english.mofcom.gov.cn/article/lawsdata/chineselaw/200211/20021100050734.shtml

- https://www.who.int/phi/publications/2081China020517.pdf
- https://redica.com/pharma-an-inside-look-at-chinas-regulatory-and-drug-approval-processes/
- https://credevo.com/articles/2021/02/25/china-drug-registration-process/
- https://www.eximbankindia.in/Assets/Dynamic/PDF/Publication-Resources/ResearchPapers/92file.pdf
- https://www.statista.com/topics/5001/pharmaceutical-industry-in-china/#dossierKeyfigures

TEXTILES

COVID-19 has challenged the textile and apparel industry drastically. Asia, which is the biggest market for the sector, has suffered from prolonged lockdowns and restrictions in most Asian countries. According to a study by the International Labour Organization (ILO), global textile trade collapsed during the first half of 2020. Exports to the major buying regions in the European Union, the USA, and Japan, fell by around 70 per cent. The industry also suffered several supply chain disruptions due to shortages of cotton and other raw materials.

Textiles and apparels are traded under HS codes 50 to 63 (Table 10), which include raw material and finished goods with total exports amounting to USD 719 billion in 2020. Apparels specifically are traded under chapters 61 and 62 and account for more than 50 per cent of the overall trade in this sector. As textiles, exports of cotton during the same period was USD 41 billion globally.

Table 10: Textile HS Codes

Chapter	*Description*
50	Silk
51	Wool, fine or coarse animal hair, horsehair yarn and woven fabric.
52	Cotton.
53	Other vegetable textile fibres; paper yarn and woven fabrics of paper yarn.
54	Man-made filaments.
55	Man-made staple fibres.
56	Wadding, felt and nonwovens; spacial yarns; twine, cordage, ropes and cables and articles thereof.
57	Carpets and other textile floor coverings.
58	Special woven fabrics; tufted textile fabrics; lace; tapestries; trimmings; embroidery.
59	Impregnated, coated, covered or laminated textile fabrics; textile articles of a kind suitable for industrial use.
60	Knitted or crocheted fabrics.
61	Articles of apparel and clothing accessories, knitted or corcheted.
62	Articles of apparel and clothing accessories, not knitted or crocheted.
63	Other made up textile articles; sets; worn clothing and worn textile articles; rags.

Among other important aspects, labelling is the most critical one. In case vital information is missing from a label or the labelling is in another language, the consignment is rejected. Therefore, an understanding of labelling requirements is crucial.

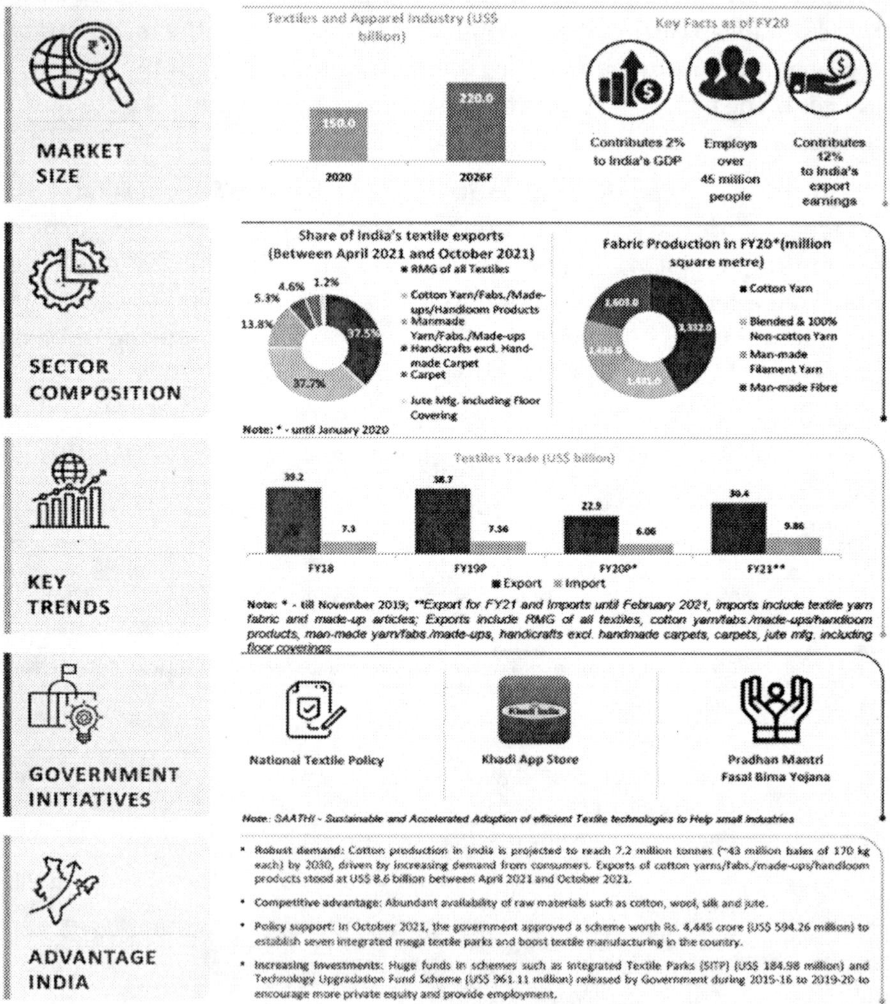

Figure 53: IBEF snapshot: textiles

India

The domestic apparel and textile industry in India contributes 5 per cent to the country's GDP, 7 per cent of industry output in value terms, and

12 per cent of the country's export earnings. India is the 6th largest exporter of textiles and apparel in the world and is one of the largest producers of cotton and jute. It is also the 2nd largest producer of silk in the world and 95 per cent of the world's hand-woven fabrics come from India. The Indian technical textiles segment is estimated at USD 16 billion, approximately 6 per cent of the global market.

The sector is the second largest employer in the country providing direct employment to 45 million people and 100 million people in allied industries.

The textiles and apparel industry in India has strengths across the entire value chain from fibre, yarn, and fabrics to apparel. The organized textile industry in India is characterized by the use of capital-intensive technology for mass production of textile products and includes spinning, weaving, processing, and apparel manufacturing.

The domestic textiles and apparel industry stood at USD 108.5 billion in 2019-20, of which USD 75 billion was domestically consumed while the remaining portion worth USD 28.4 billion was exported to the world market during the same period.

The domestic consumption of USD 75 billion was divided into apparel at USD 55 billion, technical textiles at USD 15 billion, and home furnishings at USD 5 billion. While exports comprised apparel exports at USD 12 billion; home textile exports were USD 4.8 billion; fabric exports were USD 4 billion; yarn exports were USD 3.8 billion; fibre exports were USD 1.8 billion and others were USD 2 billion.

Regulatory regime

Regulator

The Ministry of Textiles is the concerned ministry for bringing regulations in this sector, which it does through a Textile Committee. The Committee's main objective is to ensure the quality of textiles and textile machinery, both for internal consumption and export purposes.

Regulation

The import of textiles and textile articles is permitted subject to the condition that the products do not contain any of the hazardous dyes, such as AZO, whose handling, production, carriage, or use is prohibited by the Government of India under the Environment (Protection) Act, 1986. A pre-shipment certification is required declaring that the shipment is free of azo dyes. The pre-shipment certificate must be from a laboratory accredited to the National Accreditation Agency of the country of origin, certifying that the products do not contain any of the prohibited dyes.

Textile Products Imported with Pre-Shipment Inspection Certificate	**Textile Products Imported without Pre-Shipment Inspection Certificate**
• Imported textile products with a pre-shipment inspection certificate can expedite customs clearance. • If testing is required at the port of loading, samples must be collected by a third party inspector. • Mandatory testing parameters are fibre composition and azo dyes. • Testing can be carried out by a textile testing laboratory from the country of origin. The laboratory must be accredited to ISO 17025 by a national accreditation agency and the accreditation agency logo must be on the testing report. • Testing reports with "pass" results should be given to the inspection team for pre-shipment inspection certificate issuance	• For textile products imported into India without any testing, importers are required to reserve 25% of their shipment for random testing by India Customs. • Testing will be done by an Indian laboratory which is approved by the Ministry of Textiles. • Mandatory testing parameters are fibre composition and azo dyes. • Shipment will be released after a "pass" result is obtained.

Figure 54: Textile with and without PSIC (India)

As per a notification issued by the Ministry of Commerce on 24 November 2000, all pre-packaged products (intended for direct retail sale only) imported into India must carry the following declarations on the label:

- Name and address of the importer
- Generic or common name of the commodity packed
- Net quantity in terms of standard unit of weights and measurement (in metric)/size of garment
- Month and year of packing in which the commodity was manufactured, packed or imported, and the maximum retail sales price (MRP)
- Fibre content

The mandatory labelling requirements for pre-packaged commodities are not applicable to garments sold in loose form. Effective 1 July 2017, the labelling requirements for garments sold in loose form in retail stores in India may include only the following:

- Name and description of the product
- Internationally recognizable size indicators (S, M, L, XL, etc.) along with details in metric notation
- Maximum Retail Price
- Name, address, and customer care number of the manufacturer

Apart from labelling requirements, there are four mandatory standards for textile products under the Fire Retardant Textile Materials (Quality Control) Order, 2013.

- IS 15741:2007: Resistance to Ignition of Curtains and Drapes—Specification
- IS 15742:2007: Requirements for Clothing Made of Limited Flame Spread Materials and Material Assemblies Affording Protection against Heat and Flame—Specification
- IS 15748:2007: Protective Clothing for Industrial Workers Exposed to Heat (excluding clothing for fire fighters and welders)
- IS 15768:2007: Resistance to Ignition of Upholstered Composites Used for Non-domestic Furniture—Specification

United States of America

The USA is the leading producer and exporter of raw cotton, while also being the top importer of raw textiles and garments. The U.S. textile and apparel industry is a nearly USD 70 billion sector when measured by value of industry shipments. It remains one of the most significant sectors of the manufacturing industry and ranks among the top markets in the world by export value of USD 23 billion in 2018. At 341,300 jobs, the U.S. industry is a globally competitive manufacturer of textile raw materials, yarns, fabrics, apparel, home furnishings, and other textile-finished products.

The Federal Trade Commission (FTC) and the U.S. CPB are the authorities managing the labelling requirements for textile and apparel products. The FTC handles the administration of care labelling requirements, while the CPB handles the control and inspection of textile products entering the country. There are a number of regulations that need to be taken care of apart from labelling. Regulations exist at both state and central levels.

Regulatory regime

Regulation

State level: Many states have their own regulations such as the California Proposition 65. Under this regulation, the state has mandated limits for about 800 chemicals such as lead, mercury, and formaldehyde used during manufacturing. Test reports certifying the presence of these chemicals and their limit is mandatory to sell textiles or apparels in California.

Flammable Fabrics Act (FFA): This is a central act that regulates products that are highly flammable including clothing, mattresses, carpets, rugs, etc. Not all fabrics are covered under this act.

Federal Hazardous Substances Act (FHSA): This is not a textile specific act but sets limits on some substances used in the manufacturing of textiles. It regulates household products that contain potential hazards such as corrosive, reactive, and toxic substances.

Children's Clothing under Consumer Product Safety Improvement Act (CPSIA): Children in USA are those that are less than 12 years. For them, there are additional requirements for apparel:

(i) Based on the product being imported, ASTM standards[14] have to be identified and complied with
(ii) A CPSIA tracking label is to be obtained
(iii) A self-declaration is to be filled in by the manufacturer stating that the product complies with the chosen ASTM standard. This is called a Children's Product Certificate.
(iv) Tests to be done and test reports are to be obtained to prove compliance with the above

Labelling

Labelling has to be permanent in nature. It should be either a patch sewn or printed near the neck region of the apparel. Care labelling of varying strictness is present in the USA, Canada, and the EU. A care label must include:

14. In terms of textiles products, here are the standards that have been incorporated into the law:
    - Children's upper outerwear must be in conformance with ASTM F1816-97
    - Standard Guide for care symbols for care instructions on textile products – ASTM D5489

(i) Country of origin: If a garment was made in the USA from materials that were created in a different country, its label must state, "Made in the USA of Imported Materials".

(ii) ASTM Care Labels (Figure 55): These labels must be clear, legible, and designed to last the life of the garment.

(iii) English Language

(iv) Fibre Content (e.g., 99 per cent cotton, 1 per cent spandex): This is in compliance with the Wool Products Labelling Act and the Textile Fibre Products Identification Act, which are collectively known as the Textile and Wool Acts. These contents must be listed in descending order in terms of percentage, and it is not necessary to list non-fibrous materials. All fibres included in the garment that have functional significance must be listed, but non-functional fibres need not be listed if their concentrations in the final garment are less than 5 per cent each. Instead, these fibres can be declared together as a total percentage under the heading "other fibres". In addition, decorative items such as braids and belts do not need to be listed if they comprise less than 15 per cent of the garment. If ornamentation on a textile product does not exceed 5 per cent of its total composition, it can be omitted, but the phrase "Exclusive of Ornamentation" should be listed at the bottom of the label. Linings should be labelled separately, and all textile materials should be listed under their generic names instead of their trade names.

(v) Manufacturer identification: These labels must be clear, legible, and designed to last the life of the garment.

(vi) Label Placement: All the FTC's required information can be placed on one label, or split onto separate ones. These labels must remain attached to the garment until it reaches the consumer, which means that this FTC-required information cannot be included on hangtags. If a garment has a neck, the country of origin information must be located on the inside centre of the neck, and other labels must be placed in easily noticed locations.

Testing is an important function to show compliance with these regulations. They should be done in CPSIA accredited labs (e.g., TUV, SGS, UL) in the manufacturer's country.

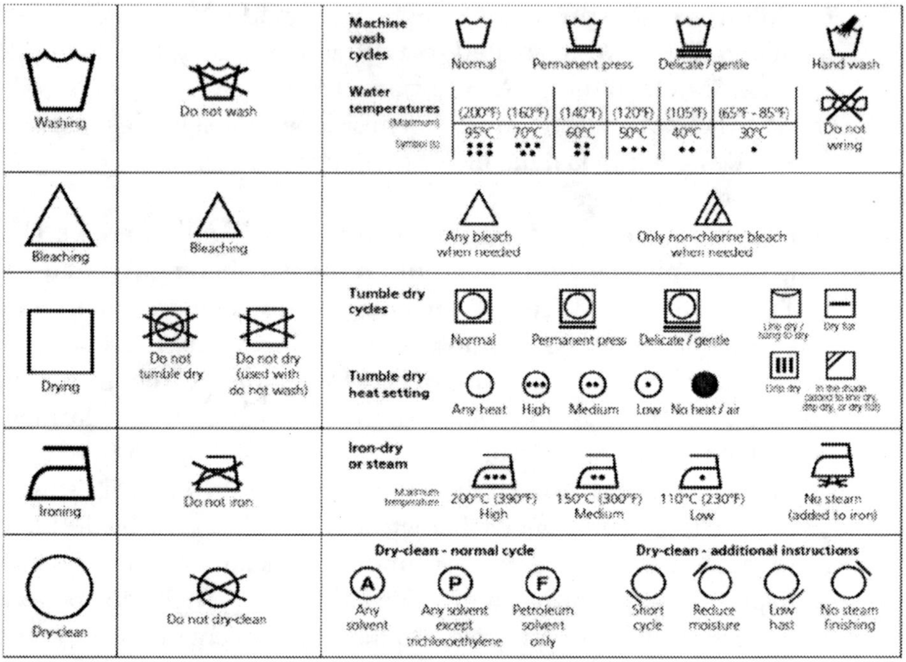

Figure 55: ASTM care labels (USA)

European Union

The textile industry of the European Union comprises Germany, Spain, France, Italy, and Portugal, at the forefront with a value of more than one-fifth of the global textile industry and is currently valued at more than USD 160 billion. Textiles and clothing is a diverse sector that plays an important role in the European manufacturing industry, employing 1.7 million people and generating a turnover of € 166 billion.

According to the European Commission, the EU textile and clothing industry is a leader in world markets. EU exports to the rest of the world represent more than 30 per cent of the world market; at the same time, the EU as a single market is important in terms of size, quality and design.

Regulatory regime

Regulation

REACH regulation: Compliance with REACH is mandatory for this sector. Appropriate tests have to be done to show that SVHCs[15] are within limits.

15. Substances of very high concern (SVHC)

Children's clothing finds special mention in the EU as in the USA. The EU children's clothing regulations are strict to prevent children from fatal incidents. These standards contain requirements to ensure that cords and drawstrings are placed safely on apparel for babies and children up to 14 years old to avoid strangulation and choking hazards. Products that fail to comply with this will face withdrawal from the EU market. Compliance with EN 14878:2007 (Burning behaviour of children's nightwear) and EN 14682:2014 (Safety of children's clothing) is required.

Labelling

EU labelling regulations are not as strict as in the USA, but still have some guidelines, depending on the country of origin. In general:

- Country of origin: Legislation regarding declaration of country of origin is not harmonized within the EU.
- Care labelling: not required under the EU but some member-countries, e.g., Austria, require it.
- Language of the target market/s must be used.
- Fibre content: The label containing this information must be securely attached and durable and should not include abbreviations except those that are internationally recognized. Any non-textile components of animal origin must be marked.
- Manufacturer identification: Not mandatory under EU law.
- Label placement: not harmonized across EU.

Ecolabel

Available for both food and natural textile products: Manufacturers must request certification from the European Ecolabelling Board.

There are some deviations from harmonization across the EU such as:

1. Flammability: There are no specific legal requirements but countries like the Netherlands and Germany have them.
2. CE marking: Mandatory if exporting personal protective equipment (PPE), for example, safety garments or gloves. For these products, compliance with specific EU safety standards for the design, manufacturing, material use, testing, and user instructions concerning PPE is required. CE marking has to be affixed at a visible location that the product conforms to PPE safety requirements.

Non-legal mandatory requirements in EU

Besides the legal requirements mentioned above, non-negotiable terms and conditions may also be levied by buyers. Such requirements are non-legal, but are still mandatory.

- *Corporate social responsibility (CSR): Many buyers in Europe are increasing their demands when it comes to corporate social responsibility. The minimum requirement is factory inspection by the buyer and signing a code of conduct stating that local labour and environmental laws are respected and corruption has been avoided. In addition, buyers may require certification concerning fair and sustainable production.*
- *Often—but not always—buyers that are strict on CSR are also strict on the quality of products. They may require rigorous testing for REACH compliance and anything from tear force to colour fastness.*

Australia

Australia imports a large quantity of apparel and exports about USD 1.5 billion worth of wool. Australia's clothing and textile regulations are overseen by Product Safety Australia (PSA), which is part of the Australian Competition & Consumer Commission (ACCC).

Regulatory regime

Regulation

Australia does not have very stringent regulations for textiles. Some chemicals are banned from use such as formaldehyde and asbestos. The following are the labelling content requirements:

- Fibre content: Not mandatory. However, New South Wales still has fibre content labelling laws.
- Country of origin: Different labelling requirements are mandated for items that are made wholly in Australia, partially in Australia, or wholly imported.
- Care labelling: Australia has comprehensive care labelling laws such as:
  - Care for textile products
  - Understand cleaning costs, such as dry cleaning, associated with the purchase of a textile product
  - Use the correct water temperature to clean products
  - Maximize the usable life of textile products
  - Avoid damage to other clothing during washing
- Manufacturer identity: Not explicitly required.

There are separate requirements for children's clothing that are mandatory. Flammability requirement is one of them. It specifies four categories for labelling children's nightclothes, depending on the degree of fire protection the garment provides.

China

China is the world's leading producer and exporter of both raw textiles and garments. Although China is exporting less apparel and more textiles to the world due to the corona virus pandemic, the country maintains its position as the top producer and exporter. Notably, China's market shares of world apparel exports fell from its peak of 38.8 per cent in 2014 to a record low of 30.8 per cent in 2019 (it was 31.3 per cent in 2018), according to the WTO. China is playing an increasingly critical role as a textile (raw material) supplier for many apparel-exporting countries in Asia.

Except for chapter 51 on wool, China has a trade surplus in all the remaining chapters under this sector. Apart from the apparel sector, in raw materials, it has a huge export of man-made fibres under chapter 54, followed by cotton.

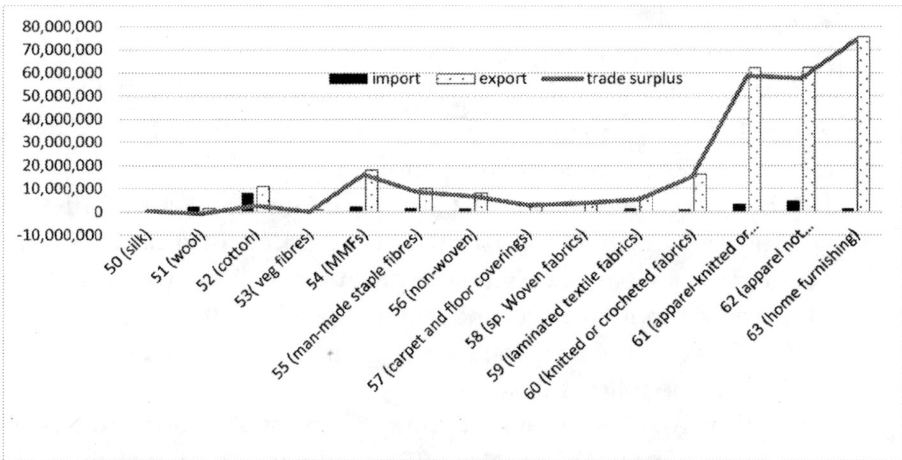

Figure 56: China's trade in textiles (2020)

Regulatory regime

Regulator

SAMR is the regulator for textiles in China.

Regulation

Like the USA and the EU, the textile sector in China is not only regulated by textile related regulations but also by its regulation on chemicals. As per GB/T 39498-2020 (The Guidelines for Controlling the Use of Key Chemical Substances in Consumer Products), effective 1 June 2021, restrictions on the use of 117 hazardous substances are in force. These standards apply to all consumer products (including their components, parts, accessories, instructions, and packaging) that are not regulated separately.

The main regulation to comply with is GB 18401 (National General Safety Technical Code for Textile Products) that sets forth the general safety technical requirements, test methods, inspection rules, and supervision as a mandatory standard applicable to apparel, decoration and home textile products. Mandatory tests include:

- formaldehyde content
- pH value
- colour fastness to water, perspiration (acid and alkaline), rubbing
- colour fastness to saliva for baby products
- determination of odour
- azo dyes

For children's safety, additional requirements have been mandated:

- GB 18401 (National General Safety Technical Code for Textile Products) mentioned above, and
- GB 31701 (Safety Technical Code for Infants and Children Textile Products) that standardises the overall safety of children's wear. Children's wear covers textile products for infants (equal to or under 36 months of age) and textile products for children between 3 and 14 years of age. The standard further categorizes children's wear as the following:
  - Category A (infant and young children's textile products),
  - Category B (children's textile products with direct contact to skin),
  - Category C (children's textile products without direct contact to skin).

Labelling

For labelling, GB 5296.4 (Instructions for Use of Products of Consumer

Interest—Part 4: Textiles and Apparel) is followed that mainly provides for general principles, label contents, and requirements in the instructions. The following information must be included in simplified Chinese on a permanent label (i.e., must be legible throughout the product's life):

- Product type and size designation—(e.g., apparel sizes in accordance with GB/T 1335.1 - 1335.3)
- Fibre content—see GB/T 29862 - Textiles-Identification of Fibre Content, and GB/T 11951-2018 - Textiles-Natural fibres - Generic names and definitions, and GB/T 4146.1-2020 - Textiles-Man-made fibres - Generic names
- Care Instruction/Washing methods - GB/T 8685 Care Labelling Code for Textiles and Apparel (based on ISO 3758). Care labels must consist of symbols and if text description is included, it must be in simplified Chinese.

Additional required information includes:

- Name and address of the manufacturer in China—in the case of imports, the registered name and address in China of the agent or importer or dealer. Also, imports must list the country of origin.
- Product name: According to national or industrial standards whenever possible.
- Effective product standards.
- Safety category (i.e., Category A, B, or C as specified in GB 18401).
- Use and storage precautions (optional).
- Certificate of quality qualification (usually declared on a hangtag).

The CCC mark is not required in apparels and fashion goods. However, for more risky products such as PPE, and clothes worn by fire fighters, CCC marking is compulsory.

Vietnam

Vietnam is the largest exporter of textiles and apparel to the world. It has overtaken Bangladesh in exports in 2020. Even though it may be a new manufacturing hub for apparels, its domestic regulations are weak.

One of the main competitive advantages of the Vietnamese manufacturing industry lies in its low labor cost, compared to its competitors such as China and Mexico. As a result, the industry has become one of the leading sectors for foreign direct investment in Vietnam. Consequently, the export of apparel products relies on the production of foreign-owned companies and local-private-owned subcontractors. Meanwhile, local production and imports address the growing domestic demand for apparel products.

Vietnam is highly dependent on imports of raw materials such as cotton, fiber, yarn, textiles, and garments for clothing production as domestic supply has not been sufficient in recent years. For instance, due to decreasing domestic production of cotton, the country has been a net importer of this material, with the United States being its largest supplier in the past years.

The apparel manufacturing sector of Vietnam has been among the hardest hit by the COVID-19 pandemic. The suspension of production in China created a raw material shortage for many Vietnamese producers in 2020. Moreover, several main import markets of textiles and garments went through a crash in demand, leading to order cancellations. This resulted in revenue loss among major textile firms in Vietnam. Textile and garment exports from Vietnam recorded the first year-on-year decrease in 25 years in 2020 but recovered in subsequent year.

Regulatory regime

Regulator

The Vietnam Industry and Trade Ministry is the regulator.

Regulation

Only in 2018 had Vietnam implemented its regulation on formaldehyde and azo dye limits. As per the regulation in force, textile products for children under three years old are allowed with 30 mg/kg of formaldehyde. Textile products, which come in direct skin contact, can have up to 75 mg/kg of formaldehyde and those without direct skin contact are allowed up to 300 mg/kg. The content of each aromatic amine derived from azo colorants shall not exceed 30 mg/kg.

The regulations also allow exemptions for certain textile products. These include unbleached or un-dyed fabrics and textile products, textile products in transit or stored in warehouses for assembling, textile products temporarily imported for re-export, foreign tourist belongings temporarily entering Vietnam and commercial samples with no market value or samples for scientific study.

All textile products that are manufactured, imported, distributed, and marketed in Vietnam are required to declare conformity with a CR mark at the point of sale and provide a conformity certificate either by self-declaration or by the appointed certifying organization.

CR mark

QCVN (Product Certification for Technical Regulation) is a mandatory certification system stipulated by Vietnam's STAMEQ (Standard Quality and Measurement Authority) for maintaining quality, stability and hygiene of all products. The mandatory items are petrol, bio-fuels, diesel, motorcycle helmets, workers' protective gear, toys, electrical and/electronic products, PVC wires and electrical appliances, concrete reinforcement steel, hot rolled steel and pre-stress steel, LPG, EMC, cement and concrete, fertilizers and insecticides, food and food additives, food packaging materials, fishery products and other food, livestock feed, and textile and apparel products.

Conformity Assessment Procedure

The certification process depends on the type of product and certification that can be determined by type test. There are eight schemes but schemes 1, 5, and 7 are most commonly used. If the product to be certified is not subject to electrical safety and mandatory certification, the applicant can decide the certification scheme.

- *Scheme 1: Process basic visual inspection and simple tests would be carried out such as resistance and short circuit tests*
- *Scheme 5: Most tests are required, such as factory inspection, type test and a posterior judgement every nine months*
- *Scheme 7: Perform type test for sample product by lot and requires a new certificate for every lot*

Labelling

Decree 89/2006/ND-CP and accompanying regulations provide for labelling of goods for sale in Vietnam. According to these regulations, product labels must include the following information:

- Name of goods
- Name and address of the organization or individual responsible for the goods
- Origin of goods

- Composition or quantitative compositions
- Technical specifications
- Hygiene, safety information, and warnings
- Instructions on use and preservation

Looking ahead

The textile sector is fraught with not just TBT issues but also labour and environment issues. Developing countries may not consider the latter as an important issue but it is important for developed countries. Manufacturing units in Bangladesh recently were involved in rows over child labour in textile factories. These non-TBT issues can also be used by developed countries as potential trade barriers to restrict trade from one country and promote in another.

Wages are also another factor that can potentially form an NTB in the textile sector. It may be made a part of the regulation and can be included in an FTA. The industry is still recovering from the effect of the COVID-19 pandemic as cotton, which is a raw material is costlier and garment manufacturers are looking for its alternative in the form of synthetic fabric. However, customers are unwilling to absorb the cost. This affects smaller manufacturers more.

REFERENCES

- https://www.ibef.org/industry/textiles/infographic
- https://www.mordorintelligence.com/industry-reports/global-textile-industry—growth-trends-and-forecast-2019—2024
- https://www.solidaritycenter.org/wp-content/uploads/2019/08/Garment-Textile-Industry-Fact-Sheet.8.2019.pdf
- https://www.investindia.gov.in/sector/textiles-apparel
- https://www.fibre2fashion.com/news/textile-news/newsdetails.aspx?news_id=165804#:~:text=According%20to%20the%20Indian%20import,(Protection)%20Act%2C%201986.
- https://www.trade.gov/textile-and-apparel-market-report-india
- https://www.fashionabc.org/global-textile-industry-overview-china-u-s-europe-dominates-market/
- https://www.fibre2fashion.com/industry-article/8788/your-guide-to-garment-labeling-requirements-for-clothing
- https://www.compliancegate.com/european-union-clothing-textiles-regulations/
- https://sewport.com/learn/garment-labeling-and-requirements
- https://www.cbi.eu/market-information/apparel/buyer-requirements
- https://www.compliancegate.com/european-union-clothing-textiles-regulations/
- https://www.compliancegate.com/united-states-clothing-textiles-regulations/
- https://www.trade.gov/textile-and-apparel-us-market-entry-requirements

- http://en.cirs-ck.com/services/gb-testing/textile-products
- https://www.trade.gov/textile-and-apparel-market-report-china
- https://www.export2asia.com/blog/exporting-clothes-to-china/
- https://www.fibre2fashion.com/news/textile-news/vietnam-has-new-rules-on-formaldehyde-and-azo-dyes-239844-newsdetails.htm
- http://otexa.trade.gov/overseas_mkts/Vietnam.pdf
- https://www.compliancegate.com/australia-new-zealand-clothing-textiles-regulations/
- https://www.iastoppers.com/articles/mains-article-indian-textile-industry-challenges-and-suggestions
- http://www.guide-cert.com/en/service/other_country/cr/
- http://ipsnews.net/business/2021/01/06/the-rise-of-bangladeshs-apparel-and-textile-industry/#:~:text=Growth%20of%20Textile%20Industry&text=In%202012%2 C%20Bangladesh's%20textile%20industry,increasing%20wages%20in%20other%20countries.
- https://www.mckinsey.com/industries/retail/our-insights/whats-next-for-bangladeshs-garment-industry-after-a-decade-of-growth
- https://www.business-standard.com/article/economy-policy/cotton-rally-squeezes-asian-garment-makers-threatens-recovery-from-covid-122060200109_1.html
- https://textilescommittee.nic.in/about-us

TOYS

Play is a child's "work" and toys are the tools children use in play. Toys do more than entertain and keep children occupied. Properly chosen, they should aid a child's physical, mental, social and emotional development. They are universally recognized as a vital part of learning and growing and are invaluable to a child's development into a mature, confident adult.

Today's toy manufacturers keep pace with the rapidly changing world and provide youngsters with correspondingly appropriate playthings for their enjoyment and to challenge their creativity and imagination.

Market growth is being fueled by video, console and computer games, with the industry also benefiting from a growing adult consumer base as this group takes a greater interest in games as a popular leisure pursuit. While traditional toys and games are losing some degree of popularity in the face of competition from interactive and intelligent toys, this market segment is expected to reach record levels of demand in some regions.

Danish company Lego, known for its interlocking plastic bricks, was the leading toy company worldwide with over USD 7.2 billion revenue in 2020. Tokyo-based Bandai Namco ranked in second place with revenue of almost USD 6.6 billion, amongst the major toy companies. Hasbro, Mattel, and Jakks Pacific complete the top five.

The U.S. is by a wide margin the leading importer in the global toy industry. In 2020, the country imported toys, dolls and sports requisites with a value of about USD 36.3 billion, the highest figure since 2011. China accounted for about 80 per cent of all imports of toys, games and sport requisites to the U.S. China is also the leading exporter in the global toy industry with about USD 71.5 billion in 2020, the global exports being USD 131 billion.

The toys are traded under chapter 95 (Toys, games and sports requisites; parts and accessories thereof.) of HS codes. At 4-digit level, the classification is given in Figure 57.

The total imports under these HS codes were USD 47.6 billion in 2020 with USA being the major importer with imports of value USD 14.3 billion. Imports worth USD 11.7 billion are from China.

HS Code	Commodity
9503	Other Toys; Rdcd-Size (Scale) Modls and Smlr Recretnl Modls, Wrkng/ Nt; Puzls of a
9504	V/Game Mach, Parlour Game and Prtbl, Billiard, Casino and Auto Bowling, Mach by Coin, B/ Note, Card, Token/other Pmt Mode
9505	Festive, Carnival or other Entertainment Articles, including Conjuring Tricks and Novelty Jokes
9506	Artcls and Eqpmnt Fr Gymnstcs,Athltcs, other Sports (Incl Tabletennis)/ Outdoor Games, N.E.S.; Swimming Pools and Paddling
9507	Fishing Rods, Fish-Hooks and other Line Fishngtckl;Fish Lndng and Smlr Nets; Decoy Birds (Excl Of 9208/9705) and Smlr Hu
9508	Trvling (Circuesand Menages) Park Ride (Amsmentandwatr); Faigrnd Amsents, Including Shting Galries; Travling Thters

Figure 57: 4-digit HS code classification of toys

The exports under HS code 9503 were valued at USD 54.1 billion with China holding the maximum share of USD 33.4 billion with the USA and the UK being its largest market. As an exporter, India is placed at the 25th position under this segment.

HS code 9503 includes the following products:

HS Code	Commodity
95030010	Dolls of wood
95030020	Dolls of metal
95030030	Dolls of plastic
95030090	Others

Figure 58: Products under HS code 9503 at 8-digit level

The toy industry is one of the most resilient industry with one of the most competitive markets. A SWOT analysis in Figure 59 shows how:

India

Indian Toys Industry is estimated to be USD 1.5 billion making up 0.5% of global market share. India exported USD 379 million of toys in 2020 and imported USD 407 million during the same period with major trade under HS codes 9506 and 9503. The major export destinations are the USA and the UK.

Strength	Weakness	Threat	Oppportunities
• A diverse base of toy producers and brands from major companies to startups. • Diverse points of sale include brick-and-mortar stores as well as online retailers. • A large capacity for the development of new products and innovations includes engineering and design firms, prototyping operations and full-scale manufacturing facilities. • Access to robust and cost-effective marketing channels at local, regional and global levels.	• New products have difficulty breaking through in terms of awareness and sales in a market dominated by well-known, popular existing products. • Slow development times and unexpected consumer responses make for a challenging forecasting environment. • Concentrated selling opportunity around the winter holidays, which creates an unusual and complex demand for more storage capacity and a larger workforce than at other times of the year.	• Parents are increasingly relying on toys to provide alternatives to "device obsession" – the tendency of children to spend inordinate amounts of time on their phones and tablets. • The rapid miniaturization and reduced costs of electronics allows manufacturers to introduce many new features into toys. • New production capacities in countries such as Vietnam are emerging as more cost-effective manufacturing centers than China, where costs have been on the rise.	• Environmental concerns. Consumers are increasingly aware of the environmental costs of excess plastic consumption and waste. • Heavily reliant on manufacturers in China.

Figure 59: SWOT analysis of toys industry

The toy manufacturers in India are mostly located in NCR, Maharashtra, Karnataka, Tamil Nadu and clusters across central Indian states. The sector is fragmented with 90% of the market being unorganized and 4,000 toy industry units from the MSME sector.

Toys are divided into following segments:

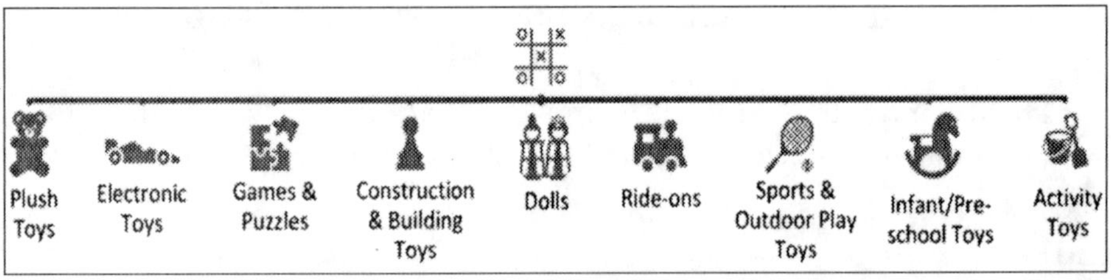

Figure 60: Toys segmentation

On the basis of the toy type, infant/pre-school toys are the most popular segment as they help develop problem-solving and motor skills among children. Other major toy types include electronic toys, games and puzzles, construction and building toys, dolls, ride-ons, sports and outdoor play toys, plush toys and activity toys.

STEM-based toys are one of the most advance trends in the toy manufacturing industry. STEM stands for science, technology, engineering, and math and such toys focus on providing fun and education to children and making it relatable to the real world. According to the Toy Association report in 2018, 67 per cent parents believe in STEM-focused toys as their primary way to encourage science and math development in young children.

Regulatory regime

Regulator

Department for Promotion of Industry and Internal Trade (DPIIT) under Ministry of Commerce and Industry is the regulator for toys in India.

The Indian toy market has advantages in the form of skilled workforce, diverse range of toys, specialization in innovation and creativity, and emphasis on learning & education.

Regulation

The Quality Council of India found in a December 2019 survey that 67 per cent imported toys were unfit and dangerous for kids in the domestic market.

To instill standardization in production and import of toys, a Toy Quality Control Order was issued on 25 February 2020 under the BIS Act, 2016 to ensure toys manufactured or imported into the country were in-line with global quality standards. Recently, an amendment to the QCO exempted handicraft artisans and MSMEs from complying with QCO norms for a period of one year to boost the domestic manufacturing ecosystem in India.

It is also interesting to note that the Confederation of All Indian Traders (CAIT) wrote to the Prime Minister's Office in September 2020, proposing formulation of a concrete toy manufacturing policy to boost the domestic toy industry.

Funskool, powered by the MRF Group, is the first Indian toy manufacturer to get certified by the BIS for Safety of Electric Toys - IS 15644 for the manufacturing plant in Goa, which also has the IS 9873-Part 1 license covering non-electric toys. Funskool has three units - one in Goa and two in Ranipet, Tamil Nadu. Each year, Funskool develops about 60-70 products comprising plastic- moulded toys, board games, puzzles, and wooden toys.

United States of America

As mentioned earlier the USA is the largest importer and exporter of toys in the world. It exported USD 5.6 billion of toys in 2020 and imported USD 36.3 billion (75 per cent of its imports are from China). Its primary export destination of toys is Canada with USD 2.7 billion.

Its largest export is of video games and consoles, followed by gym equipments and dolls/scooters/tricycled toys etc., in that order whereas its imports is primarily of dolls/scooters/tricycled toys etc.

The U.S. market size for the total toy industry in 2021 was approximately USD 38.2 billion, representing a 14.2 per cent increase vs 2020.

Three out of the five major players in the global toy industry are American companies. Led by the U.S., North America is one of the most profitable and important regional markets for these companies. The toy industry's annual total economic impact in the U.S. was USD 97.2 billion, while over 623,000 jobs directly related to the American toy industry were generated.

Regulatory regime

Regulator

The USA is very particular about safety of toys for their children. It is involved from the initial concept stage to the final product stage. The Consumer Product Safety Improvement Act (CPSIA) regulates toys and children's products sold in the USA, as part of the Consumer Product Safety Commission (CPSC). This body requires toys and children's products to carry a Children's Product Certificate or CPC to be imported and sold legally in America.

Children's Product Certificate (CPC)

Manufacturers and importers of children's products must certify, in a written Children's Product Certificate (CPC) based on test results from a CPSC-accepted laboratory, that their children's products comply with applicable children's product safety rules. The CPC and supporting test reports must be in English.

Elements Required in a CPC:

- *Identification of the product: Describe the product(s) covered by this certification in enough detail to match the certificate to each product it covers.*
- *Citation to each CPSC children's product safety rule to which this product is being certified*
- *Identification of the importer or domestic manufacturer certifying compliance of the product (name, full mailing address, and telephone number of the importer or U.S. domestic manufacturer certifying the product)*
- *Contact information for the individual maintaining records of test results (name, full mailing address, e-mail address, and telephone number of the person maintaining test records in support of the certification)*
- *Date and place where this product was manufactured: For the date(s)-at least the month and year. For the place of manufacture-at least the city and country.*
- *Provide the date(s) and place when the product was tested for compliance with the consumer product safety rule(s) cited above.*
- *Identify any third party, CPSC-accepted laboratory on whose testing the certificate depends*

Regulation

All toys sold in the U.S. must comply with a network of 100+ strict toy safety regulations, tests and requirements designed to protect children at play. The toy safety standards cover the following:

Mechanical and physical properties

- material quality, accessible points, or sharp edges. Might also include folding mechanisms and hinges, projectile toy characteristics, and more.

Small parts

- If the toy, or parts of it, is small enough to be accidentally ingested by a young child, then it presents an inherent choking hazard and would be potentially unfit for sale. For this reason, toys containing small parts are banned, if they are intended for children younger than 3 years.
- However, if the small toy (or regular toy with small parts) is intended for use by children between the age of 3 and 6 years, it has to carry a warning label noting its inherent dangers.

Chemicals and heavy metals

- Phthalates
- Lead
- Cadmium

Electrical safety

- from battery powered toys

Flammability

- for toys that can catch fire easily such as plush toys

Warning labels

- provide caution statements and symbols that help the user of the toy (or the caregivers) avoid hazards such as electrocution, accidental ingestion etc.

Figure 61: Coverage of toy standards (USA)

A mandatory set of safety rules and regulations under ASTM F963-17 – Standard Consumer Safety Specification for Toy Safety is followed. It was made mandatory by incorporation into the CPSIA. It generally covers requirements for toys used by children up to 14 years of age even though it is mandatory for toys intended for children up to 12 years of age. The toys covered by ASTM F963-17 include:

- Projectile toys
- Wheeled ride-on toys
- Magnets
- Pom-poms
- Marbles
- Rattles
- Squeeze toys
- Elastic tether toys
- Stuffed and beanbag-type toys

Following are the limits under ASTM F963-17:

Table 11: ASTM F963-17

Limits	*Requirements*
Substance restrictions	Lists different types of heavy metals and their maximum soluble migrated element limits. Some examples: • Antimony < 60 ppm • Arsenic < 25 ppm • Barium < 1000 ppm • Cadmium < 75 ppm • Chromium < 60 ppm • Lead < 90 ppm • Mercury < 60 ppm • Selenium < 500 ppm
Mechanical properties	Lists several mechanical and physical properties that might affect the safety of the product. Those properties include: • Accessible edges (excluding labelling and user manuals) • Cords, straps, and elastics • Holes, clearance, and accessibility of mechanisms • Folding mechanisms and hinges
Small parts	For an item to be considered a "small part", it has to be less than or equal to 2.25 x 1.25 inches wide, as test cylinders are purpose-built to these dimensions, matching that of a 3-year-old's fully-expanded throat. Small parts with dimensions smaller than the test cylinder are considered to be inherent choking hazards, and as such, are non-compliant and unfit for use by children under 3 years of age. However, if a toy that contains small parts is designed to be used by children between 3-6 years, it has to carry a warning label
Electrical safety	References 16 CFR Part 1505, titled "Requirements for Electrically Operated Toys or Other Electrically Operated Articles Intended for Use by Children". The standard applies to children's toys that are powered by currents of at least 120 V and it covers safety requirements such as: • Containers for heated materials • Electrical switches • Insulation • Mechanical assembly • Performance • Protective coating • Wiring
Flammability	Solids, soft toys, and fabrics are subject to flammability testing procedures.
Warning labels	To consist of the following: • An alert symbol (an exclamation mark inside an equilateral triangle); • A signal word (such as "CAUTION" or "WARNING"); • A warning phrase or sentence describing the potential hazard and how to avoid it. The standard also references 16 CFR Part 1505, which indicates that electric or electronic toys should carry a label with the following information: • Electrical rating (in volts, amperes, or watts) • Precautionary statements • Date of manufacture

UL 696 is titled the "Standard for Electric Toys". It covers electric products meant to be used as toys by children over the age of 3. It covers:

- Electrically-operated toys
- Miniatures of full-sized appliances (which are intended for use on standard 120-volt branch circuits but may not always accomplish the copied appliance's desired purpose)
- Toys that copy the function or form of an appliance that has been established for general use
- The toy's packaging, if it is meant to be used with the toy itself

It requires toys that mimic functional general-use appliances to fall under the established requirements of general-use appliances. Those requirements should supplement UL 696's requirements for electrical toys.

Testing and certification

All toys must be third party tested and be certified in a Children's Product Certificate as compliant to safety. All tests are to be done in CPSC accredited laboratory. Only certain provisions of the toy safety standard outlined in 16 CFR 1112.15 (b) (32), specify third party testing requirements. The sections of the toy safety standard that require third party testing are:

- Section 4.3.5.1, Surface Coating Materials - Soluble Test for Metals
- Section 4.3.5.2, Toy Substrate Materials
- Section 4.3.6.3, Cleanliness of Liquids, Pastes, Putties, Gels, and Powders (except for cosmetics and tests on formulations used to prevent microbial degradation)
- Section 4.3.7, Stuffing Materials
- Section 4.5, Sound Producing Toys (requirements for this section modified by 16 CFR part 1250)
- Section 4.6, Small Objects (except labeling and/or instructional literature requirements)
- Section 4.7, Accessible Edges (except labeling and/or instructional literature requirements)
- Section 4.8, Projections
- Section 4.9, Accessible Points (except labeling and/or instructional literature requirements)
- Section 4.10, Wires or Rods
- Section 4.11, Nails and Fasteners

- Section 4.12, Plastic Film
- Section 4.13, Folding Mechanisms and Hinges
- Section 4.14, Cords, Straps, and Elastics
- Section 4.15, Stability and Overload Requirements
- Section 4.16, Confined Spaces
- Section 4.17, Wheels, Tires, and Axles
- Section 4.18, Holes, Clearances, and Accessibility of Mechanisms
- Section 4.19, Simulated Protective Devices (except labeling and/or instructional literature requirements)
- Section 4.20.1, Pacifiers with Rubber Nipples/Nitrosamine Test
- Section 4.20.2, Toy Pacifiers
- Section 4.21, Projectile Toys
- Section 4.22, Teethers and Teething Toys
- Section 4.23.1, Rattles with Nearly Spherical, Hemispherical, or Circular Flared Ends
- Section 4.24, Squeeze Toys
- Section 4.25, Battery-Operated Toys (except labeling and/or instructional literature requirements)
- Section 4.26, Toys Intended to Be Attached to a Crib or Playpen (except labeling and/or instructional literature requirements)
- Section 4.27, Stuffed and Beanbag-Type Toys
- Section 4.30, Toy Gun Marking
- Section 4.32, Certain Toys with Spherical Ends
- Section 4.35, Pompoms
- Section 4.36, Hemispheric-Shaped Objects
- Section 4.37, Yo-Yo Elastic Tether Toys
- Section 4.38, Magnets (except labeling and/or instructional literature requirements)
- Section 4.39, Jaw Entrapment in Handles and Steering Wheels
- Section 4.40, Expanding Materials
- Section 4.41, Toy Chests (except labeling and/or instructional literature requirements)

For the sections of the toy safety standard that are exempt from third party testing, manufacturers are still expected to ensure that their product is compliant with those applicable sections and to certify compliance through Children's Product Certificate covering the product.

If a toy manufacturing company changes a toy's components—for example, re-designs a toy truck with faster, new wheels or uses a different color or brand of paint—then manufacturers need to get the certification again. Certification will typically involve third-party laboratory re-testing of either the new component or the whole toy.

Labelling

A tracking label has to be attached to the packaging of the products, and if possible, to the actual toy or product itself too. The tracking label is an important part of compliance for import and sale of toys, and CPSIA outlines what needs to go on the tracking label such as:

- The date and place that the product was made.
- The batch number or another identifier that displays the batch or run line, and any other marks that the manufacturer might need to be able to trace the product back to its source. This is so that any product faults or recalls can be traced quickly and accurately.
- Imported products need to have a tracking label showing the importer's details too, including their business address and contact details, and information on the materials used in the product.

Additional labeling rules for infant and toddler products

Toys designed for infants and toddlers (children aged 5 and under) have to be sold with a product registration card which must be fixed to the product itself, and display the following:

- The manufacturer's name and contact details.
- The date the item was made.
- The model name and batch number for the product, and any other relevant identifiers.
- It must include a prepaid shipping label to be used by the buyer for optional product registration and in case of recalls.
- Buyers must have the option to enter their contact details on the card and register their purchase, and the card should also give buyers the option to register their details online instead of mailing back the card.
- Records of registered buyers should be retained by the importer in case of future product recalls.

European Union

The EU imported USD 38.7 billion worth of toys in 2020 with major importers being Germany (USD 8.8 million), France (USD 5.2 million), Netherlands (USD 3.5 million) and Poland (USD 3.4 million). The total exports from the EU during the same period was USD 29.9 billion with major exporters being Germany and Netherlands.

Toys are important for the EU economy as the toy industry provides over 50,000 jobs. Most of these jobs are in small and medium-sized enterprises (SMEs) accounting for 61 per cent of the EU toy industry employment.

Regulatory regime

Regulation

The governing legislation is the Toy Safety Directive 2009/48/EC that lays down safety criteria before the toys are placed in the market. Not just this, they must also comply with other regulations, wherever applicable. The essential safety requirements are:

- general risks: health and safety of children, parents or caregivers
- particular risks: physical and mechanical, flammability, chemical, electrical, hygiene and radioactivity risks

The Directive applies to all products that are intended for use in play by children less than 14 years of age. Following is the categorization:

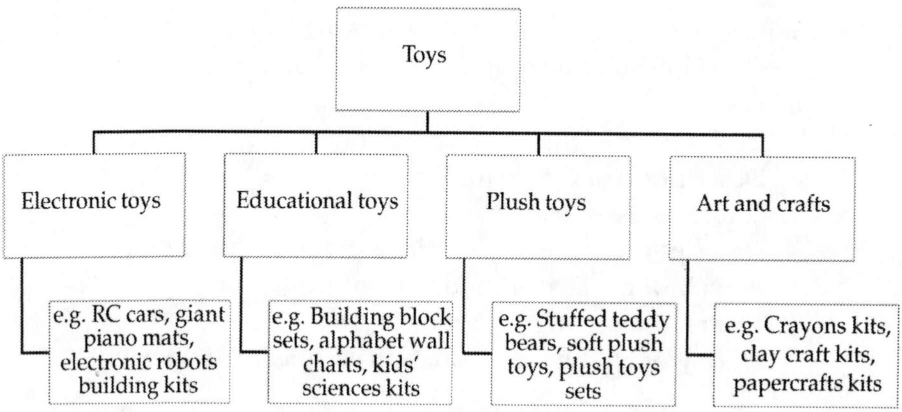

Figure 62: Categorization of toys (EU)

Certain products are exempted from the Directive even if they have "play value" such as playground equipment for public use, automatic plating machines for public use, toy vehicles equipped with engines etc.

As compared to the previous Directive, the current regulation places greater emphasis on regulation of chemicals:

- Chemicals that are susceptible to cause cancer, change genetic information, harm fertility or harm an unborn child (so-called CMR substances) are no longer allowed in the accessible parts of toys beyond the concentration limits set in the Regulation on Classification, Labelling and Packaging of substances and mixtures or unless they are considered safe following a rigorous scientific evaluation
- 19 'heavy elements' like mercury and cadmium are not allowed in toy parts accessible to children beyond the limits as mentioned in toys Directive
- 55 allergenic fragrances have been banned

EN 71 is the referenced standard that outlines the safety requirements for toys in many aspects, including physical and chemical properties, flammability, and warning requirements.

Conformity assessment

Before toys are placed on the EU market, a manufacturer (whether located in the EU or outside the EU) has to

- Prepare a Technical File as per Annex IV of the Directive that mentions information that must be included in the technical file, such as:
    - Description of the product design
    - Description of the manufacturers
    - Safety assessments
    - Description of the conformity assessment procedure
    - A copy of the Declaration of Conformity
    - Test reports
    - A copy of EC-type examination certificate (if relevant)

The Technical File must be prepared in one of the official languages of the EU and retained for 10 years.

- carry out a safety assessment: an analysis of the chemical, physical, mechanical, electrical, flammability, hygiene and radioactivity hazards, as well as an assessment of the potential exposure to those hazards
- go through one of two possible conformity assessment procedures to demonstrate that the toy complies with essential safety requirements
    - self-verification: the manufacturer applies the harmonised standard covering all relevant safety requirements for the toy and makes sure that his manufacturing process ensures compliance ('internal production control procedure').
    - third-party certification: the manufacturer submits an application for the EC-type examination to a notified body.[16] The notified body examines the toy and issues an EC-type examination certificate if the toy meets EU safety requirements. Manufacturers must ensure their manufacturing processes ensure that their toys are compliant with the approved type draw up technical documentation with all relevant details that ensure their toy complies with the essential safety requirements
- draw up the EC Declaration of Conformity stating that the fulfilment of the essential safety requirements has been demonstrated. By drawing up this document, the manufacturer assumes responsibility for the compliance of the toy with the essential safety requirements. It must be retained for 10 years after the toy has been placed in the market. Annex III of the directive outlines the information that must be included in the document
- affix the CE marking to the toy, either directly on the toy, on an affixed label or on the packaging
- affix their name and address, as well as an element allowing identification of the toy for traceability (e.g. a batch or serial number)
- ensure that the toy is accompanied by instructions and safety information and bears the required warnings

16. The NANDO database contains the names and details of notified bodies performing conformity assessments for the purposes of the Toy Safety Directive 2009/48/EC.

NANDO (New Approach Notified and Designated Organizations) Information System

Notification is an act whereby a Member State informs the Commission and the other Member States that a body, which fulfils the relevant requirements, has been designated to carry out conformity assessment according to a directive. Notification of Notified Bodies and their withdrawal are the responsibility of the notifying Member State.

The Member States, EFTA countries (EEA members) and other countries with which the EU has concluded Mutual Recognition Agreements (MRAs)[17] and Protocols to the Europe Agreements on Conformity Assessment and Acceptance of Industrial Products (PECAs) have designated Notified Bodies, established per directive. Lists of Notified Bodies can be searched on the NANDO web site. The lists include the identification number of each notified body as well as the tasks for which it has been notified, and are subject to regular update.

Labeling

The Toy Safety Directive requires that importers and manufacturers include warning labels in a clear, visible, and easily legible manner on the toy, the packaging and/or the user instructions when it is appropriate. As described in Annex V, there are two types of warnings that might apply to products:

- General warnings: mainly concern users limitations, such as minimum or maximum age of the user, minimum or maximum weight of the user, toy should be used only under adult supervision
- Specific warnings: apply to certain categories of toys such as functional toys, chemical toys, or aquatic toys. The specific warning should indicate specific precautions when using the toys, such as
  - Aquatic toys – Warning: Only to be used in water in which the child is within its depth and under adult supervision.
  - Toy masks and helmets – Warning: This toy does not provide protection.
  - Toys in food – Warning: Toy inside. Adult supervision recommended.

17. Canada, Switzerland

United Kingdom

The UK exported USD 2.2 billion worth of toys in 2020, the major destinations being Ireland, Germany, France and the USA. The imports during the same period were USD 6.7 billion with 50 per cent of them from China. India is the 17th largest exporter to the UK. The revenue of the toys market grew significantly in recent years, going from approximately £4.9 billion in 2013 to over £7.1 billion in 2021. The market size is about £ 2 billion. The industry has about 1,190 businesses and provides employment to more than 10,000 people.

The pace of digitalization of the economy picked up speed with the onset of the coronavirus pandemic in 2020. Online sales channels in the toys and games market in the UK have enjoyed a marked increase in revenue share since 2017 and are expected to overtake offline sales channels by 2024. In 2021, Smyths Toys, Waterstones, and LEGO had the highest online visibility scores among toy retailers in the UK. Despite the rise of e-commerce, the number of brick-and-mortar stores for the retail sale of games and toys continued to increase in the last decade in the UK.

Regulatory regime

Regulation

There are different provisions for Great Britain (England, Wales and Scotland) and for Northern Island under the regulation Toys (Safety) Regulations 2011. After Brexit, UK has continued to use EU regulations during the transition period. Thereafter, it has adopted those regulations, with or without changes, wherever required. The Toys (Safety) Regulations 2011 is an adoption of EU Directive 2009/48/EC. The regulation applies to those products that are intended for use by children in play under the age of 14 years.

Similar to the EU regulation, there are general requirements and particular safety requirements mentioned in Schedule 2 of the regulation.

The manufacturer is responsible for the following:

- Carrying out safety assessment
- Following the applicable conformity assessment procedure
- Drawing up a Declaration of Conformity and affix the UK Conformity Assessment (UKCA) marking visibly, legibly and

indelibly to the toy, to a label affixed to the toy or to the toy's packaging. Until 31 December 2025, the UKCA marking may be affixed to a document accompanying the toy. Where toys are too small or consist of small parts, the UKCA marking may be affixed to a label which is not affixed to the toy or a leaflet which accompanies the toy. Qualifying Northern Ireland goods can be placed on the Great Britain market with the CE and CE UKNI conformity markings.

- Drawing up the technical documentation and keep it and the Declaration of Conformity for 10 year
- Making sure the toy is accompanied by instructions for safe use, safety information and warnings as appropriate
- Carrying out sample testing of marketed toy

Manufacturers are also required to appoint an authorized representative to perform certain tasks on their behalf such as keeping technical documentation.

Conformity assessment and marking—products placed before 11 pm 31 December 2022

If a toy is completely manufactured by a manufacturer for the EU or the UK market, no additional formalities are to be followed. The UK has allowed CE marked toys uptil the date mentioned, that have been either self-declared as compliant or where compliance must and has been demonstrated through assessment by an EU-recognized conformity assessment body (notified body). Toys lawfully placed on the market with a CE marking by 11 pm 31 December 2022 can continue to circulate on the market after this date. There is no requirement to re-test or re-mark such equipment.

Products which are repaired, refurbished or exchanged without changing their original performance, purpose, or type, are not considered 'new' and therefore do not need to be recertified and remarked. If the product has been subject to important changes, substantially changing its original performance, purpose, or type, it will be considered as a 'new' product. Therefore, the modified product must comply with new regulatory requirements, including the requirement for UKCA marking from 1 January 2023.

Conformity assessment and marking – products placed from 1 January 2023

THIRD PARTY ASSESSMENT

From 1 January 2023, toys intended for the Great Britain market should be conformity assessed by a UK approved body and UKCA marked, not CE marked.

Rules around physically affixing the new UKCA marking mirror those which currently apply for the application of the CE marking, including affixing it on a label affixed to the toy or its packaging and where not possible to affix it directly on the toy because of the size or nature of the toy on a label which is not affixed to the toy or on a leaflet which accompanies the toy.

Irrespective of the latter provisions, until 31 December 2025, the UKCA marking may be affixed to a document accompanying the toy, rather than being affixed to the toy itself, its packaging or a label affixed to the toy.

SELF-DECLARATION

Manufacturers placing toys on the basis of self-declaration of conformity can affix the UKCA marking before placing a product. Alternatively, until 11pm 31 December 2022, manufacturers can affix the CE marking based on self-declaration of conformity by the manufacturer. It is possible to affix both the UKCA marking and the CE marking to the same product where conformity assessment is based on self-declaration, where the EU and UK requirements remain the same or the product conforms to the requirements of both.

Approved Bodies

The UK has established a new framework for the UK based bodies to assess products. Existing UK notified bodies have been granted the new UK 'approved body' status and are listed on a new UK database.

They are conformity assessment bodies which have been approved by the Secretary of State to carry out the procedures for conformity assessment and certification for the Great Britain market as set out in the 2011 Regulations.

These approved bodies retain their 4-digit identification number. New approved bodies will be assigned a number by the Office for Product Safety and Standards on behalf of the Secretary of State.

Approved bodies must be established in the UK and be independent of the manufacturer. They must examine the technical documentation and supporting evidence in respect of a toy to assess the adequacy of the technical design.

Japan

The toy industry in Japan is operating within a revolving market influenced by media trends, technological innovations, and fandoms in popular culture. Covering a broad range of analog and electronic products, the Japanese toy market is one of the largest worldwide, targeting children and adults alike.

However, within an aging society characterized by fertility decline and a shrinking population of children, manufacturers are looking towards adolescents and adults to stimulate growth. Addressing the interest in creating and maintaining collections of a variety of merchandise such as card games and figurines, companies supplement their standard toy series with regular releases of limited-edition merchandise.

Popular culture drives toy sales in Japan. The life cycles of licensed products are commonly tied to the serialization of a manga series or the release of anime seasons, video games, and movies in Japan. Traditional toys are mostly based on simple designs with an educational function for young people, but modern toy designs are commonly influenced by the culture of cuteness (kawaii) and current media trends. Product lines inspired by popular mascots and fictional characters in Japan are contributing to the success of licensors and licensees, being in demand among children and adults.

There are two major players in Japan's domestic toy market: Takara Tomy and Happynet/Bandai

Takara Tomy came about when two long time rivals merged in 2006. Both companies had long heritage in the toy business prior to this with Tomy's original incarnation dating back to 1924, and Takara being founded back in 1955. The company has a long-term relationship with Hasbro, distributing many Hasbro products across Japan.

The other major player in the Japanese market is Happinet/Bandai. Happinet is a toy distribution company primarily, selling Bandai's products as well as some others. Bandai owns a significant chunk of the company.

Another driver of the domestic toy market are fandoms of major franchises that are the targets of limited releases of mostly small collectibles. Ranging from time-limited figurines sold through capsule toy vending machines (gacha) to long-lasting products like character models, dedicated fans, so-called otaku, are boosting the demand in the adult population and creating new market opportunities.

It is the 5th largest destination for imports with value of USD 5.9 billion in 2020. It exported toys worth USD 3.9 billion during the same period. Its primary source of imports are from China (USD 4.5 billion).

Regulatory regime

Regulation

Toys entering the Japan market are required to comply with the Japan Food Sanitation Law (JFSL) and/or the Japan Toy Safety Standard (ST Standard). JFSL is a legislative mandatory requirement for toys intended for children up to the age of 6 years, whereas the ST standard is a popular voluntary standard established by the Japan Toy Association (JTA) for toys intended for children up to the age of 14 years.

Japan Food Sanitation Law (JFSL)

The Ministry of Health, Labor and Welfare (MHLW) is the regulator for JFSL. Enacted in 2003, this law specifically targets toys either designed to or likely to come into direct contact with children's mouths. That means products such as pacifiers, bottles, nipples, rattles, clay, masks, origami, building blocks, toy phones and dollhouse toys etc. Specific safety tests target the use of substances considered harmful when ingested, such as cadmium, lead, phthalates, arsenic and other heavy metals.

Lab-verified compliance with Sections IV and V of the JFSL is mandatory for applicable children's products before they can enter the Japanese market.

Toy Safety Standard (ST Standard)

The JTA established "Toys Safety Standard" in 1971, in consultation with the authorities concerned, academic experts and representatives of consumers. Based on the agreement between toy companies and the JTA, the toys which have been approved by the designated testing bodies of the ST standard are allowed to put the ST Mark on their products or packages.

ST mark: The JTA enters an ST Mark License Agreement with a business who manufactures, imports or sells toys. A JTA approved designated testing body conducts ST Standard conformity tests on toys manufactured, imported or sold by the business. The JTA licenses the business to place toys, or their packaging, bearing the ST Mark on the market. The JTA indemnifies ST Mark Licensees caused by defect toys bearing the ST Mark.

ST standard

- *Mechanical and Physical Properties: The standard stipulates the necessary shape and strength of toys and conformity tests shall be conducted in order to prevent children from being injured.*
- *Inflammability: Stuffed toy, toy tent, toy house, toy that children wear shall be tested to make sure whether the prohibited materials such as Celluloid are not used, or whether the materials of toys are within the scope of inflammability or not.*
- *Chemical properties: Toys are tested to make sure whether harmful substances are not used in the materials of toys.*

China

75 per cent of all toys produced worldwide are made in China, with local producers dominating the market. The primary toy production and export bases are Guangdong, Jiangsu, Shandong, Zhejiang, Fujian and Shanghai. Guangdong is the leader, with manufacturing centred around Shenzhen, Dongguan, Guangzhou, Shantou's Chenghai, and Foshan. 30 per cent of the world's toys are said to be produced in Chenghai, with production output growing at an average annual rate of 13 per cent. Chenghai is home not only to a group of welltrained toy talents specialised in various types of electronic and smart toys, but also a pool of skilled workers from China and overseas.

The bulk of toy exports are produced for foreign brands on an OEM basis.

Toys in the Chinese market can be classified broadly into four categories—electronic, mechanical, plastic and wooden. In addition to traditional products, models, licensed toys (including movie spinoffs, cartoon characters, etc), hightech toys and educational toys have continued to come onto the market. In recent years, the craze for mobile games and e-sports games has inevitably impacted on the conventional toy market. Being highly interactive and coming in a diverse range, electronic games have become a handy form of entertainment for children and adolescents in Generation Z.

China is the 12th largest importer of toys with USD 2.3 billion in 2020, whereas it is the largest exporter of toys worth USD 71.5 billion. Its biggest market is the USA (USD 23.3 billion) followed by the UK (USD 3.9 billion).

Regulatory regime

Regulator

The SAMR is the regulator for the quality monitoring of toy products. The MIIT is the authority in charge of the regulations and standards making. General Administration of Customs (GAC) is the governing body for the inspection and supervision of imported and exported toys.

Regulation

Standard

GB 6675 specifies safety requirements for majority of toys sold in China. Effective January 1, 2016, the toy standard GB 6675-2014 became effective. It consists of four parts addressing basic safety concern and physical, flammability and chemical safety as following:

- GB 6675.1-2014 Toy safety – Part 1: Basic Code
- GB 6675.2-2014 Safety of Toys – Part 2: Mechanical and Physical Properties
- GB 6675.3-2014 Safety of Toys – Part 3: Flammability
- GB 6675.4-2014 Safety of Toys – Part 4: Migration of Certain Elements

Electric toys also need to meet mandatory standard GB 19865-2005 Electric Toys - Safety.

China Compulsory Certification (CCC)

All products listed in the CCC catalogue are subject to testing by designated testing and certification centres. Only products passing CCC and granted the CCC mark can be imported. The following types of toys are subject to CCC:

- Electric toys
- Plastic toys
- Metal toys
- Projectile toys
- Doll toys
- Ride-on toys

Toys in these categories must also comply with relevant national standards and technical specifications. Other toys do not require CCC certification but can be randomly inspected by SAMR to verify their compliance to national standards and technical specifications.

The certification process includes the following process:

- Application for certification and supporting materials submitted
- For CCC toys – a CNCA Designated Test Laboratory (DTL) will test product samples for declaration of conformity
- Evaluation of certification documents, and approval/rejection of certification
- Follow-up inspection – successful applications will be subject to six-monthly follow-up inspections

Labeling

The requirements for toy labels are documented in GB 5296.5 Instructions for Use for Products of Consumer Interest – Part 5: Toys. It stipulates that the label shall include instructions for use to guide correct use of the toy and mitigate potential harm. The label must include safety warnings, or warning symbols, for the toys that may harm children during the use. The following items must be on the label:

- Product name
- Product model
- Product standard
- Appropriate age range
- Safety warnings
- Name and total content of the primary elements of the materials in stuffed toys
- Instructions for use and drawings that assembly is required
- Maintenance info
- The recommended usable lifespan
- Name and address of manufacturer and distributor

Determination of Total Lead Content in Materials of Toys and Children's Products (GB/T 22788-2016) has been implemented since 1 July 2017 to replace the Determination of Total Lead Content in Surface Coating on Toys (GB/T 22788-2008). The new national standards revise the scope of applicability and include metallic and nonmetallic materials in the determination of total lead content.

For the purpose of the Measures for the Administration of Inspection and Supervision of Toy Imports and Exports, as of 21 November 2018, the GAC has mandated requirement of original CCC certificates for the import of all toys listed in the Catalogue of Products Subject to Compulsory Product Certification. Previously, only a copy of the certificate was required.

The national standard Age Determination Guidelines for Toys (GB/T 28022-2021) was implemented on 13 April 2021 to replace the GB/T 28022-2011 version. This standard provides a guide to manufacturers to determine the lowest age suitability of children's toys. The new version has adopted the ISO standard ISO/TR 8124-8:2016.

The national standard Guideline of Determining Plasticized Materials in Toys or Parts of Toys that can be Placed in the Mouth (GB/T 40182-2021) became effective on 21 May 2021. This standard provides a template that can be compared to the size of a child's mouth, thus providing a definition for what "can be placed in the mouth" and raising the safety of children's toy products.

Canada

Toys, games and hobby supplies generated approximately almost 3.62 billion Canadian dollars in retail store sales in Canada in 2020, a large decrease from over 5.1 billion Canadian dollars in 2019. Christmas is a popular time for children to make a wish list, commonly consisting of the most popular toys and games of the year. Coinciding with the holiday and gifting season, Canadian sales of toys and games have consistently surged in the fourth quarter of each year. As of June 2021, there were over 1,400 stores in Canada to deal with this demand.

Regulatory regime

Regulator

The Consumer Product Safety Program administers and enforces the Canada Consumer Product Safety Act (CCPSA) and its regulations. Enforcement actions taken by Product Safety Officers on non-compliant products depend on the degree of hazard associated with non-compliance, and include commitment to product correction by industry, negotiation with industry for the voluntary removal of these products from the market, seizure and/or prosecution under the CCPSA.

Regulation

There are several regulations under the CCPSA that address specific hazards with children's toys. The main regulation is the Toys Regulations, which address a wide range of mechanical, flammability, toxicological, electrical, thermal and other hazards associated with children's toys. Other regulations, such as those listed below, may also apply to a specific toy, depending on the toy's design, construction, contents and, in some cases, how it is marketed:

- Consumer Products Containing Lead Regulations
- Children's Jewellery Regulations
- Glazed Ceramics and Glassware Regulations
- Tents Regulations
- Phthalates Regulations
- Science Education Sets Regulations
- Surface Coating Materials Regulations
- Textile Flammability Regulations

The CCPSA requires importers and manufacturers to prepare and maintain a copy of documentation which includes business information (i.e. manufacturers, importers, sellers, and distributors information), product information, batch coding, product test reports, product distribution location and other information required by the government. This documentation might be required by the Minister of Health when necessary.

No mandatory testing is required. However, for electric toys, some provincial and territorial legislation may require a compliance certification mark from a certification body accredited by the Standards Council of Canada to prove their compliance.

Labelling

While the Toys Regulations do not require that toys be labelled for age appropriateness or that they bear warning labels for choking hazards, such labelling is strongly encouraged by Canada.

Health Canada recommends that a choking hazard warning in both official languages (English and French) be placed on a toy, its package or its instructions for use. Such a warning is appropriate and recommended when the toy, or any of its removable components, can fit entirely into the small parts cylinder and the toy is intended for children who are at least three years of age but under six years of age.

Note that regardless of the age label on the toy, any toy considered by Health Canada as one that is or is likely to be used by a child under three years of age is subject to the strictest toy safety requirements: it must not be a small component, have a separable small component or release one with reasonably foreseeable use.

Labelling requirements for toys and related products include:

- the labelling of flexible film bags for suffocation hazards
- the safety labelling of children's play tents as detailed in the Tents Regulations
- the safety labelling of electric toys as detailed in the applicable CSA standards
- the safety labelling of chemicals as detailed in the Science Education Sets Regulations
- the French-language packaging and labelling requirements for consumer products sold in the province of Quebec
- the provincial labelling requirements for stuffed toys
- the federal labelling requirements for pre-packaged consumer products

All packaged toys must meet the requirements of the Consumer Packaging and Labelling Act and the Consumer Packaging and Labelling Regulations. This legislation:

- requires that pre-packaged consumer products bear accurate and meaningful labelling information to help consumers make informed purchasing decisions
- prohibits false or misleading representations
- sets out specifications for mandatory label information, such as the product name, net quantity and dealer identity

For toys sold in the Province of Quebec, certain language requirements for inscriptions on products, operation of products, and their packaging, instructions, etc. may be applicable under the authority of the Charter of the French Language (Charte de la langue française).

Looking ahead

The market for toys is undying. It is set to evolve further with artificial intelligence creeping into the segment and demand of the consumers for greater and safer variety. As a universal corollary, every parent wants what is best for their children and their development.

Toys are no longer restricted to traditional toys as dolls, plush toys, wooden toys etc. The creativity has expanded the scope to use artificial intelligence also in video games etc. With 'plasma parents' gaining strength, more innovative and self-involving toys are filling market that are based on responses from the children.

The developing countries have not only managed to strictly regulate the toys industry but all child related products including clothing, jewelry, strollers and carriages, furniture, car seats etc. However, developing countries are still struggling with it. Almost all countries have similar ways of regulating toys. The ISO standard 8124 related to toys is a comprehensive standard and has been adopted by many countries for preparing regulations. The Indian standard has also adopted the same standard in the QCO.

After almost a decade of efforts, India has been able to implement a regulation on toys. Given the size of its market and its unregulated nature, it was a ground for sub-standard products from other countries and even from domestic market. One could not be sure about the various kinds of chemicals being ingested by a baby when it was chewing on a toy or when it was playing with a toy with apparent choking hazard. One could hold the toy in the hand and feel that it was a low grade plastic toy or the assembly was very poor.

Although the new QCO covers everything being imported under ITC HS code 9503, it is imperative that the scope of the QCO be extended to other products being used by children. With government laying special emphasis on promoting manufacturing of toys in India, it needs to be ensured that quality is not compromised at any point of supply chain. Afterall, it's the future of the nation that we are talking about.

REFERENCES

- https://www.investindia.gov.in/sector/consumer-goods/toys-manufacturing#:~:text=The%20sector%20is%20fragmented%20with,a%20large%20potential%20growth%20opportunity.
- https://www.statista.com/topics/1108/toy-industry/#dossierKeyfigures
- https://www.statista.com/statistics/194395/revenue-of-the-global-toy-market-since-2007/
- https://smallbusiness.chron.com/industry-analysis-toys-77091.html
- https://www.ibef.org/indian-toys
- https://www.ibef.org/research/case-study/india-s-toy-story-an-overview
- https://www.toyassociation.org/ta/research/data/u-s-sales-data/toys/research-and-data/data/us-sales-data.aspx
- https://www.toyassociation.org/ta/advocacy/federal/standards/toys/advocacy/federal/us-safety-standards.aspx
- https://www.toyassociation.org/PressRoom2/IndustryStatements/ToySafety/TIA_Statement_Chemicals.aspx
- https://www.chemicalsafetyfacts.org/toys-and-chemical-safety/
- https://www.compliancegate.com/toy-safety-standards-united-states/
- https://www.cpsc.gov/Testing-Certification/Childrens-Product-Certificate-CPC
- https://www.cpsc.gov/Business—Manufacturing/Business-Education/tracking-label
- https://www.unicargo.com/everything-you-need-to-know-about-importing-toys-into-the-usa/#:~:text=CPSIA%20(the%20Consumer%20 Product%20 Safety, and%20sold%20legally%20in%20America.
- https://single-market-economy.ec.europa.eu/sectors/toys_en
- https://single-market-economy.ec.europa.eu/sectors/toys/placing-toys-eu-market_en
- https://ec.europa.eu/growth/tools-databases/nando/
- https://single-market-economy.ec.europa.eu/single-market/goods/international-aspects-single-market/mutual-recognition-agreements_en
- https://single-market-economy.ec.europa.eu/sectors/toys/placing-toys-eu-market_en
- https://single-market-economy.ec.europa.eu/sectors/toys/toy-safety_en
- https://www.compliancegate.com/toy-safety-directive/
- https://www.statista.com/topics/8815/toy-industry-in-the-uk/#dossierContents__outerWrapper
- https://www.ibisworld.com/united-kingdom/market-research-reports/toy-retailing-industry/
- https://www.gov.uk/government/publications/toys-safety-regulations-2011/toys-safety-regulations-2011-great-britain#conformity-assessment-and-marking—products-placed-on-the-gb-market-from-1-january-2023
- https://www.statista.com/topics/8446/toy-market-in-japan/#dossierKeyfigures
- https://www.spielwarenmesse.de/en/mag/markets/toy-market-in-japan
- https://www.toys.or.jp/pdf/jta_business_info_english.pdf
- https://www.sgs.com/en/services/japan-toy-st-certification
- https://www.qima.com/testing/japan-toy-safety-standard
- https://www.covue.com/japan-importer-of-record/toys-what-you-need-to-

know-about-japan-requirements-and-regulations/
- https://research.hktdc.com/en/article/MzA3ODUwOTUx
- https://www.sgs.com/en/services/china-ccc-toy-certification
- https://www.intertek.com/consumer/testing/gb/toy/
- https://www.hqts.com/requirements-for-toy-labels-in-eu-us-and-china/
- https://www.statista.com/topics/3026/toy-industry-in-canada/#dossierContents__outerWrapper
- https://www.canada.ca/en/health-canada/services/consumer-product-safety/reports-publications/industry-professionals/industry-guide-safety-requirements-children-toys-related-products-summary/guidance-document.html
- https://www.compliancegate.com/children-product-toy-safety-regulations-canada/

CHAPTER THREE

STRENGTHENING INDIA

Introduction

The previous chapters described various approaches that major import destinations have taken to regulate sectoral imports that range from technical specifications to non-legal requirements to testing necessities. Developed countries, over a period of time, have been able to leverage their economic advantages to control what is reaching their people whereas developing countries are still learning how to do so. There is also a lack of resources and expertise when it comes to developing countries. Financial and technical expertise is missing in many countries. Often, hired expertise leads to unnecessary expense for the government, which could be curtailed by harnessing talent and expertise within the country.

Rule-forming may appear to be straightforward and the procedural information may be available in the public domain to a limited extent. The detailed process, however, that goes behind formulating every regulation may not be available for countries to learn from each other's best practices. The level of involvement of various government agencies may differ from sector to sector and from country to country. Hence, there is no defined template that can be used to prepare a regulation. It has to be tailor-made to each country's regulatory environment and its market.

A TR formulation requires the collective participation of stakeholders such as consumers, manufacturers, distributors, importers, government agencies, testing facilities, etc. Not all the time do views of stakeholders converge. At times, testing infrastructure may not exist and at other times producers may support the formulation but consumers may not. It is then that an objective method is required to assess the feedback received from stakeholders to arrive at a decision to formulate a TR. Developing countries struggle with streamlining the procedure and dovetail it with each sector's requirements.

The exercise of data collection for TR formulation in larger developing countries is a major issue. Information related to the organized sector may be available but information related to the larger unorganized sector is still unrecorded. The lack of accurate data leads to challenges in policy making that is aimed at providing quality goods and services. Privacy concerns are one of the trending issues that come up while sharing confidential information with the government. Regulations like REACH that require protecting data shared by traders with the government could be a challenge in developing countries where security breaches may bring a bad name to the country.

If one looks at the notifications made to the WTO, many developed countries notify even their intent to prepare a regulation or they notify brainstorming sessions to enhance participation from stakeholders. Some even notify the outcome of such meetings. Developing countries lack such transparency, not by choice, but due to lack of experience in making and implementing regulations. It may be a decade-old exercise for developed countries but they have been in this game for much longer.

However, this does not mean that developing countries are continuing their trade with sub-standard goods and are being left behind. Many have now started opening up to the idea of using NTBs and bringing in regulations suited to their consumers' needs. This also nudges industry to change with time and adopt newer technology to stay competitive, viz-a-viz imports. Greater planning is required to not just prepare, but also enforce regulations strictly. Discipline at the regulation level is required to be followed by exporters and enforced by the government to improve the overall quality of 'Make in India' goods.

India has started its journey to regulate various sectors to improve the quality of goods available in the market with the launch of the Standards Conclave in 2014 to create awareness among various stakeholders. Since then, India has come a long way with INSS and SNAP. It has identified 371 products on which it intends to make regulations to monitor imports of sub-standard quality and non-essential goods.[18] These products range across various sectors such as iron and steel, chemicals, machinery, etc. It may, however, be noted that high imports could be considered as a criteria for preparing regulations in specific sectors but is definitely not the only criteria for formulating them. Other factors need to be taken into account for increasing the effectiveness of a regulation that is aimed at providing superior quality products to consumers.

Market Surveillance

Market Surveillance is the soul of the regulatory ecosystem. The first chapter covered the basics of a technical regulation from the trader and consumer's point of view and did not cover market surveillance as it is the government's responsibility to carry out market surveillance.

Market surveillance helps protect users against unsafe products and general non-compliance, as well as businesses from unfair competition by those who infringe the rules. It involves monitoring products placed on the market so as to ensure that they comply with applicable requirements, and taking remedial action when the products do not comply. An effective market surveillance system also implies that penalties proportionate to any infringements are in place. Market surveillance can be both pre-market and post-market. Pre-market surveillance takes the pressure off from post-market surveillance; however, this does not eliminate the necessity of having post-market surveillance.

The principle behind what activity is to be carried out (random sample testing on products picked up from the market, factory inspections, recall of products) is based on risk associated with the product. The riskier the product, the greater the surveillance. The type of conformity assessment chosen for seeking compliance with a TR is also based on risk associated with the product.

In India, there is limited post-market surveillance. The CDSCO carries out market surveillance for pharmaceuticals and the TEC is required to do the same for telecom equipment.

The BIS is required to carry out market surveillance for products that are regulated under the BIS Act 2016 because ministries/departments do

18. https://economictimes.indiatimes.com/news/economy/policy/bis-to-frame-quality-norms-for-371-items-by-march-2021-to-curb-non-essential-imports/articleshow/77203029.cms?from=mdr

not possess the infrastructure for carrying out this exercise on their own. Since regulations are made under the act, the BIS is made responsible for surveillance of regulated products. However, it is also limited by lack of manpower in carrying out market surveillance and hence, effectively, there is no proper market surveillance for a majority of non-food products regulated in India. Although there are efforts on drafting and specifying guidelines on how to carry out market surveillance, there are no clear-cut policies to define who does it. There appears to be no strict penal provisions for the same, except for those provided under the act.

Weak market surveillance leads to greater presence of spurious and sub-standard products as it allows non-compliant products also to be placed on the market despite them being certified for adherence to a standard in a TR. It increases false competition and may lead to trade distortions in the market. It increases the risk-taking behaviour of manufacturers and exporters who are aware that market surveillance in the country is weak.

The situation in India is a little different as market surveillance is not completely absent but is very limited and in certain sectors only. For example, the CDSCO has a separate market surveillance mechanism, whereas the BIS has a separate mechanism. For the BIS, it is more pronounced in the electronics sector where, along with STPI, the BIS plays an active role.

What can be done

A regulation's essence is its enforcement. Conformity assessment is a part of it but it takes market surveillance to depict a true picture of the regulation's success. There is no dedicated organization looking after market surveillance in India.

The Department of Consumer Affairs came up with its Consumer Protection Act in 2019, which is aimed at protecting the interests of consumers. The act, with amendments, could potentially act as a main source for carrying out market surveillance activities because the Central Government alone cannot carry out this task for regulated products across India. State government involvement will be required. Initially, those under the BIS Act could be taken up for establishing the infrastructure sector-by-sector, such as iron and steel, chemicals, toys, etc.

Market surveillance activities for sectors that have existing infrastructure, such as pharmaceuticals or food may be brought under the umbrella after due review of compatibility of subsuming or merging.

To carry out this activity without loss of information and to have real-time data, the market surveillance data has to be managed online with different modules for access to various stakeholders such as importers/manufacturers, state governments, central government, consumers, etc. The surveillance activity has to be carried out in accordance with the risk associated with the product. This would also guide the inspection authorities on what kind of activity needs to be carried out for surveillance. The basic source of all this information will be regulations that are made available primarily by the Central Government and, in some cases, by state governments, if their regulations exist (such as in the cosmetics sector: regulatory power to both state and centre). This information will have to be periodically updated so that the market surveillance authorities (MSAs) are updated with the tasks they have at hand.

Based on non-compliance in different sectors reported by MSAs, competent authorities may take necessary action against them as per the penal provisions available in the TR or the governing act. The regulators may also prepare reports on non-compliance observed in sectors regulated by them on a periodic basis. This report can be used as a feedback mechanism to amend the regulation to plug loopholes giving rise to non-compliance in the market.

Market surveillance closes the loop of making a technical regulation most effective. Each step of deciding what standard to mandate, stakeholder consultation, deciding on appropriate conformity assessment for stricter enforcement, and market surveillance has to be carried out after considering all available information, with the riskiness of the product being one of the most important aspects.

Regulatory Impact Assessment (RIA)

The Regulatory Impact Assessment is not a separate concept but an integral part of the entire regulation-making process. It is a term used to describe the process of systematically assessing the benefits and costs of a new regulation or an existing regulation, to improve the quality of regulatory policy. It starts with assessing different policy proposals or proposed regulations leading to achieving a definite objective. The one that is most effective and efficient is chosen.

History of RIA

In 1920, the RIA was developed in the USA and was adopted in its regulatory system in 1978. The RIA initiatives then began to develop progressively and significantly by international organizations such as the OECD (part of its Council's official policy recommendations). Today, the RIA has been widely adopted by OECD members and many non-OECD members.

RIA helps in assessing the impact that the desired regulation will make in the country based on existing market conditions. The process helps in lending objectivity to the regulatory environment in the sector with respect to a product and helps in defining a regulation's usefulness. In certain cases, it may result in no requirement of regulation.

TRs have a widespread effect. They affect consumers, manufacturers, importers, exporters, logistics, etc. For some, the effect may be hidden; for some, it may be bad. RIA helps in assessing who are affected by a regulation and how.

Cost benefit analysis

USA: A study of 15 RIAs by the US Environmental Protection Agency showed that three (out of 15) RIAs increased net benefits to society from recommended improvements in regulations, by USD 10 billion. The total cost of preparing all 15 RIAs studied was approximately USD 10 million.

EU: The REACH regulation from the EC would have imposed €10 billion in costs on the European chemicals industry, as it was first written. The regulation was revised to make it easier to comply, without significantly changing benefits. The final cost was €2 billion. The RIA cost the Commission about €1 million, producing a social return on investment of 8,000 to one, and saving thousands of jobs.

In Victoria State, Australia, a recent evaluation of RIA showed that between 2005-06 and 2009-10, the RIA process achieved an estimated gross savings of AUD 902 million over the 10-year life of the regulations.

The process is based on three initial questions: the underlying problem, the objective sought to be achieved and possible ways of achieving it. For example, the presence of sub-standard toys in the market is an underlying problem; the objective is to have safe toys for children, and possible ways could be to mandate a standard using factory inspection or self-declaration for compliance with a standard, as a required conformity assessment procedure. To arrive at a conclusion, a cost-benefit analysis is to be done for each identified process. The one with a higher benefit is likely to be the most suited in the existing scenario. However, a periodic review is necessary to maintain the effectiveness and efficiency of the regulation, given that the trade environment is highly dynamic.

Defining a regulatory problem	**Identifying different regulatory options**	**Collecting data**
This phase is the preliminary point of RIAs: identifying the regulatory or policy problem. Problems usually fall within 3 categories: market failure, regulatory inefficiencies, and new policy targets or objectives.	In this step, the need for regulatory intervention as identified in phase 1 has to be translated into concrete policy options.	This phase is crucial and the means to achieve it are diverse and vary greatly among countries. Relevant data for the RIA are collected from public consultations, telephoning and face-to-face interviews, paper questionnaires, online surveys, focus groups, etc.
Assessing alternative options	**Identifying preferred regulatory option/s**	**Communicating results of the conducted RIA**
The central phase of RIAs, most of the time, results in a cost-benefit analysis but can also be a cost-effectiveness analysis or a risk analysis. Options assessed must include the "no policy change" scenario.	Once the different options have been identified and scrutinized (usually by comparing the costs and benefits), the comparison of the different assessments will lead to the identification of the most efficient option.	Once taken into consideration by the policy makers, best practices suggest publication of the result of the RIA.This allows for further exchange with stakeholders and improves the general transparency of the regulatory process.

Figure 63: Key elements in the RIA process

Challenges faced by developing countries in implementing RIA

An increasing number of developing countries are preparing and adopting RIA systems suited to their requirements. A number of studies show that such initiatives have met with setbacks because of the targets being over-ambitious and lack of adequate expertise. Many developing countries start from scratch and reinvent the wheel rather than using existing infrastructure. This would help in cutting down costs and complete the assessments within budgetary allocations.

Owing to the technical nature of the process that may require additional data gathering, RIA poses a challenge to developing countries where data may not be easily available to the regulators. It may either not be captured in the desired form or there may be unwillingness of stakeholders to share it. Even if data is available, the required technical expertise may be absent to carry out data-crunching and churning out meaningful observations and results required for the assessment.

Developing countries sometimes lose focus on creating a robust mechanism to create apt infrastructure or governing body to implement the process and integration of the process with the complete regulation-making process.

Countries that have adopted RIA

Colombia

In 2015, Colombia introduced a new framework on regulatory impact assessments for the trade sector (Decree 1595).

European Union

Among numerous reforms undertaken in 2015-16, the European Commission adopted a Better Regulation Package. This package consolidated and strengthened the Commission's planning, consultation, evaluation, and impact assessment procedures. Specifically, a Regulatory Scrutiny Board was established to examine and issue opinions on all the Commission's draft impact assessments, major evaluations, and "fitness checks" of existing legislation. It replaced the Impact Assessment Board in July 2015 and is independent of the policy-making departments.

Kazakhstan

In October 2015, Kazakhstan passed new requirements for regulatory impact analyses in Chapter 13 of the Entrepreneurial Code (EC). The EC outlines the legal, economic, and social environment and guarantees for doing business. It also sets out the state regulation and support of business activities in Kazakhstan.

Kosovo

In 2014 and 2015, the government of Kosovo adopted the Better Regulation Strategy 2014–2020. This strategy contains guidance for improving regulatory impact assessments as part of the policy development process. The government also adopted Administrative Instruction No. 03/2015 on Budget Impact Assessment of New Government Initiatives requiring a detailed impact assessment on the budget of the Republic of Kosovo before passage.

Lithuania

The 2014 Law on the Basics of Legislation required all laws and acts applying the laws (decisions, resolutions, and court rulings) to be registered and officially published in the Register of Legal Acts. It also establishes the right of all individuals to submit proposals for legislative initiatives and legislative projects, and requires impact assessments for every new initiative to regulate non-regulated areas or when regulation is changed substantially.

Morocco

In March 2015, the Government of Morocco adopted Organic Law No. 065-13 on the organization and conduct of the government. Article 19 introduced regulatory impact assessments into Moroccan law, although the conditions and details of such assessments will need to be determined by future regulation.

Romania

In Romania, three pilot impact assessment studies were conducted under the coordination of the Prime Minister's Chancellery in order to test the new regulatory impact guidelines developed in 2015.

South Africa

In South Africa, since the Cabinet resolution of 1 October 2015, it is now compulsory to subject any proposed regulation to socio-economic impact assessment (SEIAS).

Spain

In 2015, Spain adopted a new law (Law 40) governing the formation of new regulations. It requires annual forward regulatory plans and the evaluation reports of approved regulations to be made publicly available. It also establishes a wider scope of regulatory impact assessments to include competitiveness, market unity, and SMEs analyses. Finally, Law 40 sets in place a new process for pre-consultation with the public on regulatory initiatives.

United Kingdom

In the United Kingdom, the Small Business, Enterprise and Employment Act 2015 converted a number of existing rules for rule-making within the UK's better regulation framework into a legislative requirement. In addition, it also introduced some new requirements. Specifically, the legislation put into law the requirement for an independent body to verify the costs and benefits of rules, and for that organisation to verify all the costs of measures that score toward the Business Impact Target. The existing body in the UK that scrutinizes impact assessments—the Regulatory Policy Committee—was designated as the verification body.

Vietnam

In Vietnam, a new Law on Laws came into force on 1 July 2016 (No. 85/2015/QH1). It makes regulatory impact assessments mandatory for all types of legal documents, including those issued by the local provincial people's committee. These assessments must be prepared in the early stages of the proposed rule-making.

Zambia

In Zambia, the enactment of the Business Regulatory Act No. 3 of 2014 established the Business Regulatory Review Committee and the Business Regulatory Review Agency (BRRA). The Act introduced a set of principles, procedures, and minimum requirements for the introduction of new regulatory measures. Specifically, the new law provides that a public body shall only submit to the Cabinet for approval a policy or proposed law to regulate business activity if the policy or proposed law has the prior approval of the BRRA. The regulating body must also conduct a regulatory impact assessment on the proposed intervention, which is submitted to the BRRA for review and approval.

RIA in India: Why should we adopt it?

RIA in India is not a new concept. Many committees have recommended its use in policy making including the erstwhile Planning Commission's Working Group on Business Regulatory Framework (WGBRF) (2011), Financial Sector Legislative Reforms Commission (FSLRC) (2013), Committee for Reforming the Regulatory Environment for Doing Business in India (2013), Tax Administration and Reforms Commission (2015), and the Department of Industrial Policy and Promotion's Expert Committee on Prior Permissions and Regulatory Mechanism (2016).

Besides the above recommendations, RIA is important from the financial point of view. There are no studies in the public domain, however, the cost of preparing a TR, such as setting up testing facilities and upgrading manufacturing set up, may outweigh its benefits in terms of controlling import and/or manufacture of sub-standard goods. The reality is unknown. To be able to place a finger on the exact outcome, RIA will be of great help.

It will not only help in assessing the costs involved in making and enforcing a TR but also help in reviewing the regulation to reduce costs and increase benefits. Sometimes, superficially it may appear that a TR is required to regulate a community, but the analysis may show otherwise.

RIA will bring in greater transparency in the system by involving all the stakeholders. At times, it may happen that while making a TR, not all stakeholders can be consulted. RIA will help address this problem and address the concerns involved.

It is observed that 40 per cent of India's exports is limited to just seven countries. The recent Economic Survey highlighted India's need for FTAs to diversify exports and explore new shores for promotion of its products. These FTAs have various WTO-plus provisions in different subject areas such as services, reduction of tariffs in goods, trade remedies, competition, SPS and TBT, Rules of Origin, Good Regulatory Practices (GRP), etc. From what is available in the public domain, more and more countries are taking on ambitious obligations under the FTA chapters. New chapters on GRP are also gaining traction. One of the main thrust of the GRP is RIA.

If India adopts the RIA concept in letter, it will be easier for it to take on such hard obligations under the FTAs, which will not only be beneficial to the government but to consumers as well.

To provide a uniform platform to regulatory agencies to carry out the process in a streamlined manner, an enabling legislation may be introduced by the Department of Commerce as it has been spearheading the activity of formulation TRs on 371 products and is in harmony with updates on this concept at the WTO level. The legislation is intended to lay down a step-by-step process, data collection guidelines, requirements for cost-benefit analysis, public consultation, etc. RIA should be carried out by the respective ministries for which dedicated divisions must be created in agencies/departments. The expertise in these units could be outsourced but the ultimate responsibility should lie with the government. A structure could be set up at the central and state levels.

Ultimately, it is the responsibility of the government to see that the TR it makes is effective in terms of enforcement and fully fulfils its objective.

Future: Non-tariff measures

The non-tariff measures are going to continue holding their importance. Even though there have been tariff wars between countries in recent past, but the basis of these tariff wars has resulted in NTMs in the form of anti-dumping duties, countervailing duties etc.

With more integrated trade, the nature of NTMs is also expected to get complicated. It will no longer be limited to mere standards and testing reports or factory inspections. Newer elements such as workplace conditions and man hours in factory are already creeping into the regulations. Environment and child labour are two non-trade issues that are being used by countries to restrict trade and select trading partners for imports. Few may disagree with environment being a non-trade issue but such has been the position of India at international fora uptil now. It is slowly changing with environment and sustainability being brought under the ambit of new FTAs that are under negotiation.

India now needs to work on the NTMs or technical regulations it issues. Nearly all regulations issued under the BIS Act, 2016 are of the same format. A bit of innovation or flexibility to introduce newer elements needs to be brought into the system so that the ministry / department that intends to regulate under this act are able to do so with newer elements specific to their sector.

Apart from the innovation required in the regulations, market surveillance infrastructure needs to be strengthened for closing the loop of a successful measure. This is also becoming an important part of the FTAs and we cannot take an obligation with the will to fulfil it unless the tools and the market supports its existence. Work in this arena needs to be done from scratch as market surveillance, sans food and pharmaceuticals, is dependent on the BIS. This activity cannot be outsourced as it is the duty of the government to do it. No third party will be able to do it impartially.

Another step that India needs to take forward is in the area of RIA. This will require careful planning in a phase-wise manner. There are examples from many developing countries who have made this as a part of their regulation making process and have benefitted immensely in terms of resources and saving costs. The biggest beneficiary in RIA is the industry.

NTMs ought to be used wisely to benefit the society, consumers, industry, exporters, testing facilities and other stakeholders. Continuous evolution within the country will not only benefit the domestic industry but. The exporters as well as it will give an indication to other countries that goods produced in that country follow strict quality norms and thus cannot be substandard. This will encourage exports from that country.

INDEX

*